Business Arbitration— What you need to know

by Robert Coulson
President
American Arbitration
Association

THIRD EDITION

BUSINESS ARBITRATION—WHAT YOU NEED TO KNOW

Third Edition, February 1986

For information, address American Arbitration Association,
140 West 51st Street, New York, N.Y. 10020-1203
Library of Congress Catalog Card Number: 85-48286

TABLE OF CONTENTS

PREFACE

Business Arbitration – What You Need to Know has been prepared to assist the reader in making use of alternative dispute resolution for commercial disputes, especially under the various rules of the American Arbitration Association. It contains a wealth of information on that subject. This book can help you prepare your case, eliminating uncertainty about dispute settlement procedures.

Arbitration is generally informal and businesslike – a hearing is nothing to be afraid of. Each party has the right to present its entire case. The law requires that the arbitrator hear any relevant testimony that is submitted and consider the arguments.

Most important business issues are resolved privately. The facts and arguments are considered so that a sound decision can be made. American business people use such systems because they are a sensible way to resolve disputes.

Whether you are an arbitrator, an attorney, a business executive, or a private citizen, this book will help you to understand how arbitration can be used by you to better manage your own business controversies. It is not complicated. You do not need a legal education to understand how the process works. If you add arbitration to your personal skills, you will benefit in very practical ways.

In recommending arbitration to his fellow Americans, Chief Justice Warren E. Burger of the United States Supreme Court noted: *"There are better ways of resolving private disputes, and we must in the public interest move toward taking a large volume of private conflicts out of the courts and into the channels of arbitration."*

But, of course, arbitration is not the only way to settle disputes privately. Additional material added to this third edition covers some of the other options: negotiation, mediation, fact-finding, and the mini-trial, among others. It is only when such techniques fail that arbitration need be initiated. Wherever possible, parties should settle their dispute between themselves.

CHAPTER 1

AN INTRODUCTION TO COMMERCIAL ARBITRATION

Conflict is a fact of business life, a necessary aspect of a market economy. Controversies originate for many reasons, ranging from normal market competition to honest disagreements about rights. Disputes also arise from clashes between individuals. Americans are perfectly happy to assert their legal rights. The question is how? It is not always necessary to go to court.

A free society provides many systems for resolving controversies. We think of the courts as being primary, but, of course, they are not. Most disagreements are resolved informally, without the need for judicial intervention. Settlements are worked out privately, often without lawyers and usually without judges or juries.

In the United States, the growth of litigation seems to have outrun our courts' ability to respond. Judges are finding it difficult to cope with the needs and demands of society. Most Americans no longer want to get involved in lawsuits. They are looking for alternative methods for resolving their disputes.

Voluntary procedures such as negotiation, mediation, conciliation, and arbitration are becoming our primary methods for settling disputes. The courts encourage parties to settle. In cases where the parties would benefit from a prompt decision on the merits, many judges favor alternatives to settle disputes that would otherwise end up in court.

Commercial arbitration is not a single uniform system. There are many rules and procedures applicable to various business disputes. Even under the same set of rules, arbitrators and parties may handle their cases in different ways. Some hearings may be more formal than others, depending on the relative importance of the controversy. The preferences of the participants can make a difference in the format. Arbitration, in fact, affords business the kind of flexibility it demands in other areas. This book can help you decide whether to arbitrate and which kind of arbitration is right for your dispute.

WHAT IS ARBITRATION?

Arbitration is the submission of a disagreement to one or more impartial persons. Usually, the parties agree to abide by the arbitrator's decision. Because the decision is binding, arbitration differs from mediation or conciliation, where the third party brings the parties together to discuss settlement. It also differs from fact-finding, where an impartial person studies the situation and makes a report. In most instances, arbitrators' decisions are private and only of interest to the parties involved. Few private arbitration awards come to the attention of the courts.

Arbitration is a system created by the parties themselves. When they have worked hard to settle a dispute but have failed, they submit the remaining issues to arbitration. Negotiations may have narrowed their differences, so that the negotiators can "control" the remaining issues to be submitted.

THE AMERICAN ARBITRATION ASSOCIATION

The American Arbitration Association (AAA) is a public service, not-for-profit, membership organization, founded in 1926 to encourage the use of arbitration and other techniques of voluntary dispute settlement. The AAA is based in New York City and has twenty-six dispute settlement centers located in major cities throughout the United States. The Association provides education, training, and research on all forms of out-of-court dispute settlement. The AAA offers information on private dispute resolution and helps industries to design their own systems.

LEGISLATIVE HISTORY OF ARBITRATION

Private arbitration has gained widespread acceptance since the first modern arbitration laws were passed in the late 1920s. Congress passed the U.S. Arbitration Act, which applies to most business controversies, in 1925. In 1955, Commissioners on Uniform State Laws adopted a Uniform Arbitration Act. Modern arbitration laws reflect the needs of the business community and the growing support for arbitration among lawyers and judges.

Winning the right to arbitrate future disputes has not been easy. Even today, a few states have not yet passed modern arbitration acts. (The various state arbitration statutes are listed in the appendix.) National policy favors arbitration. This is reflected in the United States Arbitration Act. Recent cases from both federal and state courts have expressed that support in strong terms.

Arbitration systems, like other voluntary institutions, are sensitive to changes in the law or to government intervention. In some cases, legislation may encourage arbitration by simplifying and reducing the issues between parties. The automobile no-fault laws are examples of this.

Many thousands of cases are arbitrated each year. Arbitration is popular with the American people. Rather than being a system of "second-class justice," it is the first choice of many people. Arbitration takes cases out of the courts. It saves public money. It puts the control of dispute settlement into the hands of the parties.

Arbitration has become an important part of the justice system. Encouraging arbitration may prevent unnecessary litigation. As officers of the court, lawyers are generally supportive of arbitration.

ARBITRATING COMMERCIAL DISPUTES

Arbitration provides an "alternative system of justice." Millions of contracts, insurance policies, leases, franchise and employment agreements, and other business and personal arrangements include arbitration clauses. Such clauses bind the parties to arbitrate disputes that may arise over the meaning or application of the language in the contract. These provisions often refer to the rules of the American Arbitration Association. (Many of these sets of rules are printed throughout this book. Write to any AAA regional office for the most up-to-date versions of these rules.)

Major arbitration systems in the United States have been created by commercial interests to resolve disputes in accordance with procedures that reflect the needs of the particular industry. Trade associations often take the lead in creating arbitration systems. Their members stand to gain by using arbitration rather than going to court. Association leaders like the idea of resolving their members' disputes without publicity or government intervention. Arbitration can avoid bad public relations that might be detrimental to the entire industry.

THE ADVANTAGES OF ARBITRATION

Why do so many executives include arbitration clauses in their contracts?

Based upon AAA surveys, the following reasons seem most persuasive. Business firms prefer to have their disagreements decided by people who are experts. Arbitrators, unlike judges, can be chosen for their business experience. AAA panels include engineers, business consultants, accountants, and many other specialized experts, as well as attorneys.

The simplicity of arbitration is also an inducement. No company wants to have its funds tied up for extended periods of time. The arbitration process can move promptly, which is especially important in disputes between builders and contractors over performance payments or between business partners who cannot agree about the division of assets.

Arbitration cases take place in a private, informal atmosphere where business people feel comfortable. There is less chance that trade secrets will be disclosed to competitors or that a firm's reputation will be placed in jeopardy. In arbitration, confidentiality is honored.

Because the award is generally not subject to appeal, arbitration results in a final and binding decision. Many parties prefer that decisions be final, rather than facing the prospect of extended appellate litigation. Again, most Americans want to stay out of court.

WHO USES ARBITRATION?

Many business disputes are resolved by arbitration. Some of the major uses are described in this book–for example, resolution of disputes in such fields as construction, textiles, insurance, and international trade. Many thousands of other controversies are also arbitrated. Collection claims, individual employee grievances, partnership and private corporation problems, patent and licensing disputes, and disagreements between authors and publishers are a few examples. Many cases originate from the real estate industry, where problems over leases, property evaluation, or brokerage fees are constantly arising.

The Construction Industry

The construction industry is a frequent user of arbitration. In earlier years, the industry used arbitration informally. This created problems, and, in 1965, a joint industry committee asked the American Arbitration Association to create an improved system. A national panel of expert arbitrators was established.

Now the AAA's Construction Industry Arbitration Rules are found in hundreds of thousands of building contracts. The caseload has grown to thousands of cases annually. Many are claims by contractors for payment, but an engineer or architect may be involved. Or several subcontractors may process claims against a prime contractor in one proceeding.

In addition, the AAA now offers an expedited arbitration system for construction claims, which can result in faster processing and reduced costs. New mediation rules for the construction industry are designed to encourage settlement before arbitration begins.

Disputes over alleged defects in new homes can be resolved under a system where an insurance-backed limited warranty is given to the purchaser of a new home by the builder. In these cases, the process takes place at the home site.

Chapter 2 describes how dispute resolution works in the construction industry.

The Textile and Apparel Industries

Years ago, leaders in the textile and apparel fields joined together to form what is now the General Arbitration Council of the Textile and Apparel Industries.

It operates as part of the American Arbitration Association. Many trade associations are represented on the council, which supervises the arbitration of textile and apparel cases. The arbitrators are active business executives. Almost all of the cases are heard in New York City, where there is the largest supply of experienced textile arbitrators.

Arbitration in the textile/apparel industries is described in chapter 3.

Insurance Claims

One of the largest consumer arbitration systems, operating in many states, involves the determination of uninsured motorist claims. Here, the claimant must prove both negligence and damages. Arbitration is used to decide liability and how much the company owes. A system is also discussed that resolves a wide variety of insurance claims by arbitration and mediation.

Arbitration also is used to resolve claims under many no-fault automobile laws. By eliminating the issue of negligence and the common-law right to compensation for pain and suffering, the injured person's claim is reduced and simplified.

The resolution of insurance claims is described in chapter 4.

International Trade

When business is carried out between parties from different countries, each party will try to avoid resolving disputes in the other party's local courts. Arbitration makes it possible to create a self-contained system where such matters can be decided by impartial experts acting under the rules and procedures of an administrative agency. The American Arbitration Association decides such cases under one or more of its commercial rules or under the UNCITRAL rules. It has issued special procedures for international cases.

International commercial arbitration is discussed in chapter 5.

Divorce Settlements

Marital separation agreements provide another example of the flexibility of arbitration. Once they have agreed on a separation, the last thing the couple wants to do is go back to court. By putting an arbitration clause in their agreement, they can avoid that eventuality. In addition to serving as arbitrators, impartial experts are also assuming new roles as family mediators, helping couples to settle their problems and converting many potential lawsuits into uncontested applications for divorce.

Community Dispute Services

Criminal complaints and controversies between individuals in a community can also be handled in mediation and arbitration. People involved in those kinds of problems may be given a chance to transfer their dispute to a community tribunal. An impartial third party appointed by the local mediation center can attempt to work out a settlement to help the parties resolve their problems. This works especially well for people who will have an ongoing relationship.

Systems have been established in many communities to deal with such conflicts. They have been widely accepted by courts and other local groups. Mediation and arbitration tribunals for community disputes, an idea whose time has come, are being created all over the country.

OTHER KINDS OF ALTERNATIVE DISPUTE RESOLUTION

Arbitration is only one of a number of alternatives that parties may use to resolve their business disputes without going to court. In recent years, other forms of dispute resolution have become popular.

Many of these techniques are private. Others are created by the courts. The primary method for resolving disputes, of course, is negotiation. Ninety-five percent of the cases filed in court are resolved without a trial. But most disputes are never filed in court; instead, lawyers and business executives constantly negotiate. Fortunately, extensive literature on that subject is available.

One elaborate negotiating technique is the *mini-trial*. It is extremely useful for corporations involved in major controversies. The parties create their own hearing, where the trial attorneys make legal presentations to a panel consisting of top executives from each organization. A neutral person presides. That kind of presentation has a sobering effect upon a corporate executive. The neutral may serve as a mediator or give an advisory opinion after the hearing. For lawyers, the mini-trial provides an arena within which to demonstrate skill as an advocate. In a mini-trial, the client's senior executive sits at the head of the table. The AAA has formulated procedures for mini-trials. These appear at the end of this chapter.

Mediation is another alternative dispute resolution technique. A mediator meets with the parties or their representatives, attempting to arrange an acceptable solution. A mediator has no authority to make decisions for the parties. Rather, a mediator helps them to analyze the issues and to exchange their perceptions about the relevant data, seeking a formula for compromise. Increasingly, attorneys are making use of professional mediation. The experience thus far has been positive.

Once parties agree to mediate, the procedure seems to take on a life of its own, leading toward a settlement. Of the many claims against insurance companies mediated under the rules of the American Arbitration Association, only a few are not settled. Under that system, the mediators are attorneys trained by the AAA.

They receive a fee. Most cases take less than a day. The settlements must be satisfactory to both attorneys. As trained professional mediators become increasingly available, people would be foolish not to take advantage of the process.

Several excellent books have been written about mediation, explaining how the process works. How do mediators bring out the facts? When do they caucus with one of the parties? How do they encourage settlement? If you are considering mediation, you should know the answers.

One kind of mediation is called *med-arb.* In this process, a neutral person is authorized to mediate but also can decide any issues the parties are unable to settle in their negotiations. This can be threatening to the parties, because they are entirely in the hands of the neutral.

Mediation is more tentative. If a party does not like the way things are going, negotiations can be terminated. A mediator has no hold on the parties. Either party can disengage at any time. In arbitration, on the other hand, the third person is given the power to make a decision. Med-arb is a combination of both techniques, but not necessarily an appropriate option. We find that few parties want to give so much power to the neutral.

COURT-ADMINISTERED ALTERNATIVE DISPUTE RESOLUTION

Arbitration has also been used by courts. For relatively small civil cases, some courts have installed court-administered arbitration. This can be done through enabling legislation or by court rule. Here, arbitration is mandatory for cases below a certain minimum dollar amount. After a case is filed in court, the parties are required to submit it to a panel of arbitrators, usually selected by rotation from a list provided by a local bar association. An arbitration hearing is held, after which the panel issues its award. Losing parties can request a trial *de novo* upon payment of certain fees.

Court-administered arbitration is neither voluntary nor binding. It is imposed by the courts to encourage the settlement of cases involving modest claims. It has been successful in that many cases are settled and the courts avoid having to provide a trial.

For civil cases, other alternative systems are available. Some courts use referees, who are appointed to hear and decide a particular case or to provide a preliminary hearing. They report back to the judge with findings of fact and conclusions of law or with a recommendation. Other courts use masters for the same purpose. In a few states, by statute, parties can submit their dispute to a retired judge or a mutually selected attorney who serves as an arbitrator, except that the award is subject to appeal to the same extent as a court judgment. This system is called rent-a-judge. The arbitrator is given much of the power and authority of an active judge and may even hold the hearing in the courthouse. The parties are expected to pay the expenses of the process. Trial attorneys represent the parties as they would in court.

Another system is the summary jury trial. It consists of a summary trial before a jury drawn from the regular panel list. The trial can be completed in a single day. A brief presentation is made by both attorneys, resulting in an advisory verdict. The verdict can be accepted by the parties, or it may provide the basis for further settlement discussions. If it is rejected by either party, a normal jury trial can be obtained.

Mediation may also take place in court. A judge may engage in direct mediation as part of a settlement conference or a referee or outside professional mediator may be used.

WHO ARE THE NEUTRALS?

To provide the business community with neutral experts from various areas of specialization, the AAA maintains a National Panel consisting of more than 60,000 people in many communities. Arbitrators are nominated by leaders in their industries or professions. They are added to the panel after the AAA has checked their qualifications and reputations.

Commercial arbitrators serve under the rules selected by the parties. Their conduct is guided by the Code of Ethics for Arbitrators in Commercial Disputes. The code is reproduced in the appendix of this book.

Arbitrators deserve respect and courtesy. In smaller cases, they may be serving without compensation. Parties can demonstrate their appreciation by facilitating the arbitrators' task and, at the same time, serve their own best interests by presenting their cases in an expeditious and orderly way.

ARE LAWYERS USED IN ARBITRATION?

Under AAA procedures, each party is guaranteed the right to be represented by an attorney. In commercial arbitration cases involving significant amounts of money or complex legal questions, lawyers will represent each party. Professional representation is important in these cases. Presenting such a case in arbitration involves the same skills of advocacy that lawyers require in litigation.

It is not always necessary for parties to negotiate through attorneys. In some situations, lawyers may even obstruct a settlement by putting an embargo upon direct communications between the parties. Being more familiar with the facts and with the personalities involved, the client may be better prepared to settle the matter.

Some lawyers see courts as the exclusive forum for civil cases, particularly if they do not have an active commercial practice. In fact, only a small percentage of business claims are decided as a result of trials in court; 95 percent are settled. More commercial claims are arbitrated than are tried before a jury.

Arbitration provides an alternative to the courthouse. Many business clients are convinced that commercial arbitration is a sensible way to resolve disputes. Attorneys tend to agree. As they gain experience in arbitration, they are pleased with its practical aspects.

Court delays and inconveniences have been particularly frustrating to the busy lawyer. For sound reasons, there has been a strong trend toward alternative systems. When selecting an attorney to represent you in arbitration, be sure that the particular system involved is familiar to your attorney.

BUSINESS PEOPLE CAN PARTICIPATE IN DISPUTE RESOLUTION

Everyone should know how to bargain. Bargaining is the key to justice in our society. The lawyer certainly needs such skills—but so does everyone else.

In the world of trade and commerce, disputes are common. Each person may understand rights and obligations differently no matter how carefully a contract is written. Different perceptions frequently lead to delayed shipments, complaints about quality of merchandise, claims of nonperformance of contracts, and similar misunderstandings. Even with good intentions, parties may perform less than they promise.

Business controversies often concern the evaluation of facts and the interpretation of contract terms. Executives make these judgments every day. When differences arise out of day-to-day commercial affairs, parties often prefer to settle through arbitration, privately and informally, in a businesslike setting that encourages continued business relationships.

Like other business functions, arbitration calls for special knowledge. The executives who were involved in creating the disputed transaction can play a useful role in settlement discussions and in arbitration. A business executive can participate actively, helping to prepare the case, selecting the arbitrator, and explaining the evidence at the hearing. The inside lawyer in a business corporation is a skilled professional who can assist in the many parts of the process that fall outside the expertise of the corporate client. A member of the firm's legal staff may provide excellent representation at the arbitration hearing. In major cases, a skilled trial lawyer may be preferred.

THE ARBITRATION AGREEMENT

An agreement to arbitrate represents an important decision. Including this provision in a contract represents a binding commitment by both parties to resort to arbitration in the event that a dispute arises about the meaning or application of the contract.

American business people are free to enter into contracts. The extent of our private rights in this regard is unique, when compared with other countries. Most contracts can be signed without prior government approval and without the payment of a tax. Freedom to contract without government interference is taken for granted.

Americans also have the right to enter into agreements to arbitrate future disputes under whichever impartial system they designate. The United States Arbitration Act and modern state arbitration laws, now broadly enacted, lend enforceability to such provisions. Only in rare instances will arbitration clauses be held unenforceable by the courts. Awards resulting from properly conducted arbitrations are enforceable in all jurisdictions. Moreover, the Federal Arbitration Act recognizes the enforceability of awards obtained in other countries.

The right to arbitrate is a fundamental part of our constitutional privilege to enter into contracts or to agree to resolve contractual obligations. Arbitration is an optional method of settlement. Parties have a right to cancel a contract without intervention by the courts. This privilege includes the right to fix the terms of such a cancellation and to submit those terms to an impartial arbitrator. The parties have the mutual right to interpret their own contract. This includes the right to authorize an impartial arbitrator to render such an interpretation for them.

In commercial relationships, parties should not be forced to go to court. They should be encouraged to arbitrate. Many arbitration clauses inserted in contracts refer to the American Arbitration Association because the parties want their agreement to be self-executing. By giving authority to an impartial administrator, they can avoid having to go to court.

In litigation, the emphasis is on procedure. The judicial machinery is designed to correct mistakes. The procedure is supposed to protect the parties against errors, with appellate review playing an important role.

In arbitration, the parties rely upon their own ability to select a wise and impartial decision maker. They waive their right to have a judge review the arbitrator's decision. The emphasis is on the integrity and experience of the decision maker. Parties select arbitration because they desire an informed judgment, applied and obtained through a simplified hearing procedure. They intend the result to be final. The emphasis is on substance rather than procedure.

When an arbitration clause names the AAA, the parties rely upon the Association to provide effective and impartial administration in accordance with its rules. You should read those rules and, if you have questions, you should ask the AAA.

STANDARD ARBITRATION CLAUSE AND SUBMISSION AGREEMENT

By including an arbitration clause in contracts, business people can choose their own dispute settlement process. They can design their own arbitration clause, but often such clauses are printed in form contracts.

The American Arbitration Association recommends the following arbitration clause for insertion in general commercial contracts:

> Any controversy or claim arising out of or relating to this contract, or the breach thereof, shall be settled by arbitration in accordance with the Commercial Arbitration Rules of the American Arbitration Association, and judgment upon the award rendered by the Arbitrator(s) may be entered in any Court having jurisdiction thereof.

Arbitration clauses should be designed to meet the specific needs of the parties. Sometimes a clause will refer to special rules. Among the AAA's rules are the Commercial Arbitration Rules (all-purpose procedures for business disputes), or, for specific industries, the Construction Industry Arbitration Rules, the Real Estate Valuation Arbitration Rules, the Rules of the General Arbitration Council of the Textile and Apparel Industries, and the Accident Claims Arbitration Rules. The tribunals employing these rules reflect modern arbitration practice. Prompt and inexpensive hearings can usually be obtained under these procedures.

Where parties fail to include an arbitration clause in their contract or where the dispute does not involve a prior contract, the dispute can still be submitted to arbitration by using the following general form:

> We, the undersigned parties, hereby agree to submit to arbitration under the Commercial Arbitration Rules of the American Arbitration Association the following controversy: (cite briefly). We further agree that the above controversy be submitted to (one) (three) Arbitrator(s) selected from the panels of Arbitrators of the American Arbitration Association. We further agree that we will faithfully observe this agreement and the Rules and that we will abide by and perform any award rendered by the Arbitrator(s) and that a judgment of the Court having jurisdiction may be entered upon the award.

STEP ONE: HOW TO INITIATE AN ARBITRATION

All that is required to begin the arbitration, regardless of how the parties agree to arbitrate, is notification to the AAA and the defending party. On receiving the initiating papers, the Association assigns the case to one of its staff members, called a tribunal administrator. From this point on, the administrator is at the disposal of the parties, assisting both sides until an award is rendered. The AAA will supply appropriate forms free of charge. A case can also be initiated through ordinary correspondence, provided the essential information is included.

Questions may arise as to where the case will be administered or where the hearings will take place. Usually the locale can be decided by the parties. But if the place of arbitration has not been designated in the contract or agreed to by the parties, the AAA will designate the place in accordance with its rules.

In appropriate cases, the AAA may schedule a prehearing conference with the parties and their counsel to arrange for the exchange of information and the stipulation of uncontested facts in an effort to expedite resolution of the dispute.

STEP TWO: SELECTION OF THE ARBITRATOR

The AAA maintains a list of experienced experts from which disputants select arbitrators. Unless the parties have chosen a different method, the AAA adheres to the following selection procedures:

1. On receiving the demand for arbitration or the submission agreement, the tribunal administrator sends each party a specially prepared list of proposed arbitrators qualified to decide the controversy. In drawing up the list, the AAA is guided by the nature of the dispute.

2. Parties are allowed seven days to study the list, to cross off objectionable names, and to number the remaining names in the order of preference. Additional information about the proposed arbitrators is available through the administrator. It is up to each party to investigate the people being suggested.

3. When the lists are returned, the tribunal administrator compares indicated preferences and notes the mutual choices. Where no mutually acceptable choice remains on a list, additional lists may be submitted at the request of both parties. If either party thinks that the wrong category of arbitrator is being listed, the matter should be discussed with the tribunal administrator.

4. If, despite efforts to arrive at a mutual choice, parties cannot agree upon an arbitrator, the AAA will make administrative appointments. No arbitrator whose name was crossed off by either party will be appointed.

STEP THREE: PREPARATION FOR THE HEARING

After the arbitrator is appointed, the tribunal administrator consults the parties in order to schedule a mutually convenient day and time for the hearing. This information is shared with the arbitrator, who makes the date official. The tribunal administrator manages the arrangements for the hearing, relieving the arbitrator of that burden and eliminating the necessity for direct communication between either party and the arbitrator except at the hearing. By discouraging communication with the arbitrator, except in the presence of both parties, there is no opportunity for one side to offer arguments or evidence that the other has no opportunity to rebut.

Because the arbitrator must reach a decision on the basis of the evidence presented at the hearing, it is essential that the parties and their attorneys carefully prepare their case. Here are a few practical suggestions.

1. Assemble all documents and papers you will need at the hearing. Make copies for the arbitrators and the other party. If some of the documents you need are

in the possession of the other party, ask that they be brought to the hearing. A checklist of your own documents and exhibits will be helpful in assuring an orderly presentation. Under some state arbitration laws, the arbitrator has authority to subpoena documents and witnesses.

2. Interview all of your witnesses. Make certain the witnesses understand the whole case and the importance of their testimony. Coordinate their testimony so that your case will seem consistent and credible. Prepare your witnesses for cross-examination. If one of your witnesses requires a translator, make arrangements in advance.

3. If there is a possibility that additional witnesses, not on your regular list, may have to appear, alert them to be available and on call.

4. Make a written summary of what each witness will prove. This will be useful as a checklist at the hearing and will help ensure that nothing is overlooked.

5. Study the case from the other side's point of view. Be prepared to answer the opposition's evidence.

6. If it will be necessary for the arbitrator to visit a building site or warehouse for an inspection, make plans in advance. The arbitrator must be accompanied by representatives of both parties, unless specifically authorized by the parties to conduct the investigation without them present.

7. If a transcript of the testimony is needed, the parties requesting such transcript should make arrangements directly with the recording agency. The expense is borne by the parties requesting the service.

In large and complex cases, the arbitrators may arrange for a prehearing conference to establish the extent of and schedule for the production of documents, to identify witnesses, and set a schedule for additional hearings.

STEP FOUR: PRESENTATION OF THE CASE

Arbitration hearings are less formal than court trials. The parties and their attorneys sit on opposite sides of a conference table. Arbitrators are expected to hear all the evidence that is relevant to the issue. Because they must determine for themselves what is relevant, arbitrators are inclined to accept evidence that might not be allowed by judges. This does not mean, however, that all evidence is of equal weight or that irrelevant or repetitious evidence will not be rejected by the arbitrator. Arbitrators are not required to follow courtroom rules of evidence. In fact, an arbitrator may become impatient with a party that keeps making technical objections.

You should bear in mind that direct testimony of witnesses tends to be more persuasive than hearsay evidence, and that facts may be better established by testimony and exhibits than by mere argument. Documentary evidence is often an essential part of any case. Most important is the contractual agreement itself, or the sections that have some bearing on the dispute. Documentary evidence may also include records of transactions between the parties, memoranda or correspondence, official minutes of meetings, medical reports, and progress-of-work reports. Every piece of documentary evidence should be properly identified and its authenticity established. The material should be physically presented to the arbitrator, and a copy made available to the other side. In many instances, key words, phrases, and sections of written documents can be underlined to focus the arbitrator's attention on the essential part. Properly presented documentary evidence can be most persuasive and merits careful handling.

Each party should depend on direct examination of witnesses for presentation of facts. After being identified and qualified as an authority on the facts, the witness should be allowed to testify largely without interruption. Although leading questions may be permitted in arbitration, testimony is more effective when the witness relates facts from knowledge. Questions from counsel may be useful in emphasizing the points being made or in keeping a witness "on the track."

Every witness is subject to cross-examination. Among the purposes of cross-examination are to bring out facts the witnesses may not have disclosed in direct testimony; to correct misstatements; to place facts in their true perspective; to reconcile apparent contradictions; and to attack the reliability and credibility of witnesses. In planning cross-examination, the objective to be achieved should be kept in mind. Each witness represents a different challenge. Cross-examination should sometimes be waived.

EVIDENCE AND PROOF

The arbitrator must provide a fair hearing, giving both parties sufficient opportunity to present their respective evidence and arguments. The AAA rules provide that "the arbitrator shall be the judge of the relevancy and materiality of the evidence offered and conformity to legal rules of evidence shall not be necessary" (except where statutes or an arbitration agreement otherwise provide).

There are many reasons why technical evidentiary rules are not suitable in arbitration. First, arbitration is intended to be an informal procedure. Second, the rules of evidence are essentially rules of exclusion. They were developed to prevent a jury from hearing or considering prejudicial or unreliable testimony and exhibits. In arbitration, however, a sophisticated person, selected by the parties for technical knowledge and good judgment, hears the case; such a person should be able to disregard evidence that is not helpful, relevant, or reliable. Third, there may be a therapeutic value in allowing the parties to vent their feelings, or to "get things off their chests," even if the testimony has little probative value.

An award will not be overturned because of a liberal admission of evidence as long as the arbitrator does not base the award on obviously irrelevant or erroneous evidence. On the other hand, refusal to hear relevant evidence may constitute grounds for vacating the award.

To say that conformity to the legal rules of evidence is not necessary does not mean that the lawyers are foreclosed from referring to them. The AAA rules recognize that arbitrators must make judgments about materiality and relevance and should not allow or consider obviously immaterial, irrelevant, or redundant testimony. The rules of evidence may help the arbitrator to decide such issues. Even if questionable evidence is admitted, an explanation of the legal rules of evidence may assist the arbitrator in deciding how much weight it should be given. For example, pointing up the likelihood of errors in hearsay evidence may warn the arbitrator not to place too much reliance upon it. The careful party will urge the arbitrator to guard against the unreliability of certain evidence.

The arbitrator has a duty to not allow testimony to stray too far afield and not to be influenced by prejudicial or unreliable testimony. The rules of evidence, flexibly applied, can assist the arbitrator in meeting this obligation. The general rule is to hear evidence that will help clarify the issues and to reach a resolution of the dispute. Even though arbitrators admit evidence or testimony over the objection of a party, they may be skeptical as to its probative value. The arbitrator can use the technical rules of evidence as aids or guidelines to help weigh the value of the evidence offered. In weighing such evidence, an arbitrator should be aware of the following concepts:

1. **Direct Evidence**–Evidence that directly proves a fact, without an inference or presumption. If true, such evidence establishes that fact. Direct evidence from one witness may be sufficient for proof of any fact.

2. **Circumstantial Evidence**–Evidence that tends to establish the "principal fact" by proving other facts from which the principal fact can be inferred. The inference is founded on experience and observed facts, establishing a connection between the proved facts and the fact to be proved.

3. **Relevant and Material Evidence**–Evidence is relevant if it reasonably tends to prove or disprove the fact at issue. Evidence is material if it will influence the decision of the case.

4. **Best Evidence**–Primary evidence as distinguished from secondary; original as distinguished from copies. Best evidence favors the presentation of original documents instead of copies.

5. Hearsay Evidence–Hearsay is second-hand evidence. It is testimony of a statement made by someone other than the witness, repeated at the hearing to show the truth of the matters contained in it. The reliability of a statement rests upon the believability of the person who made the statement. Courts tend to exclude hearsay evidence because of the risk of inaccuracy in the repetition of the story and because there is no opportunity to cross-examine the person making the original statement. There are numerous exceptions to the hearsay rule. Records kept in the ordinary course of business are one such exception. The arbitrator may give hearsay little weight where the opposing party presents contradictory evidence that is subject to cross-examination. An affidavit is a type of hearsay evidence that is explicitly authorized by AAA rules. The rules caution that the arbitrator shall give an affidavit "only such weight as the Arbitrator deems it entitled to after consideration of any objections made to its admission."

6. Parol Evidence–Testimony that seeks to explain the meaning of the contract. When a contract is expressed in language that is intended to be the complete and final expression of the rights and duties of the parties, no evidence, oral or written, of prior understandings or negotiations is admissible to contradict or vary the terms of the agreement.

7. Opinion Evidence–Evidence of what the witness thinks about the facts in dispute, as distinguished from personal knowledge of the facts, is generally not admissible in court except where the witness is an expert in the field. The importance of opinion evidence depends on whether the opinion deals with a crucial issue in the case. When a witness is asked an opinion about an important issue and the other party objects, the arbitrator will rule on admissibility. Generally, an arbitrator will allow opinions but will limit the weight given to them according to the qualifications of the witness who expressed them. On the other hand, an arbitrator may bar a witness who is not an expert from giving an opinion on the ultimate question to be decided. Greater latitude is given in arbitration because the arbitrator is likely to be an experienced person, with special knowledge, who will not be unduly influenced by the opinions or conclusions of witnesses.

8. Inference–A deduction of fact that may logically and reasonably be drawn from another fact or group of facts found or otherwise established in the matter. An inference is the result of reasoning based upon evidence.

9. Presumption–When a certain group of facts leads to a certain conclusion, the arbitrator may make a presumption.

10. Cumulative Evidence—A repetition of evidence that has been testified to previously. Evidence is not cumulative merely because it tends to establish the same ultimate fact. Cumulative evidence is additional evidence of the same kind to prove the same point. In order to conduct an orderly and expeditious hearing, an arbitrator may limit evidence that is repetitive and cumulative in nature. Generally, the arbitrator will encourage the attorney to move forward with the case.

11. Burden of Proof—There is no "burden of proof" in business arbitration. A party proves a case by providing sufficient evidence to convince the arbitrator on the relevant issues. Each party is expected to prove its case, and if the evidence does not support one of the claims submitted to arbitration, the arbitrator will simply deny that claim.

12. Leading Question—A question worded so that it suggests to the witness the desired answer, or where there is merely a yes or no answer. The danger of leading questions is that the questioner, not the witness, is testifying. Leading questions may be time saving in preliminary matters, matters that are not in dispute, or when asked during cross-examination. Leading questions about a basic matter asked of a witness, however, are improper, may be objectionable, and may be stopped by the arbitrator.

13. Objections—In arbitration, a party makes objections in order to exclude a particular question, to modify the form or manner of questioning taking place, to change momentum, or to calm a witness who is testifying on cross-examination. An objection can also warn the arbitrator about the weakness of the proffered material.

DUTY OF ARBITRATOR TO DISCLOSE

The arbitrator should have no interest, financial or otherwise, in the outcome of the case.

It is not unusual for an arbitrator, on being asked to serve, to discover some prior or present business connection with one of the parties. The Commercial Arbitration Rules require that neutral arbitrators ". . . disclose to the AAA any circumstances likely to affect impartiality, including any bias or any financial or personal interest in the result of the arbitration or any past or present relationship with the parties or their counsel."

If the contact was so close as to be disqualifying, the arbitrator should decline to serve. When the parties cannot agree as to the seriousness of challenges, the AAA has the authority to determine whether the arbitrator shall be disqualified.

Not every business relationship will cast doubt upon the impartiality of the award. In some situations, it will be enough for the arbitrator to disclose the connection before accepting the appointment.

When the parties and their witnesses assemble in the hearing room, the arbitrator may recall for the first time a past association with a person involved. Prompt disclosure at this time gives the parties an opportunity to waive their objections. Such a waiver will bar any subsequent objection to the award on the grounds of bias.

THE POWER OF THE ARBITRATOR

An arbitrator is given substantial authority by the parties and by the law. Some of these powers are procedural: the right to issue subpoenas, to fix the date of hearing, to grant postponements (either at the request of a party or on the arbitrator's own initiative), or to proceed with the hearing in the absence of a party who fails to appear after being notified. *Ex parte* awards can be enforced under federal and state laws as long as the agreement to arbitrate demonstrates the intent to allow such awards. If a contract specifies rules that permit hearings in the absence of a party, the resultant award will be valid and enforceable.

The arbitrator's authority is derived from the agreement of the parties and from the law. The authority to hear and decide any particular case exists only through the agreement of the parties to the dispute. The arbitrator must conform to standards of justice as expressed in both statutes and common law. These include an obligation to attend all of the hearings, to listen to pertinent and material evidence, and to disclose any relationship with the parties. The arbitrator should be impartial in fact and in appearance. *It is particularly important that an arbitrator avoid any direct contact with the parties except at the hearing.*

At the hearing, the arbitrator should be fair to both parties. The adversaries will argue energetically for what they believe to be their rights. A vigorous tone, a strong objection to the arbitrator's acceptance of some evidence that may be damaging, an attempt by the claimant to increase the scope of the arbitrator's authority, and the resistance of the responding party to that attempt–all these must be expected in arbitration. They are essential elements in the adversary process.

As a rule, arbitrators have no difficulty in maintaining order. An occasional emotional outburst or attempt to interrupt a witness during direct examination can be handled by the arbitrator with a reminder that the witness can be cross-examined later or that across-the-table bickering serves no useful purpose. Experienced arbitrators know that sometimes it is useful for the parties to "blow off steam"; they find that the disputants are then likely to settle down and proceed in an orderly fashion.

It is very important that arbitrators not give any indication about how they will decide the case. They should not comment on the evidence or indicate their feelings about the merits of the case. They should also avoid excessive cordiality with one of the attorneys or parties while the hearings are in progress.

The arbitrator is in charge of the hearing. The arbitrator should understand that evidence must be taken in the presence of the parties. The parties and their attorneys have the right to be present at all times. The arbitrator may permit others to attend, with due regard for the parties' right of privacy. Arbitrators may also require a witness to leave the hearing room during the testimony of other witnesses.

When the arbitrator is an expert and when the issue turns on an expert's judgment, it may seem logical for the arbitrator to resolve the matter by an examination. No difficulties are encountered when such an examination can be conducted in the hearing room with both parties present. When it is necessary to make an on-site inspection, the arbitrator should do so only with the knowledge of both parties, who have the right to accompany the arbitrator.

The arbitrator has broad powers to determine matters of fact and law as well as procedure. This authority must be exercised by the arbitrator alone, however; it may not be delegated to others. For example, the arbitrator should not seek clarification of a point of law by consulting an outside attorney. When some question of fact requires the services of an outside expert, such as a testing company or public accountants, the parties must give their permission. Parties may allow the arbitrator to engage such help, since this is not a delegation of authority. The ultimate decision still rests with the arbitrator. The arbitrator is not bound by the findings of any outside agency.

During the hearing, the parties or their lawyers may see an opportunity for settlement. They may ask for an adjournment to carry out further negotiations. The arbitrator should encourage such discussions but should take no part in them. It is permissible for the arbitrator to incorporate such a settlement in the award.

ELIMINATING DELAYS IN COMMERCIAL ARBITRATION

Arbitration is not always expeditious, but there are common reasons for delays. One or both of the attorneys may not be interested in obtaining a prompt hearing. In some situations, it may appear that neither wants the matter processed with diligence.

A respondent against whom a money award is being claimed may resist arbitration, hoping to stave off the award. Inserting special language in the arbitration clause may increase a respondent's willingness to cooperate. For example, an escrow fund may be created so that the money in issue will be withdrawn from the operating funds of the respondent, pending the outcome. The deposit would be placed in an interest-bearing account subject to the arbitrator's award. Both parties may be more eager to reach a conclusion if the fund has been placed out of their grasp during the pendency of the arbitration.

Other sources of delay have also been identified. It may be difficult to obtain mutual acceptance of neutral arbitrators familiar with the trade practices in the industry but not closely identified with either party or their attorneys. Multiple disclosures and challenges to arbitrators may take a great deal of preliminary time before a panel of acceptable, impartial arbitrators can be appointed. Discovery procedures can be an impediment, causing unnecessary delay before the attorneys are ready for their hearing. Discovery procedures are not customary in arbitration but can be arranged by the parties.

The professional staff of the American Arbitration Association can help to expedite commercial arbitration cases. The AAA will schedule a prearbitration conference with the attorneys, in an effort to streamline the hearing procedure. It may be possible to avoid any need for discovery by encouraging stipulations as to the facts or by obtaining an agreement about how evidence will be presented. In addition, parties will frequently exchange documents prior to the hearing. Prehearing conferences may also lead to negotiated settlements.

Expedited procedures are also available under the AAA's Commercial Arbitration Rules. These procedures can eliminate delays in arbitration by allowing notice by telephone, facilitating the arbitrator selection process, and by reducing the time for making the award.

MEDIATION

Prior to submitting the matter to arbitration, the parties may wish to make one final attempt at mediation. Each of the AAA's regional centers maintains a list of experienced mediators who can schedule an initial meeting with the parties to ascertain whether mediation would be productive. Using the AAA mediation rules, such a meeting can take place promptly without delaying the initial steps of appointing an arbitrator and scheduling a hearing.

DISPOSING OF PAPERWORK

Expense can be avoided if the parties reduce the amount of paperwork. Transcripts and briefs can be eliminated if the parties and their attorneys are willing to do so. In general, the AAA encourages parties to streamline their procedures. Purchasing an official transcript can be particularly expensive. In arbitration, transcripts are often a waste of money. In most cases, the arbitrator and the attorneys rely upon their own notes.

CONTROL OF SCHEDULING

In complex commercial arbitration cases, it may be difficult to schedule blocks of time when the arbitrators and the lawyers will be available. At the prearbitration conference, an effort should be made to arrange such dates. The parties should determine whether the arbitrator can devote sufficient consecutive time for hearing the case. Arbitration cases can advance rapidly if both the parties and the arbitrators will commit themselves to such a schedule. The AAA encourages the participants to begin a hearing promptly, to take a minimum lunch period, and to continue the hearing as long as possible in the afternoon.

In lengthy cases, there is some risk that an arbitrator may be called away or become disabled. Or an arbitrator may be challenged because of an undisclosed relationship with one of the parties. Under the law, it may be necessary to replace the arbitrator and reschedule hearings. Once a panel of arbitrators has been selected, the parties should conclude their case as quickly as possible.

Parties who include arbitration clauses in their contract should encourage their counsel to move expeditiously. The AAA can bring some pressures to bear. Arbitrators are told that an important part of their responsibility is to expedite the process by keeping pressure on the advocates. The tribunal administrator does everything possible to persuade attorneys to honor their scheduled hearings. A fee is imposed for postponing a hearing. Ultimately, the speed and efficiency of the arbitration process rests largely in the hands of the parties. It is necessary for the parties and their attorneys to exercise restraint in not seeking to delay arbitration.

THE HEARING PROCEDURE

The moving party ordinarily proceeds first with its case, followed by the respondent. This order may be varied, however, when the arbitrator thinks it appropriate. The "burden of proof" is not on one side more than on the other. Each party must try to convince the arbitrator of the correctness of its position. No hearing is closed until both parties have had an opportunity to present their full case. Do not allow yourself to be rushed. If you are participating in an arbitration for the first time, you should proceed carefully, asking for time to present your case.

Parties should present their case to the arbitrator in an orderly and logical manner. This usually includes the following steps:

1. An opening statement that briefly describes the controversy and indicates

what is to be proved. Such a statement helps the arbitrator understand the relevance of testimony to be presented.

2. A discussion of the remedy sought. This is important because the arbitrator's remedial power is conferred by the agreement of the parties. Each party should try to show that the relief it wants can be granted within the arbitrator's authority.

3. An orderly introduction of witnesses to clarify the nature of the controversy and to identify relevant documents and exhibits. Cross-examination of witnesses can be revealing, but each party should plan to establish its own case through the direct testimony of its own witnesses.

4. A closing statement, which should include a summary of evidence and arguments and a refutation of points made by the opposition. The arbitrator will give both sides equal time for a closing statement. This occasion should be used to summarize the relevant facts and to emphasize the issue and the decision the arbitrator is being asked to make.

Because arbitration is somewhat informal, statements may be permitted during all phases of the hearing. There may be times, however, when the arbitrator will ask parties to concentrate on presenting evidence, putting off arguments until later. In either event, all arguments should be stated fully. Above all, the presentation should be accurate and credible. Exaggeration, concealing of facts, introduction of legal technicalities with the object of delaying the proceedings, or general disregard of ordinary rules of courtesy and decorum are likely to have an adverse effect upon the arbitrators.

After both sides have had an equal opportunity to present their evidence, the arbitrator will declare the hearing closed. Under AAA rules, the arbitrator then has thirty days within which to render the award, unless the agreement provides otherwise.

THE ARBITRATION AWARD

The award is the arbitrator's decision on the matters submitted for consideration. In general, it will completely resolve the dispute. Each party has agreed beforehand to abide by the decision. Most responsible parties comply with arbitration awards. The purpose of the award is to dispose of the issues, finally and conclusively. The award must be made within the time limits of the arbitration agreement, and it should decide each claim submitted. The award should be the "end of the road."

Some judges might like to review arbitrators' awards, particularly as to legal issues. That is not possible under the American system. By referring the issues to an arbitrator, the parties have agreed to a final and nonreviewable award. Final arbitration is not compatible with judicial review. An occasional mistake by an arbitrator, left uncorrected by the courts, is the price that must be paid for a healthy system of binding arbitration.

Most arbitration systems provide for *binding* arbitration. Many parties might be unwilling to use arbitration without assurance that the decision would be final. Review of awards by a court would be contrary to the parties' expectations. Arbitration laws support this concept by providing very limited grounds for overturning an arbitration award.

Arbitrators are not required to write opinions explaining the reasons for their decisions. As a general rule, AAA commercial awards consist of a brief direction to the parties on a single sheet of paper. Written opinions can be dangerous because they identify targets for the losing party to attack.

One judge offered the following instruction to arbitrators:

> The thing we must look at is the face of the award itself, and see whether it is in excess of the powers of the arbitrator. . . . Although technical precision is not required in an award of arbitrators, I would urgently suggest that arbitrators follow the form of award provided by the American Arbitration Association. In the event they feel impelled by some uncontrollable urge, literary fluency, good conscience, or mere garrulousness to express themselves about a case they have tried, the opinion should be a separate document and not part of the award itself.

The AAA does not encourage such opinions. In some cases, both parties will request an opinion. Then the AAA has no objection. Usually, however, the parties look to an arbitrator for a decision, not an explanation.

The arbitrator has no duty to inform the parties about the arbitration award. Instead, the AAA delivers copies of the award to the parties. Once the arbitrators have signed the award, they have no further connection with the case. They should not become involved in any court actions that may follow. In fact, the arbitrators should not discuss the award or respond to a request for clarification unless requested to do so by both parties or where there is a statutory provision to that effect. The arbitrators' obligation to maintain confidence about the affairs of the parties continues indefinitely.

WHAT TO DO AFTER THE AWARD

If the award is in your favor, you should celebrate. Then, ask your adversary to comply with the award. If the losing party voluntarily performs pursuant to the terms of the award, it is not necessary to seek any confirmation. In cases of noncompliance, the winning party may move for a judgment confirming the award. Usually, the losing party will comply. Where the prevailing party requires judicial sanctions, the award will almost always be confirmed.

If the award is not in your favor and you think that it can be vacated in court, you can move for vacatur of the award. There are three general categories under which awards may be vacated: (1) arbitrator misconduct, such as corruption, fraud, or bias, (2) a showing that the arbitrators exceeded their authority, or (3) the failure to meet statutory requirements of due process. Included within the latter category are awards that contravene public policy.

Judicial review concerns itself only with defects in the arbitration procedure, not with the sufficiency of the evidence or the merits of the case. Arbitration laws draw narrow limits around the court's authority to review awards. The New York State law is typical, providing the following grounds for vacating an award:

> 1. The award shall be vacated . . . if the court finds that the rights of that party were prejudiced by:
>   - (i) corruption, fraud or misconduct in procuring the award; or
>   - (ii) partiality of an arbitrator appointed as a neutral, except where the award was by confession; or
>   - (iii) an arbitrator, or agency or person making the award exceeded his power or so imperfectly executed it that a final and definite award upon the subject matter submitted was not made; or
>   - (iv) failure to follow the procedure of this article, unless the party applying to vacate the award continued with the arbitration with notice of the defect and without objection.
> 2. The award shall be vacated . . . if the court finds that:
>   - (i) the rights of that party were prejudiced by one of the grounds specified in paragraph one; or
>   - (ii) a valid agreement to arbitrate was not made; or
>   - (iii) the agreement to arbitrate had not been complied with; or
>   - (iv) the arbitrated claim was barred by [the statute of limitations].

The New York State law also provides grounds for modifying an award. The court shall modify the award if:

> 1. there was a miscalculation of figures or a mistake in the description of any person, thing or property referred to in the award; or
> 2. the arbitrators have awarded upon a matter not submitted to them and the award may be corrected without affecting the merits of the decision upon the issues submitted; or
> 3. the award is imperfect in a matter of form, not affecting the merits of the controversy.

These narrow statutory grounds result in relatively few motions to vacate or modify arbitration awards. The laws in other states are similar, providing few opportunities to overturn arbitrators' awards.

> Where the merits of a controversy are referred to an arbitrator selected by the parties, his determination either as to law or the facts is final and conclusive, and a court will not open an award unless perverse misconstruction or positive misconduct upon the part of the arbitrator is plainly established, or there is some provision authorizing it. The award of an arbitrator cannot be set aside for mere errors of judgment, either as to the law or as to the facts. [*Matter of Wilkens*, 169 N.Y. 494, 62 N.E. 575]

Because commercial arbitrators do not write opinions explaining the reasons for their decisions, it may be difficult to determine whether an arbitrator has exceeded his or her powers. An undisclosed error of judgment is virtually immune from attack.

It is sometimes said that arbitrators are not bound by the law in reaching their decisions. This is misleading. Commercial arbitrators are carefully briefed by each opposing lawyer as to the applicable law. At the same time, attorneys argue the equitable and practical considerations that should be weighed by the arbitrator. It is improper for an arbitrator to refuse to listen to any pertinent arguments raised by either counsel. The arbitrator should carefully consider the legal arguments, even though not required to make findings on legal issues.

Many commercial arbitrators are business people who regard their service as a contribution to their industry or to society. They are not professional arbitrators. They are community leaders who are donating their time and their wisdom to their fellow citizens. If these arbitrators were required to produce comprehensive findings of fact and conclusions of law, the role of the commercial arbitrator would be changed considerably. These kinds of people will continue to participate in the process, making their services available, if courts continue to exercise restraint in reviewing awards. The privilege of arbitration, the right to design whatever system the parties prefer, is fragile. It could be destroyed if courts demanded the right to review the substance of arbitrators' awards.

After the award has been issued, the power of the arbitrator ends. The arbitrator has no further authority to modify an award, unless the parties mutually agree to reopen the proceeding and to restore his or her power. The arbitrator is *functus officio* (having no further power or authority to act in the matter). In cases where the parties agree to seek further clarification of an award or an interpretation of a disputed ruling, this agreement must be in writing. Such a request should be filed with the AAA, which then makes the necessary arrangements with the arbitrator. These petitions are rare, and if the arbitrator refuses to explain the award, the parties have no further recourse.

PARTY-APPOINTED ARBITRATION—THE DRAWBACKS

Under some arbitration clauses, each party agrees to appoint one arbitrator: these two arbitrators then select a third member of the panel. This system is a holdover from the days when administrative agencies for arbitration were not available. There are many problems with such a scheme. For example, it is not clear whether the party-appointed arbitrator is expected to be impartial. In addition, the system creates impasses because either party can refuse to proceed. The moving party must then resort to the courts. Another problem is that a compromise award may be rendered by the neutral arbitrator for the sake of obtaining a majority. When parties discover that party-appointed arbitration has been designated in their agreement, they sometimes authorize the third arbitrator to make the decision. Because of the obvious weaknesses in the party-appointed system, it seems to be dying out.

In New Jersey, the courts have held that even a party-appointed arbitrator is required to disclose any relationships with that party that might create an appearance of bias. In one case, a party-appointed arbitrator failed to report such a connection and the award was vacated.

In general, parties are well advised to avoid the party-appointed system, using a single neutral arbitrator or a totally neutral panel.

CONCLUSION

Business executives are losing patience with judicial solutions that take years to achieve results and that leave both parties exhausted by delays and legal expenses. Many people like what alternative dispute resolution can offer. They are finding that commercial arbitration and mediation are sensible ways to resolve business disputes.

The following chapters and collected materials inform the reader about some of the specialized business dispute resolution systems. Landmark law cases on commercial arbitration are summarized. Various procedural rules and the Code of Ethics are printed in full. And bibliographies describe the books and articles that you will want to examine to qualify yourself further in this rapidly expanding field.

Alternative dispute resolution is built on the belief that business people can profit by a simple and understandable system for obtaining impartial decisions. Arbitration has maintained its purpose and vitality, despite the court decisions that sometimes complicate the process. You can still face your opponent across a table and present your case to an arbitrator. The essence of commercial arbitration survives!

COMMERCIAL ARBITRATION RULES

As Amended and in Effect April 1, 1985

1. **Agreement of Parties**—The parties shall be deemed to have made these Rules a part of their arbitration agreement whenever they have provided for arbitration by the American Arbitration Association or under its Rules. These Rules and any amendment thereof shall apply in the form obtaining at the time the arbitration is initiated.

2. **Name of Tribunal**—Any Tribunal constituted by the parties for the settlement of their dispute under these Rules shall be called the Commercial Arbitration Tribunal.

3. **Administrator**—When parties agree to arbitrate under these Rules, or when they provide for arbitration by the American Arbitration Association and an arbitration is initiated thereunder, they thereby constitute AAA the administrator of the arbitration. The authority and obligations of the administrator are prescribed in the agreement of the parties and in these Rules.

4. **Delegation of Duties**—The duties of the AAA under these Rules may be carried out through Tribunal Administrators, or such other officers or committees as the AAA may direct.

5. **National Panel of Arbitrators**—The AAA shall establish and maintain a National Panel of Arbitrators and shall appoint Arbitrators therefrom as hereinafter provided.

6. **Office of Tribunal**—The general office of a Tribunal is the headquarters of the AAA, which may, however, assign the administration of an arbitration to any of its Regional Offices.

7. **Initiation under an Arbitration Provision in a Contract**—Arbitration under an arbitration provision in a contract may be initiated in the following manner:

(a) The initiating party shall give notice to the other party of its intention to arbitrate (Demand), which notice shall contain a statement setting forth the nature of the dispute, the amount involved, if any, the remedy sought, and

(b) By filing at any Regional Office of the AAA three copies of said notice, together with three copies of the arbitration provisions of the contract, together with the appropriate administrative fee as provided in the Administrative Fee Schedule. The AAA shall give notice of such filing to the other party. If so desired, the party upon whom the Demand for Arbitration is made may file an answering statement in duplicate with the AAA within seven days after notice from the AAA, in which event said party shall simultaneously send a copy of the answer to the other party. If a counterclaim is asserted it shall contain a statement setting forth the nature of the counterclaim, the amount involved, if any, and the remedy sought. If a monetary claim is made in the answer the appropriate fee provided in the Fee Schedule shall be forwarded to the AAA with the answer. If no answer is filed within the stated time, it will be assumed that the claim is denied. Failure to file an answer shall not operate to delay the arbitration.

Unless the AAA in its discretion determines otherwise, the Expedited Procedures of Commercial Arbitration shall be applied in any case where the total claim of any party does not exceed $15,000, exclusive of interest and arbitration costs. The Expedited Procedures shall be applied as described in Section 54 through 58 of these Rules.

8. Change of Claim–After filing of the claim, if either party desires to make any new or different claim, such claim shall be made in writing and filed with the AAA, and a copy thereof shall be mailed to the other party, who shall have a period of seven days from the date of such mailing within which to file an answer with the AAA. After the Arbitrator is appointed, however, no new or different claim may be submitted except with the Arbitrator's consent.

9. Initiation under a Submission–Parties to any existing dispute may commence an arbitration under these Rules by filing at any Regional Office two copies of a written agreement to arbitrate under these Rules (Submission), signed by the parties. It shall contain a statement of the matter in dispute, the amount of money involved, if any, and the remedy sought, together with the appropriate administrative fee as provided in the Fee Schedule.

10. Pre-Hearing Conference–At the request of the parties or at the discretion of the AAA a pre-hearing conference with the administrator and the parties or their counsel will be scheduled in appropriate cases to arrange for an exchange of information and the stipulation of uncontested facts so as to expedite the arbitration proceedings.

11. Fixing of Locale–The parties may mutually agree on the locale where the arbitration is to be held. If the locale is not designated within seven days from the date of filing the Demand or Submission, the AAA shall have power to determine the locale. Its decision shall be final and binding. If any party requests that the hearing be held in a specific locale and the other party files no objection thereto within seven days after notice of the request, the locale shall be the one requested.

12. Qualifications of Arbitrator–Any Arbitrator appointed pursuant to Section 13 or Section 15 shall be neutral, subject to disqualification for the reasons specified in Section 19. If the agreement of the parties names an Arbitrator or specifies any other method of appointing an Arbitrator, or if the parties specifically agree in writing, such Arbitrator shall not be subject to disqualification for said reasons.

13. Appointment from Panel–If the parties have not appointed an Arbitrator and have not provided any other method of appointment, the Arbitrator shall be appointed in the following manner: Immediately after the filing of the Demand or Submission, the AAA shall submit simultaneously to each party to the dispute an identical list of names of persons chosen from the Panel. Each party to the dispute shall have seven days from the mailing date in which to cross off any names objected to, number the remaining names to indicate the order of preference, and return the list to the AAA. If a party does not return the list within the time specified, all persons named therein shall be deemed acceptable. From among the persons who have been approved on both lists, and in accordance with the designated order of mutual preference, the AAA shall invite the acceptance of an Arbitrator to serve. If the parties fail to agree upon any of the persons named, or if acceptable Arbitrators are unable to act, or if for any other reason the appointment cannot be made from the submitted lists, the AAA shall have the power to make the appointment from among other members of the Panel without the submission of any additional list.

14. Direct Appointment by Parties–If the agreement of the parties names an Arbitrator or specifies a method of appointing an Arbitrator, that designation or method shall be followed. The notice of appointment, with name and address of the appointing party, shall be filed with the AAA by the appointing party. Upon the request of any such appointing party, the AAA shall submit a list of members of the Panel from which the party may, if it so desires, make the appointment.

If the agreement specifies a period of time within which an Arbitrator shall be appointed, and any party fails to make such appointment within that period, the AAA shall make the appointment.

If no period of time is specified in the agreement, the AAA shall notify the parties to make the appointment and if within seven days thereafter such Arbitrator has not been so appointed, the AAA shall make the appointment.

15. Appointment of Neutral Arbitrator by Party-Appointed Arbitrators—If the parties have appointed their Arbitrators or if either or both of them have been appointed as provided in Section 14, and have authorized such Arbitrators to appoint a neutral Arbitrator within a specified time and no appointment is made within such time or any agreed extension thereof, the AAA shall appoint a neutral Arbitrator who shall act as Chairman.

If no period of time is specified for appointment of the neutral Arbitrator and the parties do not make the appointment within seven days from the date of the appointment of the last party-appointed Arbitrator, the AAA shall appoint such neutral Arbitrator, who shall act as Chairman.

If the parties have agreed that their Arbitrators shall appoint the neutral Arbitrator from the Panel, the AAA shall furnish to the party-appointed Arbitrators, in the manner prescribed in Section 13, a list selected from the Panel, and the appointment of the neutral Arbitrator shall be made as prescribed in such Section.

16. Nationality of Arbitrator in International Arbitration—If one of the parties is a national or resident of a country other than the United States, the sole Arbitrator or the neutral Arbitrator shall, upon the request of either party, be appointed from among the nationals of a country other than that of any of the parties.

17. Number of Arbitrators—If the arbitration agreement does not specify the number of Arbitrators, the dispute shall be heard and determined by one Arbitrator, unless the AAA, in its discretion, directs that a greater number of Arbitrators be appointed.

18. Notice to Arbitrator of Appointment—Notice of the appointment of the neutral Arbitrator, whether appointed by the parties or by the AAA, shall be mailed to the Arbitrator by the AAA, together with a copy of these Rules, and the signed acceptance of the Arbitrator shall be filed prior to the opening of the first hearing.

19. Disclosure and Challenge Procedure—A person appointed as neutral Arbitrator shall disclose to the AAA any circumstances likely to affect impartiality, including any bias or any financial or personal interest in the result of the arbitration or any past or present relationship with the parties or their counsel. Upon receipt of such information from such Arbitrator or other source, the AAA shall communicate such information to the parties, and, if it deems it appropriate to do so, to the Arbitrator and others. Thereafter, the AAA shall determine whether the Arbitrator should be disqualified and shall inform the parties of its decision, which shall be conclusive.

20. Vacancies—If any Arbitrator should resign, die, withdraw, refuse, be disqualified or be unable to perform the duties of the office, the AAA may, on proof satisfactory to it, declare the office vacant. Vacancies shall be filled in accordance with the applicable provisions of these Rules.

In the event of a vacancy in a panel of neutral Arbitrators, the remaining Arbitrator or Arbitrators may continue with the hearing and determination of the controversy, unless the parties agree otherwise.

21. Time and Place–The Arbitrator shall fix the time and place for each hearing. The AAA shall mail to each party notice thereof at least five days in advance, unless the parties by mutual agreement waive such notice or modify the terms thereof.

22. Representation by Counsel–Any party may be represented by counsel. A party intending to be so represented shall notify the other party and the AAA of the name and address of counsel at least three days prior to the date set for the hearing at which counsel is first to appear. When an arbitration is initiated by counsel, or where an attorney replies for the other party, such notice is deemed to have been given.

23. Stenographic Record–Any party wishing a stenographic record shall make such arrangements directly with the stenographer and shall notify the other parties of such arrangements in advance of the hearing. The requesting party or parties shall pay the costs of such record.

24. Interpreter–Any party wishing an interpreter shall make all arrangements directly with an interpreter and shall assume the costs of such service.

25. Attendance at Hearings–The Arbitrator shall maintain the privacy of the hearings unless the law provides to the contrary. Any person having a direct interest in the arbitration is entitled to attend hearings. The Arbitrator shall otherwise have the power to require the exclusion of any witness, other than a party or other essential person, during the testimony of any other witness. It shall be discretionary with the Arbitrator to determine the propriety of the attendance of any other person.

26. Adjournments–The Arbitrator may take adjournments upon the request of a party or upon the Arbitrator's own initiative and shall take such adjournment when all of the parties agree thereto.

27. Oaths–Before proceeding with the first hearing or with the examination of the file, each Arbitrator may take an oath of office, and if required by law, shall do so. The Arbitrator has discretion to require witnesses to testify under oath administered by any duly qualified person or, if required by law or demanded by either party, shall do so.

28. Majority Decision–Whenever there is more than one Arbitrator, all decisions of the Arbitrators must be by at least a majority. The award must also be made by at least a majority unless the concurrence of all is expressly required by the arbitration agreement or by law.

29. Order of Proceedings–A hearing shall be opened by the filing of the oath of the Arbitrator, where required, and by the recording of the place, time and date of the hearing, the presence of the Arbitrator and parties, and counsel, if any, and by the receipt by the Arbitrator of the statement of the claim and answer, if any.

The Arbitrator may, at the beginning of the hearing, ask for statements clarifying the issues involved.

The complaining party shall then present its claim and proofs and its witnesses, who shall submit to questions or other examination. The defending party shall then present its defense and proofs and its witnesses, who shall submit to questions or other examination.

The Arbitrator has discretion to vary this procedure but shall afford full and equal opportunity to all parties for the presentation of any material or relevant proofs.

Exhibits, when offered by either party, may be received in evidence by the Arbitrator.

The names and addresses of all witnesses and exhibits in order received shall be made a part of the record.

30. Arbitration in the Absence of a Party—Unless the law provides to the contrary, the arbitration may proceed in the absence of any party which, after due notice, fails to be present or fails to obtain an adjournment. An award shall not be made solely on the default of a party. The Arbitrator shall require the party who is present to submit such evidence as the Arbitrator may require for the making of an award.

31. Evidence—The parties may offer such evidence as they desire and shall produce such additional evidence as the Arbitrator may deem necessary to an understanding and determination of the dispute. The Arbitrator, when authorized by law to subpoena witnesses or documents, may do so upon the Arbitrator's own initiative or upon the request of any party. The Arbitrator shall be the judge of the relevancy and materiality of the evidence offered and conformity to legal rules of evidence shall not be necessary. All evidence shall be taken in the presence of all the Arbitrators and of all the parties, except where any of the parties is absent in default or has waived the right to be present.

32. Evidence by Affidavit and Filing of Documents—The Arbitrator shall receive and consider the evidence of witnesses by affidavit, but shall give it only such weight as the Arbitrator deems it entitled to after consideration of any objections made to its admission.

All documents not filed with the Arbitrator at the hearing, but arranged for at the hearing or subsequently by agreement of the parties, shall be filed with the AAA for transmission to the Arbitrator. All parties shall be afforded opportunity to examine such documents.

33. Inspection or Investigation—Whenever the Arbitrator deems it necessary to make an inspection or investigation in connection with the arbitration, the Arbitrator shall direct the AAA to advise the parties of such intention. The Arbitrator shall set the time and AAA shall notify the parties thereof. Any party who so desires may be present at such inspection or investigation. In the event that one or both parties are not present at the inspection or investigation, the Arbitrator shall make a verbal or written report to the parties and afford them an opportunity to comment.

34. Conservation of Property—The Arbitrator may issue such orders as may be deemed necessary to safeguard the property which is the subject matter of the arbitration without prejudice to the rights of the parties or to the final determination of the dispute.

35. Closing of Hearings—The Arbitrator shall specifically inquire of all parties whether they have any further proofs to offer or witnesses to be heard. Upon receiving negative replies, or if satisfied that the record is complete, the Arbitrator shall declare the hearings closed and a minute thereof shall be recorded. If briefs are to be filed, the hearing shall be declared closed as of the final date set by the Arbitrator for the receipt of briefs. If documents are to be filed as provided for in Section 32 and the date set for their receipt is later than that set for the receipt of briefs, the later date shall be the date of closing the hearings. The time limit within which the Arbitrator is required to make the award shall commence to run, in the absence of other agreements by the parties, upon the closing of the hearings.

36. Reopening of Hearings—The hearings may be reopened on the Arbitrator's own motion, or upon application of a party, at any time before the award is made. If reopening the hearings would prevent the making of the award within the specific time agreed upon by the parties in the contract out of which the controversy has arisen, the matter may not be reopened, unless the parties agree upon the extension of such time limit. When no specific date is fixed in the contract, the Arbitrator may reopen the hearings, and the Arbitrator shall have thirty days from the closing of the reopened hearings within which to make an award.

37. Waiver of Oral Hearings—The parties may provide, by written agreement, for the waiver of oral hearings. If the parties are unable to agree as to the procedure, the AAA shall specify a fair and equitable procedure.

38. Waiver of Rules—Any party who proceeds with the arbitration after knowledge that any provision or requirement of these Rules has not been complied with and who fails to state objection thereto in writing, shall be deemed to have waived the right to object.

39. Extensions of Time—The parties may modify any period of time by mutual agreement. The AAA for good cause may extend any period of time established by these Rules, except the time for making the award. The AAA shall notify the parties of any such extension of time and its reason therefor.

40. Communication with Arbitrator and Serving of Notice—(a) There shall be no communication between the parties and a neutral Arbitrator other than at oral hearings. Any other oral or written communications from the parties to the Arbitrator shall be directed to the AAA for transmittal to the Arbitrator.

(b) Each party to an agreement which provides for arbitration under these Rules shall be deemed to have consented that any papers, notices or process necessary or proper for the initiation or continuation of an arbitration under these Rules and for any court action in connection therewith or for the entry of judgment on any award made thereunder may be served upon such party by mail addressed to such party or its attorney at its last known address or by personal service, within or without the state wherein the arbitration is to be held (whether such party be within or without the United States of America), provided that reasonable opportunity to be heard with regard thereto has been granted such party.

41. Time of Award—The award shall be made promptly by the Arbitrator and, unless otherwise agreed by the parties, or specified by law, no later than thirty days from the date of closing the hearings, or if oral hearings have been waived, from the date of transmitting the final statements and proofs to the Arbitrator.

42. Form of Award—The award shall be in writing and shall be signed either by the sole Arbitrator or by at least a majority if there be more than one. It shall be executed in the manner required by law.

43. Scope of Award—The Arbitrator may grant any remedy or relief which the Arbitrator deems just and equitable and within the scope of the agreement of the parties, including, but not limited to, specific performance of a contract. The Arbitrator, in the award, shall assess arbitration fees and expenses in favor of any party and, in the event any administrative fees or expenses are due the AAA, in favor of the AAA.

44. Award upon Settlement—If the parties settle their dispute during the course of the arbitration, the Arbitrator, upon their request, may set forth the terms of the agreed settlement in an award.

45. Delivery of Award to Parties—Parties shall accept as legal delivery of the award the placing of the award or a true copy thereof in the mail by the AAA, addressed to such party at its last known address or to its attorney, or personal service of the award, or the filing of the award in any manner which may be prescribed by law.

46. Release of Documents for Judicial Proceedings—The AAA shall, upon the written request of a party, furnish to such party, at its expense, certified facsimiles of any papers in the AAA's possession that may be required in judicial proceedings relating to the arbitration.

47. Applications to Court and Exclusion of Liability—(a) No judicial proceedings by a party relating to the subject matter of the arbitration shall be deemed a waiver of the party's right to arbitrate.

(b) Neither the AAA nor any Arbitrator in a proceeding under these Rules is a necessary party in judicial proceedings relating to the arbitration.

(c) Parties to these Rules shall be deemed to have consented that judgment upon the arbitration award may be entered in any Federal or State Court having jurisdiction thereof.

(d) Neither the AAA nor any Arbitrator shall be liable to any party for any act or omission in connection with any arbitration conducted under these Rules.

48. Administrative Fees—As a not-for-profit organization, the AAA shall prescribe an Administrative Fee Schedule and a Refund Schedule to compensate it for the cost of providing administrative services. The schedule in effect at the time of filing or the time of refund shall be applicable.

The administrative fees shall be advanced by the initiating party or parties, subject to final apportionment by the Arbitrator in the award.

When a matter is withdrawn or settled, the refund shall be made in accordance with the Refund Schedule.

The AAA, in the event of extreme hardship on the part of any party, may defer or reduce the administrative fee.

49. Fee When Oral Hearings are Waived—When all oral hearings are waived under Section 37, the Administrative Fee Schedule shall apply.

50. Expenses—The expenses of witnesses for either side shall be paid by the party producing such witnesses.

The cost of the stenographic record, if any is made, and all transcripts thereof, shall be prorated equally among all parties ordering copies unless they shall otherwise agree and shall be paid for by the responsible parties directly to the reporting agency.

All other expenses of the arbitration, including required traveling and other expenses of the Arbitrator and of AAA representatives, and the expenses of any witness or the cost of any proofs produced at the direct request of the Arbitrator, shall be borne equally by the parties, unless they agree otherwise, or unless the Arbitrator, in the award, assesses such expenses or any part thereof against any specified party or parties.

51. Arbitrator's Fee—Members of the National Panel of Arbitrators who serve as neutral Arbitrators do so in most cases without fee. In prolonged or in special cases the parties may agree to pay a fee, or the AAA may determine that payment of a fee by the parties is appropriate and may establish a reasonable amount, taking into account the extent of service by the Arbitrator and other relevant circumstances of the case. When neutral Arbitrators are to be paid, the arrangements for compensation shall be made through the AAA and not directly between the parties and the Arbitrators.

52. Deposits–The AAA may require the parties to deposit in advance such sums of money as it deems necessary to defray the expense of the arbitration, including the Arbitrator's fee, if any, and shall render an accounting to the parties and return any unexpended balance.

53. Interpretation and Application of Rules–The Arbitrator shall interpret and apply these Rules insofar as they relate to the Arbitrator's powers and duties. When there is more than one Arbitrator and a difference arises among them concerning the meaning or application of any such Rules, it shall be decided by a majority vote. If that is unobtainable, either an Arbitrator or a party may refer the question to the AAA for final decision. All other Rules shall be interpreted and applied by the AAA.

EXPEDITED PROCEDURES

54. Notice by Telephone–The parties shall accept all notices from the AAA by telephone. Such notices by the AAA shall subsequently be confirmed in writing to the parties. Notwithstanding the failure to confirm in writing any notice or objection hereunder, the proceeding shall nonetheless be valid if notice has, in fact, been given by telephone.

55. Appointment and Qualifications of Arbitrators–The AAA shall submit simultaneously to each party to the dispute an identical list of five members of the Commercial Arbitration Panel of Arbitrators from which one arbitrator shall be appointed. Each party shall have the right to strike two names from the list on a peremptory basis. The list is returnable to the AAA within 10 days from the date of mailing. If for any reasons the appointment cannot be made from the list, the AAA shall have the authority to make the appointment from among other members of the Panel without the submission of additional lists. Such appointment shall be subject to disqualification for the reasons specified in Section 19. The parties shall be given notice by telephone by the AAA of the appointment of the Arbitrator. The parties shall notify the AAA, by telephone, within seven (7) days of any objections to the Arbitrators appointed. Any objection by a party to such Arbitrator shall be confirmed in writing to the AAA with a copy to the other party(ies).

56. Time and Place of Hearing–The Arbitrator shall fix the date, time and place of the hearing. The AAA will notify the parties by telephone, seven (7) days in advance of the hearing date. Formal Notice of Hearing will be sent by the AAA to the parties.

57. The Hearing–Generally, the hearing shall be completed within one day. The Arbitrator, for good cause shown, may schedule an additional hearing to be held within five days.

58. Time of Award–Unless otherwise agreed to by the parties, the Award shall be rendered not later than five (5) business days from the date of the closing of the hearing.

COMMERCIAL MEDIATION RULES

Effective September 1, 1984

1. Agreement of Parties—Whenever, by stipulation or in their contract, the parties have provided for mediation of existing or future disputes under the auspices of the American Arbitration Association (AAA) or under these Rules, they shall be deemed to have made these Rules, as amended and in effect as of the date of the submission of the dispute, a part of their agreement.

2. Initiation of Mediation—Any party or parties to a dispute may initiate mediation by filing with the AAA a written request for mediation pursuant to these Rules, together with the appropriate administrative fee contained in the Administrative Fee Schedule.

3. Request for Mediation—A request for mediation shall contain a brief statement of the nature of the dispute and the names, addresses, and phone numbers of all parties to the dispute, and those who will represent them, if any, in the mediation. The initiating party shall simultaneously file two (2) copies of the request with the AAA and one copy with every other party to the dispute.

4. Appointment of Mediator—Upon receipt of a request for mediation, the AAA will appoint a qualified mediator to serve. Normally, a single mediator will be appointed unless the parties agree otherwise or the AAA determines otherwise. If the agreement of the parties names a mediator or specifies a method of appointing a mediator, that designation or method shall be followed.

5. Qualifications of a Mediator—No person shall serve as a mediator in any dispute in which that person has any financial or personal interest in the result of the mediation, except by the written consent of all parties. Prior to accepting an appointment, the prospective mediator shall disclose any circumstances likely to create a presumption of bias or prevent a prompt meeting with the parties. Upon receipt of such information, the AAA shall either replace the mediator or immediately communicate the information to the parties for their comments. In the event the parties disagree as to whether the mediator shall serve, the AAA will appoint another mediator. The AAA is authorized to appoint another mediator if the appointed mediator is unable to serve promptly.

6. Vacancies—If any mediator shall become unwilling or unable to serve, the AAA will appoint another mediator, unless the parties agree otherwise.

7. Representation—Any party may be represented by persons of their choice. The names and addresses of such persons shall be communicated in writing to all parties and to the AAA.

8. Time and Place of Mediation—The mediator shall fix the time of each mediation session. The mediation shall be held at the appropriate regional office of the AAA, or at any other convenient location agreeable to the mediator and the parties, as the mediator shall determine.

9. Identification of Matters in Dispute—At least ten (10) days prior to the first scheduled mediation session, each party shall provide the mediator with a brief memorandum setting forth its position with regard to the issues that need to be resolved. At the discretion of the mediator, such memoranda may be mutually exchanged by the parties.

At the first session, the parties will be expected to produce all information reasonably required for the mediator to understand the issues presented. The mediator may require either party to supplement such information.

10. Authority of Mediator–The mediator does not have authority to impose a settlement upon the parties but will attempt to help the parties reach a satisfactory resolution of their dispute. The mediator is authorized to conduct joint and separate meetings with the parties and to make oral and written recommendations for settlement. Whenever necessary, the mediator may also obtain expert advice concerning technical aspects of the dispute, provided the parties agree and assume the expenses of obtaining such advice. Arrangements for obtaining such advice shall be made by the mediator or the parties, as the mediator shall determine.

The mediator is authorized to end the mediation whenever, in the judgment of the mediator, further efforts at mediation would not contribute to a resolution of the dispute between the parties.

11. Privacy–Mediation sessions are private. The parties and their representatives may attend mediation sessions. Other persons may attend only with the permission of the parties and with the consent of the mediator.

12. Confidentiality–Confidential information disclosed to a mediator by the parties or by witnesses in the course of the mediation shall not be divulged by the mediator. All records, reports, or other documents received by a mediator while serving in such capacity shall be confidential. The mediator shall not be compelled to divulge such records or to testify in regard to the mediation in any adversary proceeding or judicial forum.

The parties shall not rely on or introduce as evidence in any arbitral, judicial, or other proceedings, any and all aspects of the mediation effort, including, but not limited to: (a) views expressed or suggestions made by the other party with respect to a possible settlement of the dispute; (b) admissions made by the other party in the course of the mediation proceedings; (c) proposals made or views expressed by the mediator; (d) the fact that the other party had or had not indicated willingness to accept a proposal for settlement made by the mediator.

13. No Stenographic Record–There shall be no stenographic record of the mediation process.

14. Termination of Mediation–The mediation shall be terminated: (a) by the execution of a settlement agreement by the parties; or (b) by a written declaration of the mediator to the effect that further efforts at mediation are no longer worthwhile; or (c) by a written declaration of a party or parties to the effect that the mediation proceedings are terminated.

15. Exclusion of Liability–Neither the AAA nor any mediator is a necessary party in judicial proceedings relating to the mediation.

Neither the AAA nor any mediator shall be liable to any party for any act or omission in connection with any mediation conducted under these Rules.

16. Interpretation and Application of Rules–The mediator shall interpret and apply these Rules insofar as they relate to the mediator's duties and responsibilities. All other Rules shall be interpreted and applied by the AAA.

AMERICAN ARBITRATION ASSOCIATION MINI-TRIAL PROCEDURES

The mini-trial is a structured dispute resolution method in which senior executives of the parties involved in legal disputes meet in the presence of a neutral advisor and, after hearing presentations of the merits of each side of the dispute, attempt to formulate a voluntary settlement. The following procedures have been developed by the American Arbitration Association to facilitate the use of the mini-trial in business disputes. They are available for the use of any business organization or governmental agency. Any provision, including those relating to the use of a neutral advisor and the imposition of costs, may be altered if the parties so agree.

1. The mini-trial process may be initiated by the written or oral request of either party, made to any regional office of the AAA, but will not be pursued unless both parties agree to resolve their dispute by means of a mini-trial.

2. The course of the mini-trial process shall be governed by a written agreement between the parties.

3. The mini-trial shall consist of an information exchange and settlement negotiation.

4. Each party is represented throughout the mini-trial process by legal counsel whose role is to prepare and present the party's "best case" at the information exchange.

5. Each party shall have in attendance throughout the information exchange and settlement negotiation a senior executive with settlement authority.

6. A neutral advisor shall be present at the information exchange to decide questions of procedure and to render advice to the party representatives when requested by them.

7. The neutral advisor shall be selected by mutual agreement of the parties, who may consult with the AAA for recommendations. To facilitate the selection process, the AAA will make available to the parties a list of individuals to serve as neutral advisors. If the parties fail to agree upon the selection of a neutral advisor, they shall ask that the AAA appoint an advisor from the panel it has compiled for this purpose.

8. Discovery between the parties may take place prior to the information exchange, in accordance with the agreement between the parties.

9. Prior to the information exchange, the parties shall exchange written statements summarizing the issues in the case, and copies of all documents they intend to present at the information exchange.

10. Federal or state rules of evidence do not apply to presentations made at the information exchange. Any limitation on the scope of the evidence offered at the information exchange shall be determined by mutual agreement of the parties prior to the exchange and shall be enforced by the neutral advisor.

11. After the information exchange, the senior executives shall meet and attempt, in good faith, to formulate a voluntary settlement of the dispute.

12. If the senior executives are unable to settle the dispute, the neutral advisor shall render an advisory opinion as to the likely outcome of the case if it were litigated in a court of law. The neutral advisor's opinion shall identify the issues of law and fact which are critical to the disposition of the case and give the reasons for the opinion that is offered.

13. After the neutral advisor has entered an advisory opinion, the senior executives shall meet for a second time in an attempt to resolve the dispute. If they are unable to reach a settlement at this time, they may either abandon the proceeding or submit to the neutral advisor written offers of settlement. If the parties elect to make such written offers, the neutral advisor shall make a recommendation for settlement based on those offers. If the parties reject the recommendation of the neutral advisor, either party may declare the mini-trial terminated and resolve the dispute by other means.

14. Mini-trial proceedings are confidential; no written or oral statement made by any participant in the proceeding may be used as evidence or in admission in any other proceeding.

15. The fees and expenses of the neutral advisor shall be borne equally by the parties, and each party is responsible for its own costs, including legal fees, incurred in connection with the mini-trial. The parties may, however, in their written agreement alter the allocation of fees and expenses.

16. Neither the AAA nor any neutral advisor serving in a mini-trial proceeding governed by these procedures shall be liable to any party for any act or omission in connection with the mini-trial. The parties shall indemnify the AAA and the neutral advisor for any liability to third parties arising out of the mini-trial process.

BIBLIOGRAPHY

American Arbitration Association. *Commercial Arbitration Rules: As Amended and in Effect April 1, 1985*. New York: 1985.

______. *Commercial Mediation Rules: Effective September 1, 1984.* New York: 1984.

______. *A Manual for Commercial Arbitrators.* New York: 1983.

______. *Mini-Trial Procedures.* New York: 1985.

Arbitration and the Law: AAA General Counsel's Annual Report. New York: American Arbitration Association, 1981–present (ongoing publication).

Bernstein, Merton C. *Private Dispute Settlement: Cases and Materials on Arbitration.* New York: Free Press, 1968.

Center for Public Resources. *Corporate Dispute Management 1982: A Manual of Innovative Corporate Strategies for the Avoidance and Resolution of Legal Disputes.* New York: Matthew Bender, 1982.

Coulson, Robert. *How to Stay Out of Court*. 2d ed. New York: American Arbitration Association, 1984.

______. *Professional Mediation of Civil Disputes.* New York: American Arbitration Association, 1984.

Domke, Martin. *Domke on Commercial Arbitration (The Law and Practice of Commercial Arbitration)*. Rev. ed. by Gabriel M. Wilner. Wilmette, Ill.: Callaghan & Co., 1984. Has 1985 Cumulative Supplement.

Eager, Samuel W. *The Arbitration Contract and Proceedings.* Buffalo: Dennis, 1971.

Fisher, Roger, and William Ury. *Getting to Yes: Negotiating Agreement Without Giving In*. Boston: Houghton Mifflin, 1981.

Goldberg, George E. *A Lawyer's Guide to Commercial Arbitration.* 2d ed. Philadelphia: ALI–ABA, 1983.

Kreindler, Donald L., and George E. Goldberg. *What the Businessman Should Know about Commercial Arbitration.* New York: New York Credit & Financial Management Association, 1973.

Lawyers' Arbitration Letter. New York: American Arbitration Association, 1960–present (ongoing publication).

Lazarus, Stephen *et al. Resolving Business Disputes: The Potential of Commercial Arbitration.* New York: American Management Association, 1965.

Marks, Jonathan B., Earl Johnson, Jr., and Peter L. Szanton. *Dispute Resolution in America: Processes in Evolution.* Washington, D.C.: National Institute for Dispute Resolution, 1984.

Poppleton, Allen. "The Arbitrator's Role in Expediting the Large and Complex Commercial Case." *The Arbitration Journal*, vol. 36, no. 4 (December 1981), pp. 6–10.

Raiffa, Howard. *The Art and Science of Negotiation.* Cambridge, Mass.: Belknap Press, 1982.

Rodman, Robert M. *Commercial Arbitration with Forms.* St. Paul: West Publishing, 1984.

Widiss, Alan I., ed. *Arbitration: Commercial Disputes, Insurance, and Tort Claims.* New York: Practising Law Institute, 1979.

Williston, Samuel A. *A Treatise on the Law of Contracts. Volume 16.* 3d ed. by Walter H. E. Jaeger. Rochester: Lawyers Co-operative Publishing, 1976. Has 1984 Cumulative Supplement.

CHAPTER 2

THE CONSTRUCTION INDUSTRY

HISTORY OF CONSTRUCTION ARBITRATION

Arbitration of construction disputes is not a new concept. As early as 1871, when arbitration was first introduced into standard-form construction agreements, attorneys representing architects, contractors, and engineers were using arbitration. When the American Institute of Architects (AIA) first began using printed forms, arbitration clauses were part of its recommended owner-architect contracts. The procedures outlined in AIA's Article 40 of "The General Conditions of the Contract for the Construction of Buildings" provided for arbitration in accordance with either the AIA rules, which specified a party-appointed system, or the Commercial Arbitration Rules of the American Arbitration Association.

The choice of a party-appointed system or arbitration under AAA rules may have seemed ideal because it gave the parties an option, but this dual option created difficulties in initiating a claim. Neither procedure was completely satisfactory to all parties. In practice, setting up a party-appointed panel causes lengthy delays. And to some construction industry professionals, the AAA commercial rules were undesirable because the AAA had not yet recruited a nationwide panel of expert construction arbitrators.

In 1964, an AIA-AGC (Associated General Contractors) liaison committee studied the problem. After reviewing their members' experience under both systems, the committee recommended the adoption of the AAA as the sole administrator but suggested that an expanded committee help the AAA develop procedures and panels of arbitrators custom-tailored to the construction industry. By 1965, the National Construction Industry Arbitration Committee (NCIAC) included representatives of the following organizations: American Consulting Engineers Council (then Consulting Engineers Council); American Institute of Architects; Associated General Contractors; Associated Specialty Contractors, Inc. (then Council of Mechanical Specialty Contracting Industries); and National Society of Professional Engineers. After a thorough study, Construction Industry

Arbitration Rules were adopted providing a uniform nationwide procedure for the construction industry. A specialized panel, made up of business people and professionals, was screened and selected by local advisory committees. More than 30,000 arbitrators, representing all segments of the industry, now serve on the AAA's national construction panel, and there are over 100 different categories represented on that panel.

The construction industry rules are recommended for use throughout the building and construction industry. With the expansion of NCIAC membership to include the American Society of Civil Engineers, American Society of Landscape Architects, American Subcontractors Association, Associated Builders and Contractors, Inc., Construction Specifications Institute, and National Association of Home Builders, eleven national construction associations have been participating in sponsoring this arbitration system.

THE ARBITRATION CLAUSE

The modern construction project–with its multiplicity of participants, highly technical procedures, and new techniques and materials available–requires complex planning, bid documents, and contracts. The potential for controversy is always present. Including a reliable arbitration clause in your agreement can help to resolve these disputes more quickly and efficiently. The ingredients of a properly formulated arbitration clause are: (1) a delineation of which disputes are arbitrable; (2) reference to a standard procedure under which the arbitration will be conducted; and (3) a commitment that the parties will be bound by the ultimate award. A frequently used contract provision is found in AIA Document A201 (1980), subparagraph 7.9.1 of the General Conditions:

> All claims, disputes and other matters in question between the Contractor and the Owner arising out of or relating to the Contract Documents or the breach thereof, except as provided in Subparagraph 2.3.14 with respect to the Architect's decisions on matters relating to artistic effect, and except for claims which have been waived by the making or acceptance of final payment as provided by Subparagraphs 9.9.4 through 9.9.6, inclusive, shall be decided by arbitration in accordance with the Construction Industry Arbitration Rules of the American Arbitration Association then obtaining unless the parties mutually agree otherwise. . . . The foregoing agreement to arbitrate and any other agreement to arbitrate with an additional person or persons duly consented to by the parties to the Owner-Contractor agreement shall be specifically enforceable under the prevailing arbitration law. The award rendered by the arbitrators shall be final, and judgment may be entered upon it in accordance with applicable law in any court having jurisdiction thereof.

By referring to the AAA's Construction Industry Arbitration Rules, a well-tested procedure is made available to the parties, backed up by an experienced professional administrator. Section 11 allows the AAA to determine the appropriate locale of hearings when the parties are unable to agree and have not specified a place of hearing in their agreement. Section 40 of the rules provides for the mailing of all notices.

Participants in a construction project should check the arbitration clauses in their various interlocking contracts. For example, AIA's Standard Form of Agreement between Owner and Contractor (Document A101) provides that the General Conditions of the Contract will be applicable to other contract documents. The arbitration provision between prime contractor and subcontractor, however, may not be identical to the provision in the General Conditions, although sometimes the arbitration clause between the owner and prime contractor will "flow down" to the subcontractor. The AIA subcontract form (Document A401, 1978) provides an example of this type of clause commonly used by the industry:

> 13.1 All claims, disputes and other matters in question arising out of, or relating to, this Subcontract, or the breach thereof, shall be decided by arbitration, which shall be conducted in the same manner and under the same procedure as provided in the Contract Documents with respect to disputes between the Owner and the Contractor, except that a decision by the Architect shall not be a condition precedent to arbitration. If the Contract Documents do not provide for arbitration or fail to specify the manner and procedure for arbitration, it shall be conducted in accordance with the Construction Industry Arbitration Rules of the American Arbitration Association then obtaining unless the parties mutually agree otherwise.

SPECIAL PROVISIONS

Sometimes a construction contract should be tailor-made. For instance, some public works contracts specify that, although the hearing must be held within the jurisdiction involved, the arbitrators may not be from that area; or the parties might designate that claims over a certain dollar amount must be heard by a panel of three arbitrators; or they may specify the qualifications and backgrounds of the individuals on their panel. Arbitration is flexible. Even where the parties specify the construction rules, they can add special provisions.

Consider the case of an owner and contractor who had enjoyed a long and profitable working relationship. When they encountered a disagreement that they could not resolve through negotiations, they decided to tailor their arbitration. They were able to stipulate to many of the facts. Their contract provided that damages for delay would be borne by the contractor. But they were unable to negotiate the amount of liability. In order to facilitate the process, they agreed that the hearing should take no more than one day. They also instructed the arbitrator to issue the award within seven days from the date of the hearing. Finally.

they agreed to use a method called "final-offer arbitration," a technique developed in the labor field. At the close of the hearing, each party gives its "final offer" to the arbitrator, who selects one of the offers, based on the merits of the case. No compromise is permitted, and the rejected offer remains confidential.

Because the arbitration process is flexible, the parties can devise a system that they believe will be fair and will not damage their working relationship. An arbitration clause may specify the location of hearings, the qualifications of the arbitrator, provisions for prehearing discovery procedures, or expedited hearing schedules. The parties control the process. They should discuss these procedural issues. With the aid of their lawyers, the parties should design a convenient and appropriate procedure. Often this is done at a prearbitration conference with a representative of the AAA.

The AAA administers arbitration cases in accordance with the parties' arbitration agreement. In most cases, specific administrative details need not be described in the contract. By using a standard arbitration clause specifying the AAA's Construction Industry Arbitration Rules, the parties can obtain an orderly and expeditious arbitration. Even where parties do not use a printed form contract, they may refer to the Construction Industry Arbitration Rules by using the following clause in their contract:

> Any controversy or claim arising out of or relating to this contract, or the breach thereof, shall be settled by arbitration in accordance with the Construction Industry Arbitration Rules of the American Arbitration Association, and judgment upon the award rendered may be entered in any Court having jurisdiction thereof.

ENFORCEABILITY OF ARBITRATION CLAUSES

The construction industry was in the vanguard lobbying for modern legislation. Prior to the passage of modern arbitration laws, many courts had refused to enforce agreements to arbitrate future disputes under building contracts. In the absence of a statute, the courts looked to the common law decisions of England. And at the time of the American Revolution, the English courts were refusing to enforce arbitration agreements in contracts because they "ousted the courts of jurisdiction."

Although this did not mean that arbitration was not being used by parties, it did mean that a party could refuse to arbitrate and thus force the contractor into court. During the 1920s, public policy began to shift in favor of arbitration. Courts were already becoming crowded, and legislators became convinced that arbitration offered a suitable tribunal for the determination of business disputes.

Contractual arbitration reduced the increasing burden on court calendars. Legislation to encourage arbitration was urged by the construction industry. Modern laws first appeared in the important commercial states. At the same time, a movement to pass a national arbitration law began to take shape.

In general, construction projects involve interstate movement of materials and personnel. Disputes are therefore arbitrated under federal law and are covered by the United States Arbitration Act. Under this act, a written arbitration provision in a contract involving "commerce" is "valid, irrevocable, and enforceable." Federal policy favors arbitration. When a question arises about whether an issue is subject to arbitration, a federal court will enforce a contract clause providing for arbitration. For the construction contract that involves interstate commerce, there need be little concern about state arbitration statutes. The federal law will apply, and that law supports arbitration.

Even for purely *intra*state construction contracts, the lack of a modern state arbitration law does not prevent the voluntary submission of a dispute under the standard AIA form. Under common law, the parties always have the right to submit an existing dispute to arbitration. The courts will enforce the arbitrator's award. Fortunately, most state laws now enforce arbitration clauses.

MOTIONS TO STAY

Attempts to compel arbitration against a resisting party involve a showing that there is an agreement to arbitrate, that an arbitrable dispute exists, and that the other party has been notified of the demand for arbitration. If the opposing party initiates litigation, a motion can be filed to stay that proceeding on the grounds that the lawsuit is in violation of the arbitration clause. In rendering a decision on arbitrability, the courts will look to the arbitration clause and not to the merits of the dispute.

Once a construction claim has been filed for administration, the AAA acknowledges receipt and sends both parties a list of potential arbitrators. If the respondent objects to the arbitration, the AAA will ask both parties for their comments. If the contract authorizes the AAA to proceed, it will continue to administer the case and will so advise the parties. If the matter is not contested in court, the arbitrator can decide the arbitrability issue at the first hearing.

The AAA always follows court orders. Unless a court orders the Association to stop proceedings or unless the parties agree otherwise, the AAA will continue with the administration of the case while a motion is pending. If the moving party obtains a temporary stay from the courts, however, the arbitration will be held in abeyance until the motion to stay is resolved. Sometimes, a moving party will appeal a lower court's decision. Again, the AAA will proceed unless both parties agree to suspend administration or until a temporary stay is granted pending the appeal by the court. In other words, the AAA will follow the directions of the court.

There is no need to make the Association a party to such litigation. Section 47 of the construction rules states that "Neither the AAA nor any arbitrator in a proceeding under these Rules is a necessary party in judicial proceedings relating to the arbitration." Parties should keep the tribunal administrator advised of pending litigation. A copy of any court order should be forwarded promptly to the AAA, and it will immediately comply.

HOW TO INITIATE AN ARBITRATION

When a construction contract contains an arbitration clause, either party may initiate a claim by filing an AAA demand form or a letter that contains the required information. The demand should be accompanied by the appropriate filing fee, based upon the amount in issue. This fee pays the cost of administration and also helps to maintain this industrywide system of arbitration. The demand for arbitration should describe the dispute in enough detail so that the AAA can select appropriate names from its panel of arbitrators.

THE PREHEARING CONFERENCE—HOW IT HELPS THE PARTIES

Section 10 of the Construction Industry Arbitration Rules provides for a prehearing conference at the request of the parties or at the discretion of the AAA. Such conferences are particularly useful in complex cases where several days of hearings are anticipated. The prehearing conference brings the attorneys and their clients together with a senior AAA representative to exchange information or to stipulate to uncontested facts. Sometimes procedural disagreements can be resolved. The parties are informed that any discussion of the merits will be confidential. The prehearing conference is entirely separate from the hearings themselves, and the arbitrator does not participate.

Various administrative details are also discussed. A list of items that can be raised at the prehearing conference includes: the parties' estimate of the number of hearings that will be required; the desired timetable for scheduling hearings; the rate and terms of arbitrator compensation, if any; the arrangements for an on-site inspection; hearing room size; description of claims and counterclaims; exchange of witness lists and brief outline of testimony; arrangements for the exchange and marking of exhibits; whether briefs are to be submitted; and any other special arrangements in connection with the arbitration.

Parties are not always able to reach agreement on every point raised, but experience has shown that the prehearing conference facilitates the arbitration process. Many construction cases involve lines of testimony and schedules and documents that are complicated and difficult to organize. Anything that can be done to simplify the parties' presentations will help ensure a better understanding of the case. Moreover, many a case has been settled at a prehearing conference, as the attorneys and principals take advantage of this opportunity to share their perceptions with one another. The administrator can also assist in searching for a solution to their problem.

SELECTING AN ARBITRATOR

The specialized arbitration panel constitutes one of the major advantages that arbitration enjoys over litigation. The parties have the opportunity to select individuals who understand the construction industry because they have been a part of it. Thus, there is no need to "educate the bench." The arbitrator is likely to show a lively interest in the case, and he or she can request additional documentation or inspect the work site in order to better understand the issues in dispute.

Every effort is made by the AAA to ensure that the list sent to the parties contains experienced arbitrators – practical experts with good reputations in their fields – who are likely to be acceptable to all parties. The demand form asks for the industry category of each party (subcontractor, contractor, architect, engineer, or owner). It should be emphasized that the claimant's description of the dispute in the demand, and the respondent's answering statement, should contain enough information for the Association to suggest an appropriate list of potential arbitrators. For example, a statement that "claimant seeks damages in the amount of $10,000.00 for delays" is not very helpful. The more information that is supplied about the nature of the work involved, the better prepared the AAA will be to compile a suitably balanced list. Each arbitrator card in the AAA's construction panel contains information about the individual's educational background, specialization, membership in professional associations, and years of experience. A synopsis of this information is included on the list that is sent to the parties. If more information is requested, it will be supplied by the AAA.

In a recent survey of the AAA's panel of construction arbitrators, many indicated that they would be willing to make themselves available for a long case. If multiple hearings will be required, the AAA should be notified in advance so it can submit a list of arbitrators available to serve for as long as necessary. Parties are also encouraged to allocate consecutive dates so that the matter can proceed without delays in the hearing process. In addition, when returning the lists of preferred selections, parties should also return the calendar forms and witness list. These reduce the possibility of administrative delay, since the AAA can more easily determine whether prospective arbitrators are willing to serve on the case.

CHALLENGING THE ARBITRATOR FOR BIAS

Many people in the construction industry become acquainted through various jobs. Individuals selected as arbitrators may discover that they know one or both parties involved in the dispute. Section 19 of the construction rules requires a neutral arbitrator to disclose "any circumstances likely to affect his or her impartiality." A 1981 New Jersey case imposed the same obligation on a party-appointed arbitrator. This would include a personal or financial relationship, past or present, with any party, counsel, or witness. Such information is communicated by the

AAA to the parties, who are asked for their comments. Sometimes, a party will challenge the arbitrator, who may then be asked to resign. In those cases where the grounds seem insubstantial, however, the AAA may decide that the arbitrator should continue to serve. That decision is conclusive.

Where such determinations have been tested in the courts, one standard that has applied is whether the arbitrator had an interest in the proceeding that was "direct, definite and capable of demonstration rather than remote, uncertain or speculative." The courts recognize that, in some situations, many people in an industry do business together. The AAA follows a pragmatic standard but tries to avoid the possibility that an award will be vacated because of a claim of bias.

WHERE SHOULD THE CASE BE HEARD?

The location of the hearing is seldom a problem in construction arbitration. If the parties anticipate that this issue might arise, however, they should specify in their contract a suitable site for hearings. Occasionally, if the locale has not previously been designated, when the case is filed one party may wish the hearing to take place near its office, and the other may want it at the site.

If the arbitration clause does not specify a place of hearing and the parties cannot agree, the AAA must decide. In such cases, both parties will be requested, by the regional office where the claim was filed, to explain their reasons, and a determination will then be made by the AAA. Under section 11 of the construction arbitration rules, this decision is final. Factors that are considered when making a decision on locale include: (1) location of the parties; (2) location of witnesses and documents; (3) location of the work site; (4) relative cost to the parties; (5) laws applicable to the contract; (6) previous court actions; and (7) availability of the most appropriate panels. The location requested by the filing party is often given a preference.

THE POWERS OF THE ARBITRATOR

An arbitrator has broad powers under the Construction Industry Arbitration Rules. These include the authority to: consider amendments to the claim or counterclaim (section 8); schedule, close, and reopen hearings (sections 21, 35, and 36); determine whether any person not directly involved can attend the hearing (section 25); grant or deny hearing adjournments (section 26); and conduct an arbitration in the absence of a party after due notice (section 30). Where authorized to do so by law, the arbitrator may subpoena witnesses or documents independently or at the request of a party (section 31). The arbitrator can also receive, consider, and weigh any evidence including evidence of witnesses by affidavit (sections 31 and 32); conduct a viewing of the project site (section 33); order the safeguarding of any property subject to the dispute during the pendency of the arbitration hearings (section 34); grant interest on the award (section 43); assess arbitrator fees and expenses equally or in favor of any party (section 51); and determine issues of arbitrability (section 53).

As you ponder these procedural powers and recall that arbitrators can make their decisions without giving any reasons, you must realize that the authority of the arbitrator is extensive, but only as to those issues designated by the parties.

CONSOLIDATING CLAIMS

One of the most troublesome procedural issues pertains to the consolidation of construction arbitration claims involving a single project site. This is a major subject of debate within the industry. Some contend that consolidation of claims would avoid inconsistent results. Others reply that multiparty cases serve only to complicate the process and lead to unnecessary delays. Court opinions also vary. Some of the factors that may be considered by a court when reaching a decision on a particular case are: (1) the various arbitration clauses; (2) the similarity of issues between the various parties; (3) the similarity of method of selecting arbitrators in the various contracts; and (4) the participation in the selection of arbitrators that preceded the motion to consolidate. Some jurisdictions are liberal in granting consolidation where common issues are involved. Others seem to favor separate arbitrations.

The National Construction Industry Arbitration Committee has considered whether the construction rules should provide for consolidation. Thus far, this decision has been left to the parties. Consolidation may be accomplished by stipulation or by a provision in the arbitration agreement. At the present time, the AIA's owner-architect agreement prohibits consolidation or joinder without the written consent of all parties. On the other hand, agreements between owners and prime contractors often provide that subcontractor claims in the same construction project may be consolidated in the owner-contractor arbitration. Some subcontractor agreements contain provisions allowing consolidation of two or more related controversies involving the contractor, subcontractor, or other persons having contractual relations with the contractor.

The AAA will administer each case as filed unless directed by the courts to do otherwise. If all parties agree to consolidate a case or to split up a case, the AAA will follow their direction. Where a demand for arbitration is filed against multiple parties, the case will be initiated in that form; and if one of the respondents objects and there are separate contracts, the claims will be separated unless a party obtains an order of consolidation. When the parties named in the demand are signatories of the same contract, the AAA will combine the claims. The parties control the design and the operation of their own contractual system. The AAA's role is to try to determine what services have been requested. In general, the AAA attempts to expedite the arbitration, but always subject to direction from the courts.

EXPEDITED CONSTRUCTION ARBITRATION PROCEDURES

For those interested in further reducing the costs and delays in settling a construction dispute, expedited procedures are also available under AAA rules. These procedures are applied in any case where the total claim of any party does not exceed $15,000, exclusive of interest and arbitration costs. If both parties agree, expedited procedures may also be applied to cases involving claims of more than $15,000.

Under the expedited procedures, as a time-saving device, all notices and announcements are transmitted by the AAA to the parties by telephone and are subsequently confirmed in writing. The AAA also notifies the parties by telephone of the appointment of the arbitrator.

The date, time, and place of hearing are set by the arbitrator. The AAA will notify parties of these decisions by telephone seven days before the hearing, and will follow up with a Formal Notice of Hearing sent to each party.

The hearing and presentations of the parties are generally completed within one day. An additional hearing may be scheduled by the arbitrator, if necessary, to be held within five days. The award shall be rendered not later than five business days from the close of the hearing, unless otherwise agreed to by the parties.

IS MEDIATION THE ANSWER?

Experience under the construction industry rules indicates that although arbitration may provide a more attractive alternative in construction cases than litigation, it would be preferable for the parties to negotiate their own settlement without having to devote the time and effort required in arbitration.

What prevents successful negotiation? Sometimes the parties hesitate to initiate direct discussions. Mediation can encourage parties to institute discussions or to narrow their differences. Mediation involves the use of a third party to help the parties in reaching a mutual settlement.

The AAA's voluntary construction mediation program provides for the appointment of one or more mediators "with expertise in the area of the dispute and knowledge of the mediation process." The construction industry committee has established a panel of trained mediators. When drawing up a construction contract, parties can refer to the AAA's mediation program by agreeing to attempt mediation before going to arbitration. The following clause can be used:

> The parties hereby submit their dispute to mediation under the Construction Industry Mediation Rules of the American Arbitration Association. The requirement of filing a notice of claim shall be suspended until the conclusion of the mediation process.

In addition, the agreement can designate the mediators and any other details of the process.

Mediation is a voluntary process. The parties can withdraw and proceed to arbitration at any time. The rules provide that nothing that transpires during the mediation proceeding is intended in any way to affect the rights or prejudice the position of any of the parties to the dispute, whether in arbitration or in a court of law.

If the mediation is successful, the agreement is accomplished by the parties themselves. The mediator cannot force a settlement but, by encouraging meetings, can guide the parties and assist the negotiations. The mediator can help the parties to clarify issues and to set priorities. He or she can meet with each party separately when joint sessions have reached an impasse. During this pause in direct negotiations, a mediator may "shuttle" back and forth between the parties, bringing them together whenever further discussions would be productive.

The AAA's mediation procedures are simple and flexible. Mediation can take place at the project site or at any other location agreeable to the parties, and the AAA will make its hearing rooms available. The National Construction Industry Arbitration Committee encourages industry professionals to make use of mediation as a means of bringing about settlements.

HOME OWNER WARRANTY CLAIMS

The arbitration of claims under Home Owners Warranty (HOW) programs demonstrates the flexibility of the modern arbitration process. Patterned upon a system developed by home builders in England, it was adapted for this country by industry leaders. Home builders were concerned about increasing state legislation imposing liability upon builders for faulty construction. They were convinced that their members and the home building industry would benefit from the creation of a responsible warranty program. A program was established in 1974 to offer protection from certain construction defects to new home buyers. Each participating builder would agree to comply with approved building standards and would offer new home purchasers a warranty agreement. An important part of the agreement was a commitment by the builder to accept the judgment of impartial arbitrators.

The agreement to arbitrate is signed by the participating builder and the home owner. Some major builders have created their own systems. Others subscribe to the HOW program. In New Jersey, the state has a mandatory program for builders who are not part of a private system. The AAA provides administrative services. In any case, the warranty agreement is controlled by the approved standards, including local government codes that define performance. Quality standards set minimum levels that the finished house must meet.

The How of Home Owner Arbitration

Before attempting to arbitrate, the owner should check the standards and warranty to see if the particular defect is covered. He or she then discusses the problem with the builder.

If the parties are unable to settle their differences, the owner can file a request for dispute settlement. The local council will encourage the parties to settle their differences. If this is unsuccessful, a neutral will attempt to persuade the parties to resolve their problem, suggesting a formula for settling the dispute. The conciliator cannot force the parties to accept a proposed settlement, however, and where efforts at settling the dispute have been unsuccessful, the matter may be referred to arbitration.

The Arbitration Procedure

Home warranty arbitrations follow the administrative steps of selecting an arbitrator and hearing date. The arbitrator will be experienced in the home construction field and will be appointed, not selected, from lists. Retired builders, construction attorneys, independent structural engineers, civil engineers, architects, or real estate appraisers might serve as arbitrators. The arbitration takes place at the home, so that the arbitrator can examine the alleged defects with both parties present.

The hearing itself is informal, but may involve opening statements, witnesses, cross-examination, and closing statements. Parties to home warranty arbitrations can be represented by counsel; usually, however, they decide to present their own cases without an attorney.

The Award

The arbitrator's award must be mailed to the parties by the tribunal administrator. Each issue raised by the parties is decided in the award. The award describes what defects are to be remedied by the builder. The powers of the arbitrator are limited to the terms of the warranty. For example, the arbitrator cannot order the builder to repair or replace something that is not covered in the agreement.

The award is not binding on the owner. If the owner does accept the award, however, it is binding on the builder. If the award has been accepted by the owner, the builder must acknowledge that the award is accepted.

The rules provide that any party may request modification or clarification of the award within twenty days after it has been sent to them by the AAA. The tribunal administrator will then invite the other party to file comments regarding the request. The administrator forwards the correspondence to the arbitrator, who will consider the request and issue a written determination that is sent to the parties.

If the owner's claims are denied by the arbitrator, the industry pays the entire fee. But if the owner prevails, the builder must pay part of the fees. The owner does not pay any part of the cost.

Enforcement of Awards

The AAA's services are completed when it transmits a final award or modification. Inquiries regarding compliance with the award are sent to the other party. If a builder fails to abide by the award, satisfaction may be obtained through the insurance coverage included as part of the agreement. Arbitration serves several purposes. The owner of the home obtains a prompt and effective review of complaints. The builder knows that a businesslike dispute settlement mechanism will be available when needed. In addition, the courts are relieved of thousands of potential lawsuits.

CONCLUSION

The construction industry serves every segment of our society. It brings together more diverse groups than any other industry, so inevitably it faces many problems. By providing a modern mechanism for the resolution of construction contract disputes, arbitration is making a valuable contribution to a dynamic industry. As they gain wider acceptance, mediation and other alternative dispute resolution techniques may play an equally significant role in bringing about settlements and reducing the frequency of disputes on the construction site.

CONSTRUCTION INDUSTRY ARBITRATION RULES

As Amended and in Effect January 1, 1986

1. **Agreement of Parties**–The parties shall be deemed to have made these Rules a part of their arbitration agreement whenever they have provided for arbitration under the Construction Industry Arbitration Rules. These Rules and any amendment thereof shall apply in the form obtaining at the time the arbitration is initiated.

2. **Name of Tribunal**–Any Tribunal constituted by the parties for the settlement of their dispute under these Rules shall be called the Construction Industry Arbitration Tribunal, hereinafter called the Tribunal.

3. **Administrator**–When parties agree to arbitrate under these Rules, or when they provide for arbitration by the American Arbitration Association, hereinafter called AAA, and an arbitration is initiated hereunder, they thereby constitute AAA the administrator of the arbitration. The authority and duties of the administrator are prescribed in the agreement of the parties and in these Rules.

4. **Delegation of Duties**–The duties of the AAA under these Rules may be carried out through Tribunal Administrators, or such other officers or committees as the AAA may direct.

5. **National Panel of Arbitrators**–In cooperation with the National Construction Industry Arbitration Committee, the AAA shall establish and maintain a National Panel of Construction Arbitrators, hereinafter called the Panel, and shall appoint an arbitrator or arbitrators therefrom as hereinafter provided. A neutral arbitrator selected by mutual choice of both parties or their appointees, or appointed by the AAA, is hereinafter called the arbitrator, whereas an arbitrator selected unilaterally by one party is hereinafter called the party-appointed arbitrator. The term arbitrator may hereinafter be used to refer to one arbitrator or to a Tribunal of multiple arbitrators.

6. **Office of Tribunal**–The general office of a Tribunal is the headquarters of the AAA, which may, however, assign the administration of an arbitration to any of its Regional Offices.

7. **Initiation under an Arbitration Provision in a Contract**–Arbitration under an arbitration provision in a contract shall be initiated in the following manner:

The initiating party shall, within the time specified by the contract, if any, file with the other party a notice of an intention to arbitrate (Demand), which notice shall contain a statement setting forth the nature of the dispute, the amount involved, and the remedy sought; and shall file three copies of said notice with any Regional Office of the AAA, together with three copies of the arbitration provisions of the contract and the appropriate filing fee as provided in Section 48 hereunder.

The AAA shall give notice of such filing to the other party. A party upon whom the demand for arbitration is made may file an answering statement in duplicate with the AAA within seven days after notice from the AAA, simultaneously sending a copy to the other party. If a monetary claim is made in the answer the appropriate administrative fee provided in the Fee Schedule shall be forwarded to the AAA with the answer. If no answer is filed within the stated time, it will be treated as a denial of the claim. Failure to file an answer shall not operate to delay the arbitration.

Unless the AAA in its discretion determines otherwise, the Expedited Procedures of Construction Arbitration shall be applied in any case where the total claim of any party does not exceed $15,000, exclusive of interest and arbitration costs. Parties may also agree to the Expedited Procedures in cases involving claims in excess of $15,000. The Expedited Procedures shall be applied as described in Sections 54 through 58 of these Rules.

8. Change of Claim or Counterclaim—After filing of the claim or counterclaim, if either party desires to make any new or different claim or counterclaim, same shall be made in writing and filed with the AAA, and a copy thereof shall be mailed to the other party who shall have a period of seven days from the date of such mailing within which to file an answer with the AAA. However, after the arbitrator is appointed no new or different claim or counterclaim may be submitted without the arbitrator's consent.

9. Initiation under a Submission—Parties to any existing dispute may commence an arbitration under these Rules by filing at any Regional Office two copies of a written agreement to arbitrate under these Rules (Submission), signed by the parties. It shall contain a statement of the matter in dispute, the amount of money involved, and the remedy sought, together with the appropriate filing fee as provided in the Fee Schedule.

10. Pre-Hearing Conference and Preliminary Hearing—At the request of the parties or at the discretion of the AAA, a pre-hearing conference with the administrator and the parties or their counsel will be scheduled in appropriate cases to arrange for an exchange of information and the stipulation of uncontested facts so as to expedite the arbitration proceedings.

In large and complex cases, unless the parties agree otherwise, the AAA may schedule a preliminary hearing with the parties and the arbitrator(s) to establish the extent of and schedule for the production of relevant documents and other information, the identification of any witnesses to be called, and a schedule for further hearings to resolve the dispute.

11. Fixing of Locale—The parties may mutually agree on the locale where the arbitration is to be held. If any party requests that the hearing be held in a specific locale and the other party files no objection thereto within seven days after notice of the request is mailed to such party, the locale shall be the one requested. If a party objects to the locale requested by the other party, the AAA shall have power to determine the locale and its decision shall be final and binding.

12. Qualifications of Arbitrator—Any arbitrator appointed pursuant to Section 13 or Section 15 shall be neutral, subject to disqualification for the reasons specified in Section 19. If the agreement of the parties names an arbitrator or specifies any other method of appointing an arbitrator, or if the parties specifically agree in writing, such arbitrator shall not be subject to disqualification for said reasons.

13. Appointment from Panel—If the parties have not appointed an arbitrator and have not provided any other method of appointment, the arbitrator shall be appointed in the following manner: Immediately after the filing of the Demand or Submission, the AAA shall submit simultaneously to each party to the dispute an identical list of names of persons chosen from the Panel. Each party to the dispute shall have seven days from the mailing date in which to cross off any names to which it objects, number the remaining names to indicate the order of preference, and return the list to the AAA. If a party does not return the list within the time specified, all persons named therein shall be deemed acceptable. From among the persons who have been approved on both lists, and in accordance with the designated order of mutual preference, the AAA shall invite the acceptance of an arbitrator to serve. If the parties fail to agree upon any of the persons named, or if acceptable arbitrators are unable to act, or if for any other reason the appointment cannot be made from the submitted lists, the AAA shall have the power to make the appointment from other members of the Panel without the submission of any additional lists.

14. Direct Appointment by Parties–If the agreement of the parties names an arbitrator or specifies a method of appointing an arbitrator, that designation or method shall be followed. The notice of appointment, with name and address of such arbitrator, shall be filed with the AAA by the appointing party. Upon the request of any such appointing party, the AAA shall submit a list of members of the Panel from which the party may make the appointment.

If the agreement specifies a period of time within which an arbitrator shall be appointed, and any party fails to make such appointment within that period, the AAA shall make the appointment.

If no period of time is specified in the agreement, the AAA shall notify the parties to make the appointment, and if within seven days after mailing of such notice such arbitrator has not been so appointed, the AAA shall make the appointment.

15. Appointment of Arbitrator by Party-Appointed Arbitrators–If the parties have appointed their party-appointed arbitrators or if either or both of them have been appointed as provided in Section 14, and have authorized such arbitrator to appoint an arbitrator within a specified time and no appointment is made within such time or any agreed extension thereof, the AAA shall appoint an arbitrator who shall act as Chairperson.

If no period of time is specified for appointment of the third arbitrator and the party-appointed arbitrators do not make the appointment within seven days from the date of the appointment of the last party-appointed arbitrator, the AAA shall appoint the arbitrator who shall act as Chairperson.

If the parties have agreed that their party-appointed arbitrators shall appoint the arbitrator from the Panel, the AAA shall furnish to the party-appointed arbitrators, in the manner prescribed in Section 13, a list selected from the Panel, and the appointment of the arbitrator shall be made as prescribed in such Section.

16. Nationality of Arbitrator in International Arbitration–If one of the parties is a national or resident of a country other than the United States, the arbitrator shall, upon the request of either party, be appointed from among the nationals of a country other than that of any of the parties.

17. Number of Arbitrators–If the arbitration agreement does not specify the number of arbitrators, the dispute shall be heard and determined by one arbitrator, unless the AAA, in its discretion, directs that a greater number of arbitrators be appointed.

18. Notice to Arbitrator of Appointment–Notice of the appointment of the arbitrator, whether mutually appointed by the parties or appointed by the AAA, shall be mailed to the arbitrator by the AAA, together with a copy of these Rules, and the signed acceptance of the arbitrator shall be filed prior to the opening of the first hearing.

19. Disclosure and Challenge Procedure—A person appointed as neutral arbitrator shall disclose to the AAA any circumstances likely to affect his or her impartiality, including any bias or any financial or personal interest in the result of the arbitration or any past or present relationship with the parties or their counsel. Upon receipt of such information from such arbitrator or other source, the AAA shall communicate such information to the parties and, if it deems it appropriate to do so, to the arbitrator and others. Thereafter, the AAA shall determine whether the arbitrator should be disqualified and shall inform the parties of its decision, which shall be conclusive.

20. Vacancies—If any arbitrator should resign, die, withdraw, refuse, be disqualified or be unable to perform the duties of office, the AAA shall, on proof satisfactory to it, declare the office vacant. Vacancies shall be filled in accordance with the applicable provisions of these Rules. In the event of a vacancy in a panel of arbitrators, the remaining arbitrator or arbitrators may continue with the hearing and determination of the controversy, unless the parties agree otherwise.

21. Time and Place—The arbitrator shall fix the time and place for each hearing. The AAA shall mail to each party notice thereof at least five days in advance, unless the parties by mutual agreement waive such notice or modify the terms thereof.

22. Representation by Counsel—Any party may be represented by counsel. A party intending to be so represented shall notify the other party and the AAA of the name and address of counsel at least three days prior to the date set for the hearing at which counsel is first to appear. When an arbitration is initiated by counsel, or where an attorney replies for the other party, such notice is deemed to have been given.

23. Stenographic Record—Any party wishing a stenographic record shall make such arrangements directly with the stenographer and shall notify the other parties of such arrangements in advance of the hearing. The requesting party or parties shall pay the cost of such record.

24. Interpreter—Any party wishing an interpreter shall make all arrangements directly with an interpreter and shall assume the costs of such service.

25. Attendance at Hearings—Persons having a direct interest in the arbitration are entitled to attend hearings. The arbitrator shall otherwise have the power to require the retirement of any witness or witnesses during the testimony of other witnesses. It shall be discretionary with the arbitrator to determine the propriety of the attendance of any other persons.

26. Adjournments—The arbitrator may adjourn the hearing, and must take such adjournment when all of the parties agree thereto.

27. Oaths—Before proceeding with the first hearing or with the examination of the file, each arbitrator may take an oath of office, and if required by law, shall do so. The arbitrator may require witnesses to testify under oath administered by any duly qualified person or, if required by law or demanded by either party, shall do so.

28. Majority Decision—Whenever there is more than one arbitrator, all decisions of the arbitrators must be by at least a majority. The award must also be made by at least a majority unless the concurrence of all is expressly required by the arbitration agreement or by law.

29. Order of Proceedings—A hearing shall be opened by the filing of the oath of the arbitrator, where required, and by the recording of the place, time, and date of the hearing, the presence of the arbitrator and parties, and counsel, if any, and by the receipt by the arbitrator of the statement of the claim and answer, if any.

The arbitrator may, at the beginning of the hearing, ask for statements clarifying the issues involved. In some cases, part or all of the above will have been accomplished at the preliminary hearing conducted by the arbitrator(s) pursuant to Section 10.

The complaining party shall then present its claims, proofs and witnesses, who shall submit to questions or other examination. The defending party shall then present its defenses, proofs and witnesses, who shall submit to questions or other examination. The arbitrator may vary this procedure but shall afford full and equal opportunity to the parties for the presentation of any material or relevant proofs.

Exhibits, when offered by either party, may be received in evidence by the arbitrator.

The names and addresses of all witnesses and exhibits in order received shall be made a part of the record.

30. Arbitration in the Absence of a Party or Counsel–Unless the law provides to the contrary, the arbitration may proceed in the absence of any party or counsel, who, after due notice, fails to be present or fails to obtain an adjournment. An award shall not be made solely on the default of a party. The arbitrator shall require the party who is present to submit such evidence as is deemed necessary for the making of an award.

31. Evidence–The parties may offer such evidence as is pertinent and material to the controversy and shall produce such additional evidence as the arbitrator may deem necessary to an understanding and determination of the controversy. An arbitrator authorized by law to subpoena witnesses or documents may do so upon the request of any party, or independently.

The arbitrator shall be the judge of the relevance and the materiality of the evidence offered, and conformity to legal rules of evidence shall not be necessary. All evidence shall be taken in the presence of all of the arbitrators and all of the parties, except where any of the parties is absent in default or has waived the right to be present.

32. Evidence by Affidavit and Filing of Documents–The arbitrator shall receive and consider the evidence of witnesses by affidavit, giving it such weight as seems appropriate after consideration of any objections made to its admission.

All documents not filed with the arbitrator at the hearing, but arranged for at the hearing or subsequently by agreement of the parties, shall be filed with the AAA for transmission to the arbitrator. All parties shall be afforded opportunity to examine such documents.

33. Inspection or Investigation–An arbitrator finding it necessary to make an inspection or investigation in connection with the arbitration shall direct the AAA to so advise the parties. The arbitrator shall set the time and the AAA shall notify the parties thereof. Any party who so desires may be present at such inspection or investigation. In the event that one or both parties are not present at the inspection or investigation, the arbitrator shall make a verbal or written report to the parties and afford them an opportunity to comment.

34. Conservation of Property–The arbitrator may issue such orders as may be deemed necessary to safeguard the property which is the subject matter of the arbitration without prejudice to the rights of the parties or to the final determination of the dispute.

35. Closing of Hearings–The arbitrator shall specifically inquire of the parties whether they have any further proofs to offer or witnesses to be heard. Upon receiving negative replies, the arbitrator shall declare the hearings closed and a minute thereof shall be recorded. If briefs are to be filed, the hearings shall be declared closed as of the final date set by the arbitrator for the receipt of briefs. If documents are to be filed as provided for in Section 32 and the date set for their receipt is later than that set for the receipt of briefs, the later date shall be the date of closing the hearing. The time limit within which the arbitrator is required to make the award shall commence to run, in the absence of other agreements by the parties, upon the closing of the hearings.

36. Reopening of Hearings–The hearings may be reopened by the arbitrator at will, or upon application of a party at any time before the award is made. If the reopening of the hearing would prevent the making of the award within the specific time agreed upon by the parties in the contract out of which the controversy has arisen, the matter may not be reopened, unless the parties agree upon the extension of such time limit. When no specific date is fixed in the contract, the arbitrator may reopen the hearings, and the arbitrator shall have thirty days from the closing of the reopened hearings within which to make an award.

37. Waiver of Oral Hearings–The parties may provide, by written agreement, for the waiver of oral hearings. If the parties are unable to agree as to the procedure, the AAA shall specify a fair and equitable procedure.

38. Waiver of Rules–Any party who proceeds with the arbitration after knowledge that any provision or requirement of these Rules has not been complied with and who fails to state an objection thereto in writing, shall be deemed to have waived the right to object.

39. Extensions of Time–The parties may modify any period of time by mutual agreement. The AAA for good cause may extend any period of time established by these Rules, except the time for making the award. The AAA shall notify the parties of any such extension of time and its reason therefor.

40. Communication with Arbitrator and Serving of Notices–There shall be no communication between the parties and an arbitrator other than at oral hearings. Any other oral or written communications from the parties to the arbitrator shall be directed to the AAA for transmittal to the arbitrator.

Each party to an agreement which provides for arbitration under these Rules shall be deemed to have consented that any papers, notices or process necessary or proper for the initiation or continuation of an arbitration under these Rules and for any court action in connection therewith or for the entry of judgment on any award made thereunder may be served upon such party by mail addressed to such party or its attorney at its last known address or by personal service, within or without the state wherein the arbitration is to be held (whether such party be within or without the United States of America), provided that reasonable opportunity to be heard with regard thereto has been granted such party.

41. Time of Award–The award shall be made promptly by the arbitrator and, unless otherwise agreed by the parties, or specified by law, no later than thirty days from the date of closing the hearings, or if oral hearings have been waived, from the date of transmitting the final statements and proofs to the arbitrator.

42. Form of Award–The award shall be in writing and shall be signed either by the sole arbitrator or by at least a majority if there be more than one. It shall be executed in the manner required by law.

43. Scope of Award–The arbitrator may grant any remedy or relief which is just and equitable and within the terms of the agreement of the parties. The arbitrator, in the award, shall assess arbitration fees and expenses as provided in Sections 48 and 50 equally or in favor of any party and, in the event any administrative fees or expenses are due the AAA, in favor of the AAA.

44. Award upon Settlement–If the parties settle their dispute during the course of the arbitration, the arbitrator, upon their request, may set forth the terms of the agreed settlement in an award.

45. Delivery of Award to Parties–Parties shall accept as legal delivery of the award the placing of the award or a true copy thereof in the mail by the AAA, addressed to such party at its last known address or to its attorney, or personal service of the award, or the filing of the award in any manner which may be prescribed by law.

46. Release of Documents for Judicial Proceedings–The AAA shall, upon the written request of a party, furnish to such party, at its expense, certified facsimiles of any papers in the AAA's possession that may be required in judicial proceedings relating to the arbitration.

47. Applications to Court and Exclusion of Liability–(a) No judicial proceedings by a party relating to the subject matter of the arbitration shall be deemed a waiver of the party's right to arbitrate.

(b) Neither the AAA nor any arbitrator in a proceeding under these Rules is a necessary party in judicial proceedings relating to the arbitration.

(c) Parties to these Rules shall be deemed to have consented that judgment upon the award rendered by the arbitrator(s) may be entered in any Federal or State Court having jurisdiction thereof.

(d) Neither the AAA nor any arbitrator shall be liable to any party for any act or omission in connection with any arbitration conducted under these Rules.

48. Administrative Fees–As a not-for-profit organization, the AAA shall prescribe an administrative fee schedule and a refund schedule to compensate it for the cost of providing administrative services. The schedule in effect at the time of filing or the time of refund shall be applicable.

The administrative fees shall be advanced by the initiating party or parties in accordance with the administrative fee schedule, subject to final apportionment by the arbitrator in the award.

When a matter is withdrawn or settled, the refund shall be made in accordance with the refund schedule.

The AAA, in the event of extreme hardship on the part of any party, may defer or reduce the administrative fee.

49. Fee When Oral Hearings are Waived–Where all oral hearings are waived under Section 37, the Administrative Fee Schedule shall apply.

50. Expenses–The expenses of witnesses for either side shall be paid by the party producing such witnesses.

The cost of the stenographic record, if any is made, and all transcripts thereof, shall be prorated equally between the parties ordering copies, unless they shall otherwise agree, and shall be paid for by the responsible parties directly to the reporting agency.

All other expenses of the arbitration, including required traveling and other expenses of the arbitrator and of AAA representatives, and the expenses of any witness or the cost of any proofs produced at the direct request of the arbitrator, shall be borne equally by the parties, unless they agree otherwise, or unless the arbitrator in the award assesses such expenses or any part thereof against any specified party or parties.

51. Arbitrator's Fee—Unless the parties agree to terms of compensation, members of the National Panel of Construction Arbitrators will serve without compensation for the first day of service.

Thereafter, compensation shall be based upon the amount of service involved and the number of hearings. An appropriate daily rate and other arrangements will be discussed by the administrator with the parties and the arbitrator(s). If the parties fail to agree to the terms of compensation, an appropriate rate shall be established by the AAA, and communicated in writing to the parties.

Any arrangement for the compensation of an arbitrator shall be made through the AAA and not directly by the arbitrator with the parties. The terms of compensation of neutral arbitrators on a Tribunal shall be identical.

52. Deposits—The AAA may require the parties to deposit in advance such sums of money as it deems necessary to defray the expense of the arbitration, including the arbitrator's fee, if any, and shall render an accounting to the parties and return any unexpended balance.

53. Interpretation and Application of Rules—The arbitrator shall interpret and apply these Rules insofar as they relate to the arbitrator's powers and duties. When there is more than one arbitrator and a difference arises among them concerning the meaning or application of any such Rules, it shall be decided by a majority vote. If that is unobtainable, either an arbitrator or a party may refer the question to the AAA for final decision. All other Rules shall be interpreted and applied by the AAA.

EXPEDITED PROCEDURES

54. Notice by Telephone—The parties shall accept all notices from the AAA by telephone. Such notices by the AAA shall subsequently be confirmed in writing to the parties. Notwithstanding the failure to confirm in writing any notice or objection hereunder, the proceeding shall nonetheless be valid if notice has, in fact, been given by telephone.

55. Appointment and Qualifications of Arbitrators—The AAA shall submit simultaneously to each party to the dispute an identical list of five members of the Construction Arbitration Panel of Arbitrators from which one arbitrator shall be appointed. Each party shall have the right to strike two names from the list on a peremptory basis. The list is returnable to the AAA within ten days from the date of mailing. If for any reason the appointment cannot be made from the list, the AAA shall have the authority to make the appointment from among other members of the Panel without the submission of additional lists. Such appointment shall be subject to disqualification for the reasons specified in Section 19. The parties shall be given notice by telephone by the AAA of the appointment of the arbitrator. The parties shall notify the AAA, by telephone, within seven days of any objections to the arbitrator appointed. Any objection by a party to such arbitrator shall be confirmed in writing to the AAA with a copy to the other party(ies).

56. Time and Place of Hearing–The arbitrator shall fix the date, time, and place of the hearing. The AAA will notify the parties by telephone, seven days in advance of the hearing date. Formal Notice of Hearing will be sent by the AAA to the parties.

57. The Hearing–Generally, the hearing and presentations of the parties shall be completed within one day. The arbitrator, for good cause shown, may schedule an additional hearing to be held within five days.

58. Time of Award–Unless otherwise agreed to by the parties, the award shall be rendered not later than five business days from the date of the closing of the hearing.

CONSTRUCTION INDUSTRY MEDIATION RULES

As Amended and in Effect May 1, 1985

1. Agreement of Parties–Whenever, by stipulation or in their contract, the parties have provided for mediation of existing or future disputes under the auspices of the American Arbitration Association (AAA) or under these Rules, they shall be deemed to have made these Rules, as amended and in effect as of the date of the submission of the dispute, a part of their agreement.

2. Initiation of Mediation–Any party or parties to a dispute may initiate mediation by filing with the AAA a written request for mediation pursuant to these Rules, together with the appropriate administrative fee contained in the Administrative Fee Schedule.

3. Request for Mediation–A request for mediation shall contain a brief statement of the nature of the dispute and the names, addresses, and phone numbers of all parties to the dispute, and those who will represent them, if any, in the mediation. The initiating party shall simultaneously file two (2) copies of the request with the AAA and one copy with every other party to the dispute.

4. Appointment of Mediator–Upon receipt of a request for mediation, the AAA will appoint a qualified mediator to serve. Normally, a single mediator will be appointed unless the parties agree otherwise or the AAA determines otherwise. If the agreement of the parties names a mediator or specifies a method of appointing a mediator, that designation or method shall be followed.

5. Qualifications of a Mediator–Any mediator appointed shall be a member of the AAA's Construction Mediation Panel, with expertise in the area of the dispute and knowledgeable in the mediation process.

No person shall serve as a mediator in any dispute in which that person has any financial or personal interest in the result of the mediation, except by the written consent of all parties. Prior to accepting an appointment, the prospective mediator shall disclose any circumstances likely to create a presumption of bias or prevent a prompt meeting with the parties. Upon receipt of such information, the AAA shall either replace the mediator or immediately communicate the information to the parties for their comments. In the event the parties disagree as to whether the mediator shall serve, the AAA will appoint another mediator. The AAA is authorized to appoint another mediator if the appointed mediator is unable to serve promptly.

6. Vacancies–If any mediator shall become unwilling or unable to serve, the AAA will appoint another mediator, unless the parties agree otherwise.

7. Representation–Any party may be represented by persons of their choice. The names and addresses of such persons shall be communicated in writing to all parties and to the AAA.

8. Time and Place of Mediation–The mediator shall fix the time of each mediation session. The mediation shall be held at the appropriate regional office of the AAA, or at any other convenient location agreeable to the mediator and the parties, as the mediator shall determine.

9. Identification of Matters in Dispute–At least ten (10) days prior to the first scheduled mediation session, each party shall provide the mediator with a brief memorandum setting forth its position with regard to the issues that need to be resolved. At the discretion of the mediator, such memoranda may be mutually exchanged by the parties.

At the first session, the parties will be expected to produce all information reasonably required for the mediator to understand the issues presented. The mediator may require either party to supplement such information.

10. Authority of Mediator—The mediator does not have authority to impose a settlement upon the parties but will attempt to help the parties reach a satisfactory resolution of their dispute. The mediator is authorized to conduct joint and separate meetings with the parties and to make oral and written recommendations for settlement. Whenever necessary, the mediator may also obtain expert advice concerning technical aspects of the dispute, provided the parties agree and assume the expenses of obtaining such advice. Arrangements for obtaining such advice shall be made by the mediator or the parties, as the mediator shall determine.

The mediator is authorized to end the mediation whenever, in the judgment of the mediator, further efforts at mediation would not contribute to a resolution of the dispute between the parties.

11. Privacy—Mediation sessions are private. The parties and their representatives may attend mediation sessions. Other persons may attend only with the permission of the parties and with the consent of the mediator.

12. Confidentiality—Confidential information disclosed to a mediator by the parties or by witnesses in the course of the mediation shall not be divulged by the mediator. All records, reports, or other documents received by a mediator while serving in such capacity shall be confidential. The mediator shall not be compelled to divulge such records or to testify in regard to the mediation in any adversary proceeding or judicial forum.

The parties shall maintain the confidentiality of the mediation and shall not rely on, or introduce as evidence in any arbitral, judicial or other proceedings: (a) views expressed or suggestions made by the other party with respect to a possible settlement of the dispute; (b) admissions made by the other party in the course of the mediation proceedings; (c) proposals made or views expressed by the mediator; (d) the fact that the other party had or had not indicated willingness to accept a proposal for settlement made by the mediator.

13. No Stenographic Record—There shall be no stenographic record of the mediation process.

14. Termination of Mediation—The mediation shall be terminated: (a) by the execution of a settlement agreement by the parties; or (b) by a written declaration of the mediator to the effect that further efforts at mediation are no longer worthwhile; or (c) by a written declaration of a party or parties to the effect that the mediation proceedings are terminated.

15. Exclusion of Liability—Neither the AAA nor any mediator is a necessary party in judicial proceedings relating to the mediation.

Neither the AAA nor any mediator shall be liable to any party for any act or omission in connection with any mediation conducted under these Rules.

16. Interpretation and Application of Rules—The mediator shall interpret and apply these Rules insofar as they relate to the mediator's duties and responsibilities. All other Rules shall be interpreted and applied by the AAA.

17. Expenses—The expenses of witnesses for either side shall be paid by the party producing such witnesses. All other expenses of the mediation, including required travelling and other expenses of the mediator and representatives of the AAA, and the expenses of any witness, or the cost of any proofs or expert advice produced at the direct request of the mediator, shall be borne equally by the parties unless they agree otherwise.

BIBLIOGRAPHY

Acret, James. *Construction Arbitration Handbook.* Colorado Springs: Shepard's/McGraw-Hill, 1985.

Allen, Randall C. "Construction Arbitration: Some Practical Considerations." *Construction Claims Monthly*, vol. 3, no. 6 (June 1981), pp. 1–8.

American Arbitration Association. *Construction Industry Arbitration Rules: As Amended and in Effect January 1, 1986.* New York: 1986.

______. *Construction Industry Mediation Rules: As Amended and in Effect May 1, 1985.* New York: 1985.

______. *A Guide for Construction Industry Arbitrators.* New York: 1985.

______. *An Outline of the Law and Practice of Arbitration under the Construction Industry Arbitration Rules of the American Arbitration Association.* New York: 1984.

American Institute of Architects. *Architect's Handbook of Professional Practice.* Washington, D.C.: 1980–Present (ongoing publication).

Callahan, Michael T. "Advocacy in Construction Arbitration." *Trial Diplomacy Journal*, vol. 3, no. 3 (Fall 1980), pp. 26–29.

______. "Discovery in Construction Arbitration." *The Arbitration Journal*, vol. 37, no. 1 (March 1982), pp. 3–9.

______. "Procedures in Construction Arbitration: From an Arbitrator's View." *Construction Law*, vol. 3, no. 2 (Spring 1982), p. 3.

Coulson, Robert. "Dispute Management under Modern Construction Systems." *Law and Contemporary Problems*, vol. 46, no. 1 (Winter 1983), pp. 127–135.

Cushman, Robert F., ed. *The McGraw-Hill Construction Business Handbook: A Practical Guide to Accounting, Credit, Finance, Insurance, and Law for the Construction Industry.* New York: McGraw-Hill, 1978.

Cushman, Robert F., Michael S. Simon, and McNeil Stokes. *The Construction Industry Formbook: A Practical Guide to Reviewing and Drafting Forms for the Construction Industry.* Colorado Springs: Shepard's, 1979.

"Effect of Arbitration Agreements on Assignees, Guarantors and Other Non-Parties." *Lawyers' Arbitration Letter*, vol. 1, no. 17 (March 1977), p. 6.

Engineering News-Record and Conference and Exposition Management Company. *Construction Claims and Disputes for Owners and Contractors: Everything You Must Know about Presenting and Defending a Claim.* New York: Engineering News-Record, 1982.

Gallagher, Gerard B. "The Case for Writing in an Arbitration Clause." *Building Design and Construction*, vol. 25 (January 1984), p. 45.

Gibbons, Margaret, and Linda M. Miller, eds. *Construction Arbitration: Selected Readings.* New York: American Arbitration Association, 1981.

Guidelines for Improving Practice: Architects and Engineers Professional Liability. Washington, D.C.: Office for Professional Liability Research of Victor O. Schinnerer, n.d.

Hauf, Harold D. *Building Contracts for Design and Construction.* 2d ed. New York: John Wiley, 1976.

Hoellering, Michael F. "Construction Arbitration and Mediation." *Journal of the American Water Works Association*, February 1984, pp. 34–38.

______. "New Approaches to Resolving Disputes in Building Industry." *New York Law Journal*, April 12, 1979, p. 1.

Little, David C. "The Architect's Immunity as Arbiter." *Saint Louis University Law Journal*, vol. 23, no. 2 (1979), pp. 339–350.

O'Brien, James Jerome. *Construction Delay: Responsibilities, Risks and Litigation.* Boston: Cahners Books International, 1976.

Page, Rosemary S. "Construction Cases." *New York Law Journal*, May 15, 1984, p. 1.

______. "Legal Aspects of Arbitration." In *Construction Contracts 1977.* New York: Practising Law Institute, 1977, pp. 411–434.

______. "Subcontractors and Arbitration." *New York Law Journal*, June 12, 1980, p. 1.

Reiss, Jerome. "Construction Industry Disputes." In Alan I. Widiss, ed., *Arbitration: Commercial Disputes, Insurance, and Tort Claims*. New York: Practising Law Institute, 1979, pp. 69–111.

Richards, Bradley J. "Enforceability of Arbitration Provisions in Construction Contracts." *Federation of Insurance Counsel Quarterly*, vol. 34 (Fall 1983), pp. 95–110.

Richter, Irv, and Jeffrey B. Kozek. "Construction Arbitration Procedures: Basic Principles and Guidelines." *Construction Briefings*, October 1978, pp. 1–14.

______. "Proving Damages in Arbitration: Basic Principles and Guidelines." *Construction Briefings*, July 1979, pp. 1–14.

Richter, Irv, and Roy S. Mitchell. *Handbook of Construction Law and Claims*. Reston, Va.: Reston Publishing, 1982.

Schwartz, Max. "Evidence in Construction Arbitration." *The Arbitration Journal*, vol. 31, no. 4 (December 1976), pp. 248–253.

______. "Selection of Engineering Experts." *The Arbitration Journal*, vol. 32, no. 3 (September 1977), pp. 195–202.

Stokes, McNeil. *Construction Law in Contractors' Language*. New York: McGraw-Hill, 1977.

Walker, Nathan, Edward N. Walker, and Theodor K. Rohdenburg. *Legal Pitfalls in Architecture, Engineering and Building Construction (with Special Forms)*. 2d ed. New York: McGraw-Hill, 1979.

CHAPTER 3

THE TEXTILE AND APPAREL INDUSTRIES

In no other industries do fashion and technology play such an important role as in the textile and apparel trades. When business executives and designers guess correctly about the public's preference for the coming season, almost anything sells. The industry prospers. When the consumer demand moves elsewhere, the picture changes. Mills, converters, and cutters drown in unsold goods. Manufacturers glare at their unpaid bills. Controversies multiply, and insolvency beckons.

How can such controversies best be settled? Who should decide whether a fabric was rejected because quality standards had not been met or because the purchaser bought similar goods elsewhere at a lower price? When goods are only somewhat inferior, but still saleable, who is to fix a fair price?

HISTORY OF TEXTILE ARBITRATION

In 1920, the New York legislature enacted the first modern arbitration law in the United States. New York was particularly important because arbitrations in the textile and apparel industries are almost always heard in New York City.

Arbitration has been an important part of the textile industry for many years. Each historical strand contributed to the present system. Many years ago, for example, the needle trades concluded that their disagreements did not belong in court. The issues were often technical, calling for knowledge and expertise that could not be found among judges or jurors.

The New England Cotton Manufacturers Association, formed in 1854, is now known as the Northern Textile Association. In the South, the American Cotton Manufacturers Association took shape. These groups then represented the northern and southern cotton mills. Their members sold their products through sales firms based in New York, organized through the Association of Cotton Textile Merchants of New York since 1918. These firms were then based in and around Worth Street in lower New York City. The famous Worth Street Rules were an attempt to bring quality, uniformity, and reliable performance to the industry. A committee on arbitration formed by the textile merchants demonstrated that it was possible for an industry to regulate its own commercial standards through voluntary, contractual methods.

The history of arbitration was much the same in wool, silk, yarn, and man-made fibers. Each of these industries first attempted to create its own system of uniform contracts and arbitration procedures, and then joined with the industry-wide General Arbitration Council of the Textile and Apparel Industries (GAC). For example, in 1971, the National Association of Wool Manufacturers merged into the Association of Textile Manufacturers Institute (ATMI), one of the leading members of GAC. In the same way, the National Federation of Textiles, which had established an arbitration bureau for silk and rayon trade disputes, joined the other segments of the industry in ATMI and became part of GAC. A similar merger took place with the American Yarn Spinners Association.

Encouraged by the New York law, the industry's interest in voluntary arbitration grew rapidly. After the General Arbitration Council of the Textile Industry was formed in 1930, the caseload increased. In 1958, the Arbitration Bureau of the National Federation of Textiles was merged into the General Arbitration Council.

At the same time, some contracts in the textile and apparel industries provided for arbitration under the AAA's commercial rules. In May 1964, the GAC became a division of the AAA, making use of its hearing rooms, research facilities, and administrative skills. GAC retains a separate identity so that arbitrations can still be administered under its rules. Parties to disputes involving cloth and yarn mills, converters, dyers, printers, garment manufacturers, and any other aspect of the industry now have a choice–they can agree to arbitration under GAC rules or AAA commercial rules. In either case, the AAA staff and services are available.

BRINGING A DISPUTE TO ARBITRATION

In the textile and apparel industries, most documents contain a "future disputes clause." These are found on the face of contracts, purchase orders, and confirmation-of-order forms. These clauses refer to the Rules of the General Arbitration Council of the Textile and Apparel Industries or to AAA's Commercial Arbitration Rules.

Some arbitration clauses give the party bringing the matter to arbitration the option of selecting either the GAC or the AAA, and read as follows:

> Any controversy or claim arising under, or in relation to, this contract shall be settled by arbitration which shall be held in the City of New York in accordance with the laws of the State of New York, and the rules then obtaining of the General Arbitration Council of the Textile and Apparel Industries, or the American Arbitration Association, as the party first referring the matter to arbitration shall elect. The parties consent to the personal jurisdiction and venue of the Supreme Court of the State of New York, and the United States District Court for the Southern District of New

> York, and further consent that any process or notice of motion or other application to the court or a judge thereof may be served outside of the State of New York by registered or certified mail or by personal service, provided a reasonable time for appearance is allowed. Judgment upon the award rendered by the arbitrator(s) may be entered in any state or federal court having jurisdiction thereof.

The textile department of the AAA's New York regional office administers all kinds of textile and apparel disputes. This group administers cases under both the GAC and AAA rules. Although most cases conducted under the GAC rules are administered by the New York City regional office, there have been some cases administered in other AAA regional offices. The same rules apply, but the specified locale is different.

THE BATTLE OF THE FORMS

The arbitration clause in the purchase order does not always match the clause in the confirmation form. Although both parties may wish to arbitrate, they have not agreed on the procedure. In such circumstances, the parties can still designate their choice by filling out a "submission agreement," setting forth the issue in dispute and containing the following language:

> We, the undersigned parties, hereby agree to submit to arbitration under the Rules of [the AAA or the GAC] the following controversy: (state briefly). We further agree that we will faithfully observe this agreement and the Rules, and that we will abide by and perform any award and that a judgment of the court having jurisdiction may be entered upon the award.

A problem can arise if the parties have not explicitly agreed to arbitrate. A 1978 case in the Court of Appeals in New York, *Marlene Industries Corp.* v. *Carnac Textiles*, 45 N.Y.2d 327, 380 N.E.2d 239, 408 N.Y.S.2d 410 (1978), concerned such a situation. The parties entered into an oral agreement for the purchase and sale of some fabric. Marlene sent a printed purchase order to Carnac that did not contain an arbitration clause and stated that its terms could not be superseded by an unsigned contract. Carnac sent an Acknowledgment of Order with the usual arbitration clause. Neither party signed the other's document. The fabric was delivered. Some was accepted and paid for—some was rejected.

When Carnac commenced arbitration under the terms of its form, Marlene moved in court to stay the arbitration. The lower court and intermediate appellate courts ordered the arbitration to proceed, noting that arbitration was the norm in the industry. But the Court of Appeals reversed the lower courts. Ignoring the long history of arbitration in the textile industry, the court held that an arbitration clause was a material alteration in a contract of sale that could not be inferred without a clear agreement.

More recent court decisions, however, have helped refine the *Marlene* doctrine, even in cases involving unsigned documents. Among these are *Schubtex, Inc.* v. *Allen Snyder, Inc.*, 49 N.Y.2d 1, 399 N.E.2d 1154, 424 N.Y.S.2d 133 (1980), and *Ernest J. Michel & Co.* v. *Anabasis Trade, Inc.*, 50 N.Y.2d 951, 409 N.E.2d 931, 431 N.Y.S.2d 459 (1980). Although again finding that arbitration was not agreed to by both parties, and thus was not compelled, the court in *Schubtex* suggested that, in appropriate cases, an agreement to arbitrate could be inferred "from a course of past conduct or the custom and practice in the industry."

This exception was brought to the fore in *Michel*, a case involving seven confirmation contracts (with arbitration clauses), one of which was signed by the buyer and returned to the seller. The court affirmed the order compelling arbitration, stating that an "agreement to arbitrate was manifested" by the buyer's acceptance and confirmation of one of the seven order forms.

Where there is a prior agreement to arbitrate, either party can file a demand for arbitration. The AAA commercial rules specify that one copy of the demand be served on the other party, and that two copies be filed with the Association together with the appropriate administrative fee. The GAC rules state that the party initiating the arbitration must serve a copy of the demand for arbitration and the document containing the arbitration agreement to the other party, and that three copies of the demand and agreement be sent, with the administrative fee, to the Council.

THE PANEL OF ARBITRATORS

Textile arbitrators are drawn from more than twenty branches of the textile and apparel industries, including mill workers, garment manufacturers, finishers, credit executives, converters, purchasing agents, retailers, wholesalers, and executives in other specialized fields. They generally know and do business with many people within the industry. Textile arbitrators usually serve on a voluntary basis, and they view their service as a contribution to their industry. Cases usually require no more than one day of hearing. From time to time, however, a lengthy case may require particularly dedicated service from a panel. Arbitrators are highly regarded by their peers in the textile industry.

SELECTING AN ARBITRATOR

In textile/apparel cases administered under the AAA's commercial rules, the policy is now to assign three arbitrators if the claim exceeds $40,000. This is somewhat different than the GAC rules, which require three arbitrators where the amount in dispute is greater than $20,000, exclusive of interest and arbitration costs. Disputes involving less than the threshold amount are assigned one arbitrator under either set of rules.

Single-Arbitrator Cases

In a single-arbitrator case, an identical list of proposed arbitrators is submitted to the parties, who are allowed several days to indicate their preferences and return the list. A party can strike names off this list. GAC rules provide ten days for this procedure, and the commercial rules allow seven. Extensions of time may be granted for good cause. If a party does not return its list on time, all names are deemed acceptable. The Association compares the lists returned by the parties and then attempts to appoint a mutually acceptable arbitrator from among the remaining names. If no names are agreeable to both parties or if the acceptable candidates cannot serve, the Association may send another list or may appoint an arbitrator from its panel, other than one whose name had appeared on the list.

In single-arbitrator cases, the person selected to hear the dispute is not selected from the segment of the industry of either party. Thus, a sole arbitrator in a case between an apparel manufacturer and a textile mill would not be from a manufacturer or a mill.

Three-Arbitrator Panels

When three arbitrators are to be selected, the procedures differ. The AAA rules provide for selection of all three arbitrators by the parties, initially from lists or, if that proves impossible, by administrative appointment. Under the GAC rules, the first two arbitrators are selected from an initial list of names from the parties' own segment of the industry. The chairperson is selected by the first two appointments, who are furnished a list of proposed arbitrators. The third arbitrator can be administratively appointed if the first two arbitrators cannot agree on a name contained on the list or if the persons they select are unable to serve. Attorneys and accountants are not eligible to serve as arbitrators. Only people active in the industry are acceptable.

CHALLENGING THE ARBITRATOR FOR BIAS

If a party has a factual objection to the continued service of an arbitrator, the AAA or the General Arbitration Council can decide whether to remove that arbitrator on the basis of a challenge. Factual objections may include the arbitrator's past or present business or personal relationships with the parties or their attorneys. Arbitrators as well as the parties and their attorneys are urged to disclose any such relationships promptly. Failure of the participants to disclose a business or social relationship may constitute a waiver. Even if the challenge is made and granted at a later time, the delay may have resulted in extra cost and inconvenience for all concerned. The Code of Ethics for Arbitrators in Commercial Disputes and the applicable rules reflect the leading court decisions on this subject; they should be studied to see what kinds of relationships must be disclosed. In general, anything that might indicate potential bias should be disclosed.

THE ARBITRATION HEARING

The arbitrator will attempt to select a hearing date that is convenient for both parties. But if it appears that a party is seeking to delay the proceeding, the arbitrator will schedule a date. The arbitrator possesses broad discretion under the rules, including the authority to issue subpoenas, to grant adjournments, and to rule on procedural issues. The arbitrator can proceed with a hearing if a party does not appear after being duly notified, but the party who is present must demonstrate to the arbitrator that its claim is valid.

Although informal, arbitration hearings in the textile field are not without structure. Parties to arbitration cases have the right to be represented by counsel. This was not always the case. When arbitration was first adopted by industry groups, it was conceived as a merchants' tribunal. But as issues became more complicated, often depending upon complex legal and contractual considerations, the parties saw the need for professional representation. A sophisticated arbitration bar has emerged, and today most textile parties make use of the highly skilled lawyers who practice textile arbitration.

THE TYPICAL CASE

In the typical case, when the parties arrive at the hearing place they are introduced to the arbitrators, who will have been briefed by an AAA tribunal administrator. Sometimes attorneys will submit an opening brief or memorandum to assist the arbitrators in following the case. The chairperson will swear in those witnesses who intend to testify. The hearing then follows a familiar pattern of opening statements, introduction of the initiating documents, examination and cross-examination of witnesses, presentation of exhibits, and final summations. The parties "bring the case to the arbitrator," presenting such evidence and arguments as they deem pertinent. In cases involving the quality of fabric, it may be necessary for the panel to inspect the goods.

THE AWARD

After the parties have completed their presentation, the arbitrator must declare the hearings closed. Under the AAA's commercial rules, the award must be sent to the parties within thirty calendar days after the close of the hearings. The GAC rules provide for five business days in an expedited case, and ten business days in a regular case. If the arbitration board consists of more than one arbitrator, a majority decision is required.

The award must fall within the limits of the arbitration agreement and must decide each claim and counterclaim submitted. In a typical case, the award may direct that a party accept delivery of the goods and pay for them; or it may order the buyer to return defective goods to the seller; or it may permit an offset for goods that did not measure up to contract specifications. In general, the overall effect of the award should be to finally and conclusively end the controversy. Under the arbitration laws of some states a party may apply to the arbitrator, within a limited time, for a modification of the award. This request may be based on a mistake in designating a party or property, or a miscalculation of figures.

As noted earlier, in most instances, parties abide by the decision of the arbitrator. If they lose, they pay. But in the event that a party refuses to comply with the terms of an award, both the GAC and AAA rules provide that judgment on the award may be entered in the state or federal court having jurisdiction over such matters. An agreement to that effect should be contained in the arbitration clause. When the award is confirmed into a judgment, it can be used as the basis for collection.

GAC EXPEDITED PROCEDURES

In addition to the regular arbitration procedures, the rules of the GAC provide for an expedited procedure for cases involving less than $15,000. This procedure enables parties with smaller claims to have their disputes resolved quickly and inexpensively.

For this expedited procedure, a single arbitrator is appointed by the GAC from among its official panel of arbitrators. Hearings are scheduled and announced by telephone, as are all other notices from the Council to the parties. All such notices and announcements are subsequently confirmed in writing.

The hearing is generally completed within one day, and the award is rendered within five business days of the close of the hearing. The administrative fee for this GAC procedure is $200 for claims of $5,000 or less, $250 for claims from $5,000 to $10,000, and $300 for claims from $10,000 to $15,000.

CONCLUSION

Textile and apparel industry members have greatly benefited from submitting their disagreements to arbitration. As Frederic P. Houston explained in *The Arbitration Journal*:

> This development in the [New York] law of arbitration would not have occurred as early as 1920 were its only justification the establishment of a substitute for litigation to relieve congestion in the courts. The 1925 enactment of the United States Arbitration Act was initiated by merchants, trade associations, and chambers of commerce.

It became an accepted principle that disputes between merchants be resolved by arbitrators from within the same industry. Arbitration statutes reflect the demand by merchants that their disputes be resolved by arbitrators who possess knowledge of trade practices in the industry in which the dispute has arisen.

The textile industry has its own definitions:

> The standards of acceptability of particular shipments of fabric vary by the practice, usage, and custom of the trade, from (a) "mill standard" (what can be expected from particular sellers as their major and minor defect count to distinguish firsts from seconds), (b) "by sample" (whether the production delivery is a fair match to the sample which the seller furnished to the buyer) and (c) "end use standards" (standards established by buying trade practices, which may or may not have been incorporated in the "agreement" in the particular case). A similar peculiarity of the textile industry is the "perishability" of the merchandise, in the sense that "season," "style," and general economic conditions can make a fabric that was of substantial value when purchased of far less value at the time of the dispute or its resolution. Arbitrators, actively engaged in the textile industry, can more expeditiously and more accurately understand and apply these principles than can judges and juries, who must, of necessity, rely solely on so-called "expert-witness" testimony.

Merchantability is particularly important in the textile industry. Price fluctuations are frequent. And manufacturers must be alert to opportunities in the market. Yarn may be knitted or woven to serve whatever purpose the knitter or weaver selects to meet the demand. The fabric may be dyed, printed, laminated, or converted for a different use. The layperson is incapable of understanding these complexities. An arbitrator from the trade can determine whether claimed defects justify the return of the goods or a price allowance, or whether they are so minimal as to warrant no adjustment at all.

Arbitration has made a substantial contribution to the operating efficiency of the textile industry. The combined backgrounds, expertise, and energetic support of industry arbitrators, together with the cooperation of the parties, have greatly contributed to the success of the process. The textile procedures have served as a model for other industries that have decided to use arbitration.

ARBITRATION RULES OF THE GENERAL ARBITRATION COUNCIL OF THE TEXTILE AND APPAREL INDUSTRIES

As Amended and in Effect April 1, 1984

1. The General Arbitration Council–The Council as presently constituted is composed of one representative from each of the organizations listed below. The membership may be expanded at the Council's discretion, upon application by a trade association serving the textile or apparel industries. The Council shall have general charge of all matters referred for resolution under these Rules, and shall be authorized to amend such Rules or adopt special Rules as hereafter provided.

The member organizations of the Council are: American Apparel Manufacturers Association; American Textile Manufacturers Institute, Inc.; American Yarn Spinners Association, Inc.; Association of Yarn Distributors; Knitted Textile Association; Narrow Fabrics Institute, Inc.; National Association of Hosiery Manufacturers; National Association of Textile and Apparel Wholesalers; National Knitwear Manufacturers Association; National Knitwear and Sportswear Association; National Outerwear and Sportswear Association, Inc.; Northern Textile Association; Silk and Rayon Printers and Dyers Association of America, Inc.; Textile Distributors Association, Inc.; and The Thread Institute, Inc.

2. Agreement of Parties–Any party to an agreement for arbitration pursuant to these Rules, unless the parties thereto have otherwise agreed in writing, consents that such arbitration shall be held in the City of New York and in accordance with the laws of the State of New York and further consents to the jurisdiction of the Supreme Court of the State of New York and the United States District Court for the Southern District of New York and agrees that any process or notice of motion or other application to the Court or a judge thereof may be served within or outside the State of New York by registered or certified mail or by personal service providing a reasonable time for appearance is allowed.

3. The Tribunal–Wherever the word "party" or "parties" is used in these Rules it shall refer to the parties to the Submission or the parties to a controversy; and wherever the word "Arbitrator" or "Arbitrators" is used it shall refer to the Arbitrator or Arbitrators, as the case may be, whether there are one or more. Wherever the word "Council" is used, it shall refer to the General Arbitration Council of the Textile and Apparel Industries. Wherever the word "AAA" is used it shall refer to the American Arbitration Association, of which the Council is a Division. Wherever the word "Chairperson" or "Secretary" is used it shall refer to the Chairperson or Secretary of the Council. Wherever the words "Major Division of the Textile and Apparel Industries" or "Industry Division" are used they shall refer to any of the following: Apparel Manufacturers; Brokers; Coated Fabric Suppliers; Converters; Credit Men; Factors; Finishers; Importers/Exporters; Jobbers/Wholesalers; Knit Goods Manufacturers; Knitted Outerwear Manufacturers; Narrow Fabric Manufacturers; Retailers; Textile Mill and Mill Selling Agents; Thread Manufacturers; Throwsters; and Yarn Manufacturers, Selling Agents and Distributors.

4. Delegation of Duties–The duties of the Council under these Rules may be carried out through the Secretary or such other administrators, officers or committees as the Council may direct.

5. The Panel of Arbitrators—The Council shall appoint and maintain an official Panel of Arbitrators which shall include, but not be limited to, members of the various divisions of the textile/apparel industries represented in the Council.

6. Initiation under an Arbitration Provision in a Contract—Arbitration under an arbitration provision in a contract shall be initiated in the following manner:

(a) The initiating party (Claimant) shall give notice to the other party of its intention to arbitrate (Demand), which notice shall contain a statement setting forth the nature of the dispute, a sufficient description of the merchandise or service, the amount involved, and the remedy sought. A copy of each of the document(s) containing the arbitration clause(s) shall accompany the Demand filed with the other party (Respondent), and,

(b) By filing with the Council three (3) copies of said notice, together with three (3) copies of the document or documents containing the arbitration clause(s), together with the appropriate administrative fee as provided in the Administrative Fee Schedule.

The Council shall give notice of such filing to the other party. A party upon whom the Demand for Arbitration is made, within ten (10) days of mailing of notification by the Secretary, shall file with the Claimant and with the Secretary an answer and/or counterclaim in writing, setting forth in concise form the claims and contentions of such party with respect to the document(s) submitted by Claimant for arbitration. If a monetary claim is made in the answer, the appropriate fee provided in the Fee Schedule shall be forwarded to the Council with the answer. If no answer is filed within the stated time, it will be assumed that the claim is denied. Failure to file an answer shall not operate to delay the arbitration.

7. Expedited Procedures of Arbitration—The Expedited Procedures of Arbitration of the Council shall be applied in any case where the *total* claim of *any* party does not exceed $15,000, exclusive of interest and arbitration costs. The Council shall utilize its Expedited Procedures as described in Sections 45 through 50 of these Rules.

8. Initiation under a Submission—Parties to any existing dispute may commence an arbitration under these Rules by filing with the Council three (3) copies of a written agreement to arbitrate under these Rules (Submission), signed by the parties. It shall contain a statement of the matter in dispute, a detailed description of the merchandise or service, the amount involved, and the remedy sought, together with the appropriate filing fee as provided in the Fee Schedule.

9. Change of Claim—After filing of the claim, if either party desires to make any new or different claim, such claim shall be made in writing and filed with the Secretary, and a copy thereof shall be mailed to the other party, who shall have a period of seven (7) days within which to file an answer with the Secretary. However, after the appointment of the Arbitrator no new or different claim may be submitted except with the Arbitrator's consent.

When arbitration proceedings involving common questions are pending before the Council, the Secretary may, upon consent of all parties or upon Court order, consolidate the proceedings in a joint hearing on any or all the matters in dispute.

10. Pre-Hearing Conference—At the request of the parties or at the discretion of the Secretary, a pre-hearing conference with the administrator and the parties or their counsel will be scheduled in appropriate cases to arrange for an exchange of information and the stipulation of uncontested facts so as to expedite the arbitration proceedings.

11. Number of Arbitrators–In any case where the claim of a party does not exceed $20,000, exclusive of interest and arbitration costs, the dispute shall be heard and determined by one Arbitrator, unless the Secretary directs that a greater number of Arbitrators be appointed.

In all other cases the dispute shall be heard and determined by three Arbitrators, unless the parties agree that a single Arbitrator serve, or unless the Secretary determines that a greater number of arbitrators shall be appointed.

12. Qualifications of Arbitrator–Any Arbitrator appointed pursuant to Section 13 shall be neutral, subject to disqualification for the reasons specified in Section 15.

13. Appointment of Arbitrator(s)–(1) Where a case is to be heard by a sole Arbitrator, the Secretary shall submit simultaneously to each party an identical list of proposed Arbitrators selected from the official Panel of Arbitrators. All such proposed Arbitrators must be active, or have been active, within the five-year period prior to appointment, in the textile/apparel industries, but should not be, or have been during the said five-year period, actively engaged in the industry division of any party to the dispute. Each party shall have ten (10) days from the mailing date to return the list to the Secretary, crossing off the names of persons to whom it objects, and consecutively numbering remaining names in the order of preference. The Secretary shall invite those persons from the respective lists returned by the parties, in accordance with their order of preference, to serve as Arbitrator. If a party fails to return the list within the time specified, all persons named therein shall be deemed acceptable to such party. If the parties fail to agree upon any of the persons named, or if for any other reason the appointment cannot be made from the submitted list, the Secretary shall have the power to make the appointment from other members of the Panel without the submission of an additional list.

(2) Where a case is to be heard by three Arbitrators, the Secretary shall submit simultaneously to each party an identical list of proposed Arbitrators selected from the official Panel of Arbitrators. The list shall contain only proposed Arbitrators selected, in equal number, from an industry division in which each party is engaged. If the official Panel does not contain names of available Arbitrators engaged in, allied with, or formerly active in the industry division in which a party is engaged, the Secretary may submit to the parties names of qualified persons who are not on the official Panel.

Each party shall have ten (10) days from the mailing date to return the list to the Secretary, crossing off the names of persons to which it objects, and consecutively numbering the remaining names on the list submitted from each industry division in the order of preference. The Secretary shall invite one person on each list from each industry division to serve as Arbitrator in accordance with the order of preference of the parties, provided the names acceptable to a party have not been crossed off by another party. If a party does not return the list within the time specified, all persons named therein shall be deemed acceptable. If the parties fail to agree upon any of the persons named, or if acceptable Arbitrators are unable to act, or if for any other reason the appointment cannot be made from the submitted lists, the Secretary will have the power to make the appointment from other members of the Panel without the submission of additional lists.

After two Arbitrators have been appointed, the Secretary shall submit simultaneously to each such Arbitrator a list of names of Arbitrators selected from Panel Groups other than those from which the appointed Arbitrators shall be chosen. Each such Arbitrator shall have ten (10) days from the mailing of such list to return the list to the Secretary, crossing off any objectionable names, and numbering the remaining names in order of preference. If an Arbitrator fails to return the list within the time specified, all names thereon shall be deemed acceptable to such Arbitrator. From among the names so approved, and in accordance with the order of mutual preference, if any, the Secretary shall invite an Arbitrator to serve. The Arbitrator so selected shall serve as Chairperson of the Panel. If the Arbitrators fail to agree upon any of the persons named, or if acceptable Arbitrators are unable to act, or if for any other reason the appointment cannot be made from the submitted list, the Secretary shall have the power to make the appointment from other members of the Panel without the submission of additional lists.

14. Notice to Arbitrator(s) of Appointment—Notice of the appointment of the Arbitrator shall be mailed to the Arbitrator by the Secretary, and the signed acceptance of the Arbitrator shall be filed prior to the opening of the first hearing.

15. Disclosure and Challenge Procedure—A person appointed as Arbitrator shall disclose to the Secretary any circumstances likely to affect his impartiality, including any bias or any financial or personal interest in the result of the arbitration or any past or present relationships with the parties or their counsel. The Secretary shall also request, and each party and their attorneys shall disclose to the Secretary, any such circumstances known to them. Upon receipt of such information from such Arbitrator or other source, the Secretary shall communicate such information to the parties and, if deemed appropriate, to the Arbitrator and others. Thereafter, the Secretary shall determine whether the Arbitrator should be disqualified and shall inform the parties of the decision, which shall be conclusive.

16. Vacancies—If any Arbitrator should resign, die, withdraw, refuse, be disqualified or be unable to perform the duties of office, the Secretary may, on satisfactory proof, declare the office vacant. In the event of such vacancy, the appointment of the remaining Arbitrators shall stand and the vacancy shall be filled in accordance with the applicable provisions of these Rules. If any such vacancy should occur after the submission of evidence and completion of hearings, the award shall be made by the remaining Arbitrators, unless the parties otherwise agree.

17. Time and Place of Hearing—The Arbitrator shall fix the time and place for each hearing. The Secretary shall mail to each party notice thereof at least ten (10) days in advance, unless the parties by mutual agreement waive such notice or modify the terms thereof.

18. Representation by Counsel—Any party may be represented by counsel. A party intending to be so represented shall notify the other party and the Secretary of the name and address of counsel as soon as possible prior to the date set for the hearing at which counsel is first to appear. When an arbitration is initiated by counsel, or where an attorney replies for the other party, such notice is deemed to have been given.

19. Attendance at Hearings—Only the parties to the arbitration, their authorized representatives, witnesses and counsel, the Secretary, and any other persons authorized by the Council or the Secretary or required by the Arbitrator may be present at any of the hearings. The Arbitrator shall have the power to require the retirement of any witness or witnesses during the testimony of other witnesses.

20. Oaths–Before proceeding with the first hearing or with the examination of the file, each Arbitrator may take an oath of office, and if required by law, shall do so. The Arbitrator may, in his discretion, require witnesses to testify under oath administered by any duly qualified person or, if required by law or demanded by either party, shall do so.

21. Stenographic Record–Any party wishing a stenographic record shall make such arrangements directly with the stenographer and shall notify the other parties of such arrangements in advance of the hearing. The requesting party or parties shall pay the cost of such record.

22. Adjournments–The Arbitrators or a majority of them, in their discretion, may postpone or adjourn any hearing on their own motion, or upon the motion of a party for good cause. The Arbitrators shall make such adjournments when all the parties agree thereto.

23. Majority Decision–Whenever there is more than one Arbitrator, all decisions of the Arbitrators must be by at least a majority. The award must also be made by at least a majority unless the concurrence of all is expressly required by the arbitration agreement or by law.

24. Order of Proceedings–A hearing shall be opened by the filing of the Oath of the Arbitrator, where required, and by the recording of the place, time and date of the hearing, the presence of the Arbitrator and the parties, and counsel, if any, and by the receipt by the Arbitrator of the statement of the claim, answer and/or counterclaim, if any.

The Arbitrator may, at the beginning of the hearing, ask for statements clarifying the issues involved.

The complaining party shall then present its claim, proofs, and witnesses who shall submit to questions or other examination. The defending party shall then present its questions and examination. The Arbitrator may vary this procedure but shall afford full and equal opportunity to all parties for the presentation of any material or relevant proofs.

Exhibits, when offered by either party, may be received in evidence by the Arbitrator.

The names and addresses of all witnesses and exhibits, in the order received, shall be made a part of the record.

25. Arbitration in the Absence of a Party–Unless the law provides to the contrary, the arbitration may proceed in the absence of any party who, after due notice, fails to be present or fails to obtain an adjournment. An award shall not be made solely on the default of a party. The Arbitrator shall require the party who is present to submit such evidence as may be required for the making of an award.

26. Evidence–The parties may offer such evidence as they desire and shall produce such additional evidence as the Arbitrator may deem necessary to an understanding and determination of the dispute. The Arbitrator, when authorized by law to subpoena witnesses or documents, may do so upon his/her initiative or upon the request of any party. The Arbitrator shall be the judge of the relevancy and materiality of the evidence offered and conformity to legal rules of evidence shall not be necessary. All evidence shall be taken in the presence of all of the Arbitrators and of all the parties, except where any party is absent in default or has waived the right to be present.

27. Evidence by Affidavit and Filing of Documents–The Arbitrator shall receive and consider the evidence of witnesses by affidavit, but shall give it only such weight as the Arbitrator deems it entitled to after consideration of any objections made to its admission.

All documents not filed with the Arbitrator at the hearing, but arranged for at the hearing or subsequently by agreement of the parties, shall be filed with the Secretary for transmission to the Arbitrator. All parties shall be afforded opportunity to examine such documents.

28. Closing of Hearings—The Arbitrator shall specifically inquire of the parties whether they have any further proofs to offer or witnesses to be heard. Upon receiving negative replies, or if satisfied that the record is complete, the Arbitrator shall declare the hearings closed and a minute thereof shall be recorded. If briefs are to be filed, the hearings shall be declared closed as of the final date set by the Arbitrator for the receipt of briefs. If documents are to be filed as provided for in Section 27 and the date set for their receipt is later than that set for the receipt of briefs, the later date shall be the date of closing the hearings. The time limit within which the Arbitrator is required to make his award shall commence to run, in the absence of other agreements by the parties, upon the closing of the hearings.

29. Reopening of Hearings—The hearings may be reopened on the Arbitrator's own motion, or upon application of a party at any time before the award is made. If the reopening of the hearing would prevent the making of the award within the specific time agreed upon by the parties in the contract out of which the controversy has arisen, the matter may not be reopened, unless the parties agree upon the extension of such time limit. When no specific date is fixed in the contract, the Arbitrator may reopen the hearings, and the Arbitrator shall have ten (10) business days from the closing of the reopened hearings within which to make an award.

30. Waiver of Oral Hearings—If the parties to a controversy agree in writing to waive oral hearings, they shall submit to the Secretary their contentions in writing, including a statement of the facts, all written documents, abstracts from books of account or other evidence, all properly verified under oath, and samples of merchandise (if any be involved). Upon receipt of the statement of facts and written arguments, the Secretary shall submit immediately a copy thereof to the respective parties and each shall have the right to make reply thereto. If either party shall fail to make such reply within fifteen (15) days from the receipt thereof, that party shall be deemed to have waived the right to reply. Such statement of facts and arguments, together with all the evidence, shall be submitted to the Arbitrator.

31. Waiver of Rules—Any party who proceeds with the arbitration after knowledge that any provision or requirement of these Rules has not been complied with and who fails to state objection thereto in writing shall be deemed to have waived the right to object.

32. Extensions of Time—The parties to an arbitration may modify any period of time set forth in these Rules by mutual agreement. The Secretary for good cause may extend any period of time established by these Rules except the time for making the award. The Secretary shall notify the parties of any such extension of time and the reason therefor.

33. Communication with Arbitrator and Serving of Notices—(a) There shall be no communication between the parties and the Arbitrator other than at oral hearings. Any other oral or written communications from the parties to the Arbitrator shall be directed to the Secretary for transmittal to the Arbitrator.

(b) The parties further consent that any papers, notices or process necessary or proper for the initiation or continuation of an arbitration under these Rules, other than as provided in Section 2, may be served upon such party by mail addressed to such party or, if such party has appeared in such arbitration with an attorney, to the attorney's last known address, or by personal service, within or outside the United States of America, provided that reasonable opportunity to be heard by the Arbitrator with regard thereto has been granted such party.

34. Time of Award—The award shall be made by the Arbitrator at the close of the hearing or as soon thereafter as may be practicable and, unless otherwise agreed by the parties or specified by law, no later than ten (10) business days from the date of closing of the hearings, or if oral hearings have been waived, from the date of transmitting the final statements and proofs to the Arbitrator.

35. Form of Award—The award shall be in writing and shall be signed either by the sole Arbitrator or by at least a majority if there be more than one. It shall be executed in the manner required by law.

36. Scope of Award—The Arbitrator may grant any remedy or relief which the Arbitrator deems just and equitable and within the scope of the agreement of the parties. The award may require specific performance of a contract; require the acceptance or replacement of merchandise; fix allowances for defective merchandise; declare a contract breached in whole or in part; and/or award money damages in the alternative or otherwise. The Arbitrator, in the award, shall assess arbitration fees and expenses in favor of any party and, in the event any administrative fees or expenses are due the AAA, in favor of the AAA.

If, in the opinion of the Arbitrator, an award which is not for money only has not been complied with fully within a reasonable time, the Arbitrator may make a supplemental award for money only, and the powers of the Arbitrator shall continue for this purpose.

37. Award Upon Settlement—If the parties settle their dispute during the course of the arbitration, the Arbitrator, upon their request, may set forth the terms of the agreed settlement in an award.

38. Delivery of Award to Parties—Parties shall accept as legal delivery of the award the placing of the award or a true copy thereof in the mail by the Secretary, addressed to such party at its last known address or to its attorney, or personal service of the award, or the filing of the award in any manner which may be prescribed by law.

39. Release of Documents for Judicial Proceedings—The Council shall, upon the written request of a party, furnish to such party, at its expense, certified facsimiles of any papers in the file that may be required in judicial proceedings relating to the arbitration.

40. Applications to Court—(a) No judicial proceedings by a party relating to the subject matter of the arbitration shall be deemed a waiver of the party's right to arbitrate.

(b) Neither the Council, the AAA nor any Arbitrator is a necessary party in judicial proceedings relating to the arbitration.

(c) Parties to these Rules shall be deemed to have consented that judgment upon the arbitration award may be entered in any Federal or State Court having jurisdiction thereof.

(d) Neither the Council, the AAA nor any Arbitrator shall be liable to any party for any act or omission in connection with any arbitration conducted under these Rules.

41. Interpretation and Application of These Rules—The Arbitrator shall interpret and apply these Rules insofar as they relate to the Arbitrator's powers and duties, in a manner best calculated to obtain a just and speedy determination of the controversy. When there is more than one Arbitrator and a difference arises among them concerning the meaning or application of any such Rules, it shall be decided by a majority vote. If that is unobtainable, either an Arbitrator or a party may refer the question to the Council for final decision. All other Rules shall be applied and interpreted by the Council.

42. The Standing Committee – The Chairperson of the Council shall appoint a Standing Committee of five member representatives of whom not less than three shall constitute a quorum. The Standing Committee is empowered to hear and make decisions in matters involving interpretations of these Rules. Whenever, in the opinion of the Council or of a majority of the Arbitrators, the foregoing Rules are not fully applicable or whenever an unusual or unforeseen situation arises, the Council, in its judgment, may adopt Special Rules to cover such conditions and in case of conflict between the foregoing Rules and such Special Rules, the Special Rules shall prevail.

The Standing Committee, in its absolute discretion, may refuse to extend the arbitration services of the Council in any case which it deems appropriate, or may discontinue such services during the pendency of any proceedings, and in such event shall notify the parties in writing of such action.

Actions taken by the Standing Committee hereunder shall be reported to the other members of the Council at the Annual Meeting thereof or in such other manner as the Council from time to time may direct. In all other matters, the Council may delegate all of its power under these Rules to the Chairperson or to the Standing Committee or any three members thereof.

43. Administrative Fees – As a not-for-profit organization, the AAA shall prescribe an Administrative Fee Schedule and a Refund Schedule to compensate it for the cost of providing administrative services to parties proceeding under these Rules. The Administrative Fee Schedule in effect at the time of filing or the time of refund shall be applicable to proceedings under these Rules.

The administrative fees shall be advanced by the initiating party or parties, subject to final apportionment by the Arbitrator in the award. If a claim is made in the answer, the appropriate fee shall be forwarded with that answer.

When a matter is withdrawn or settled, the refund shall be made in accordance with the Refund Schedule.

The Council, in the event of extreme hardship on the part of any party, may defer or reduce the administrative fee.

44. Expenses – The expenses of witnesses for either side shall be paid by the party producing such witnesses.

The cost of the stenographic record, if any is made, and all transcripts thereof, shall be prorated equally among all parties ordering copies unless they shall otherwise agree and shall be paid for by the responsible parties directly to the reporting agency.

All other expenses of the arbitration, including the expenses of the Arbitrator and of the Council representatives, if any, and the expenses of any witness or the cost of any proofs produced at the direct request of the Arbitrator, shall be borne equally by the parties, unless they agree otherwise, or unless the Arbitrator in the award assesses such expenses or any part thereof against any specified party or parties.

EXPEDITED PROCEDURES

45. Notice by Telephone—The parties shall accept all notices from the Council by telephone. Such notices by the Council shall subsequently be confirmed in writing to the parties.

46. Appointment and Qualification of Arbitrators—Upon the Council's receipt of the Demand for Arbitration or Submission to Arbitration, in accordance with Sections 6, 7, or 8 of these Rules, the Council shall, without the submission to the parties of a list of proposed Arbitrators, appoint one Arbitrator from its official Panel of Arbitrators, as provided in Section 5. The Arbitrator appointed must be active, or have been active, within the five-year period prior to appointment, in the textile/apparel industries, but should not be, or have been during the said five-year period, actively engaged in the industry division of any party to the dispute. Such appointment shall be subject to disqualification for the reasons specified in Section 15.

The parties shall be given notice, by telephone, from the Council, of the appointment of the Arbitrator. The parties shall notify the Council, by telephone, within ten (10) days, of any objections to the Arbitrator appointed. Any objections by a party to such Arbitrator shall be confirmed in writing to the Council, with a copy to the other party(ies).

47. Time and Place of Hearing—The Arbitrator appointed shall fix the date, time and place of the hearing. The Council will notify the parties, by telephone, ten (10) days in advance of the hearing date. Formal Notice of Hearing will be sent by the Council to the parties.

48. The Hearing—Generally, the hearing shall be completed within one day. The Arbitrator, for good cause shown, may schedule an additional hearing to be held within five (5) days.

49. Time of Award—Unless otherwise agreed to by the parties, the award shall be rendered not later than five (5) business days from the date of the closing of the hearings.

50. GAC Expedited Procedures Administrative Fee Schedule—

Amount of Claim	*Fee*
Up to $5,000	$200
$5,000 to $10,000	$250
$10,000 to $15,000	$300

The Other Service Charges and Postponement Fees set forth in the Administrative Fee Schedule of these Rules shall also apply to cases administered under the Expedited Procedures.

No refund will be made in cases administered under the Expedited Procedures.

BIBLIOGRAPHY

American Arbitration Association. *Arbitration Rules of the General Arbitration Council of the Textile and Apparel Industries: As Amended and in Effect April 1, 1984.* New York: 1984.

______. *General Arbitration Council of the Textile Industry*. New York: 1981.

______. *A Guide to Arbitration for the Textile and Apparel Industries*. New York: 1983.

Bonn, Robert L. "Arbitration: An Alternative System for Handling Contract Related Disputes." *Administrative Science Quarterly*, vol. 17 (1972), pp. 254–264.

______. "The Predictability of Non-Legalistic Adjudication in the Textile Industry." *The Arbitration Journal*, vol. 27 (March 1972), pp. 29–34.

Friedman, George H. "Textile Arbitration—Recent Cases." *New York Law Journal*, December 10, 1981, p. 1.

______. "Textile Arbitration—Recent Developments." *New York Law Journal*, November 21, 1984, p. 1.

Houston, Frederic P. "A Barrier to Arbitration." New York: New York Board of Trade, 1983.

______. "A Barrier to Arbitration in the Textile Industry." *The Arbitration Journal*, vol. 34, no. 2 (June 1979), pp. 9–18.

CHAPTER 4

INSURANCE CLAIMS

The insurance industry in the United States has been concerned about the cost and inefficiency of litigation. The industry has been eager to move its disputes into more modern channels. For intercompany disagreements, it has established a broad range of internal arbitration procedures under the administration of the Committee on Insurance Arbitration.

Bernard L. Hines's book, *Arbitration: A Guide to Insurance Industry Forums*, contains a comprehensive description of these programs. Insurance companies participate in the prompt settlement of intercompany claims through a network of arbitration committees. This industrywide system has been a boon to the courts, relieving them of the burden of many thousands of subrogation and other claims between insurance companies. In addition, the casualty industry has participated in the creation of major uninsured motorist and no-fault arbitration systems, under which the claims of individuals against their own automobile insurance companies are settled by impartial arbitrators.

The AAA has also instituted the Alternative Dispute Resolution (ADR) program for insurance liability cases. Initiated in mid-1983 on a pilot basis, the ADR program has been found to speed up claims resolution and to help control litigation costs.

This chapter will describe some of the systems used to resolve insurance claims.

UNINSURED MOTORIST CLAIMS

Uninsured motorist coverage has become well accepted in the United States. It helps to protect insured motorists by providing damages when they suffer personal injuries because of the negligence of an uninsured or hit-and-run driver. This coverage is required by law in most states. A typical uninsured motorist endorsement promises

> . . . to pay all sums which the insured shall be legally entitled to recover as damages from the owner or operator of an uninsured automobile because of bodily injury sustained by the insured, caused by an accident arising out of the ownership, main-

> tenance, or use of such uninsured automobile, provided determination as to whether the insured is legally entitled to recover such damages, and if so, the amount therefor, shall be made by agreement between the insured and the company or, if they fail to agree, by arbitration.

This endorsement usually describes an arbitration procedure. A typical insurance policy endorsement contains the following language:

> If any person making claim hereunder and the company do not agree that such person is legally entitled to recover damages from the owner or operator of such uninsured automobile because of the amount of payment which may be owing under this endorsement, then, upon written demand of either, the matter or matters upon which such person and the company do not agree shall be settled by arbitration in accordance with the Accident Claims Rules of the American Arbitration Association. Judgment upon the award rendered by the arbitrators may be entered in any court having jurisdiction thereof. Such person and the company each agree to consider itself bound and to be bound by any award made by the arbitrator(s) pursuant to this endorsement.

The AAA's accident claims arbitration system was established in 1956 at the request of the insurance industry. It relies upon a panel of lawyers with negligence experience who have been nominated by bar associations or by other attorneys and have volunteered to serve as arbitrators in uninsured motorist cases. The AAA helps the parties to select an arbitrator and provides administrative assistance in accordance with the Accident Claims Arbitration Rules. The AAA rules also offer the parties an option to submit the claim to mediation, which has proven to be a prompt, fair, and economical method of settling insurance claims. These services are supported by fees paid by both the filing party and the insurance carrier. Each year thousands of cases are resolved under such procedures.

The Arbitration Procedure

The injured person can initiate the claim by serving a demand for arbitration on the insurance company, with copies to the nearest AAA office. The demand should describe the nature of the injury, the amount of the claim, other information required by the rules, and a copy of the arbitration provision of the policy.

Arbitrators are appointed by the AAA, in most cases from a list of names submitted to the parties. Cases involving claims exceeding the minimum uninsured motorist coverage available in a jurisdiction, either because of multiple policies ("stacking") or because of optional additional coverage, are heard by a panel of three arbitrators unless local law provides otherwise. Other cases are heard by a single arbitrator unless the AAA determines that more arbitrators would be appropriate.

The injured individual may designate the place of hearing. If no objection is raised by the insurance carrier, the case will be heard at that location. If a dispute about the locale originates prior to the arbitrator's appointment, the AAA will decide the question. The date and place of the hearing are set after considering the mutual convenience of the parties. A notice of at least twenty days must be given. The parties may be represented at the hearing by counsel.

Uninsured motorist arbitration hearings tend to be brief and informal. Each side is given an opportunity to convince the arbitrator through the testimony of witnesses and the presentation of exhibits. Cross-examination of opposing witnesses is encouraged, and the lawyers present and argue cases in their own way. The arbitrator is required by law to hear the case and to determine the issues submitted for resolution. A written award must be signed by the arbitrator within thirty days after the hearing is declared closed. Prompt decisions are encouraged. It is not customary for the arbitrator to explain the reasoning behind the award. The award is prepared by the AAA and, when signed by the arbitrator, is mailed simultaneously to the parties.

Arbitration provides an expedited method of dispute settlement. This is advantageous to everyone concerned. Claimants need not face court delays, and insurers do not have to maintain files for long periods of time. The lawyers give better service to their clients, as well. The arbitration of uninsured motorist claims has demonstrated how private voluntary arbitration can work in the public interest. The lawyers who serve as arbitrators are providing an important service.

Mediation

In mediation, the mediator assists the parties in reaching their own settlement, but does not have the authority to make a binding decision or award.

Mediators appointed in accident claims cases are experienced attorneys. They have mediation training or experience and are required to inform the AAA of any circumstances that might prevent a prompt hearing or create a presumption of bias. Upon the objection of either party, the AAA will replace the mediator.

Because mediation is voluntary, all parties to the dispute must consent to participate. Upon request, a mediation submission form will be provided by the AAA, or you may indicate your willingness to mediate by placing a check mark in the appropriate box on the Demand for Arbitration form. The AAA will contact the other parties and attempt to obtain their agreement to mediate.

If there is no agreement or mediation proves unsuccessful, the parties can continue with the arbitration.

NO-FAULT INSURANCE CLAIMS

Prior to the enactment of no-fault laws, someone injured through the use or operation of a motor vehicle had to show that the other driver's negligence caused the accident. For example, if a car ran off the road into a tree, an injured passenger might have a negligence claim against the driver or owner; if another vehicle was involved in the accident, an injured person might have the right to recover against the driver or owner of either vehicle. Ordinarily, the driver or owner would be insured. Where the other vehicle was not covered by insurance, injured claimants could obtain relief under the uninsured motorist provision of their policy. In all of these examples, however, injured claimants would have to establish the other party's negligence and their own freedom from contributory negligence. If such negligence could be established, the claimant could collect for actual damages and for pain and suffering.

No-fault operates on a different principle. The underlying theory is that it is most important for victims of automobile accidents to be reimbursed for their economic loss and that it should be unnecessary to determine negligence. The no-fault statutes provide protection for anyone—driver, passenger, pedestrian—who sustains injuries arising out of the use or operation of the insured vehicle, without regard to fault, from the insurer or self-insurer of that vehicle, regardless of whether another vehicle was involved.

Coverage varies from state to state. The federal government has not required a uniform approach. Some states have not adopted the no-fault principle. In general, no-fault laws provide compensation for medical expenses, lost wages, and other reasonable and necessary expenses arising out of the personal injuries sustained in an accident. Disputes still arise between insurers and claimants as to whether coverage exists and as to the extent of coverage, but the issues tend to be less complicated than they were under the prior law. On the other hand, injured persons no longer have a right to collect for pain and suffering.

Unlike arbitration of uninsured motorist claims, which is based solely upon the agreement of the insurer and policyholder to arbitrate any disputes, no-fault arbitration arises out of provisions in the law. Five states—Hawaii, Minnesota, New Jersey, New York, and Oregon—have no-fault automobile insurance laws that provide for arbitration of disputes between claimants and carriers.

NEW YORK NO-FAULT ARBITRATION

The New York No-Fault Law provides that:

> Each insurer shall provide a claimant with the option of submitting any dispute involving the insurer's liability to pay first-party benefits. . . to arbitration pursuant to simplified procedures to be promulgated or approved by the superintendent.

The New York No-Fault Law became effective February 1, 1974. The arbitration procedures initially provided for arbitration by the AAA of all legal and medical claims. These procedures were applicable to injuries sustained prior to December 1, 1977. Amendments of the law in 1977 contained several revisions of the optional arbitration procedures. Medical and attorneys' fee schedules were established, and awards could be appealed to a master arbitrator. These amended procedures apply to claims for no-fault benefits for injuries suffered on and after December 1, 1977.

Under revised New York regulations, the AAA is the administrator of no-fault arbitrations concerning the threshold questions of entitlement to coverage and nonmedical issues such as wage loss.* Under the revised procedures, all requests for arbitration of claims for injuries must be filed with the state Insurance Department. The department reviews these claims and refers unresolved disputes to either the Insurance Department Arbitration (IDA), the AAA, or the Health Service Arbitration (HSA) forums. The arbitration forum is selected based upon the nature of the claim. Four issues are available for arbitration: (1) disputes where the only issue is whether a claim was overdue when it was paid; (2) expedited arbitration of coverage issues; (3) disputes over health services; and (4) all other issues, including lost wages. The AAA administers all disputes except those involving health services, which are handled by the HSA panel, and those involving timeliness of payment of benefits, which are administered by the IDA panel. AAA arbitrations are conducted in accordance with the Rules for New York State No-Fault Arbitration and No-Fault Expedited Arbitration, which were adopted pursuant to insurance department regulations. (Up-to-date copies of these rules can be obtained from any of the New York State offices of the AAA.)

AAA Expedited Arbitration of Coverage Issues

The following issues are subject to expedited arbitration:

(1) whether a policy was in force on the date of the accident;
(2) whether the claimant qualifies as an "eligible injured person" under the law;
(3) whether the claimant violated policy conditions resulting in exclusion from coverage;
(4) whether the claimant is excluded from coverage under policy conditions or exclusions;
(5) whether the claimant's injuries arose out of the use or operation of a motor vehicle;
(6) whether a valid assignment of no-fault benefits exists, or whether the absence of same precludes the applicant's standing in the arbitration; or

*Cases involving health services rendered in New York are arbitrated under the administration of the Health Service Arbitration Panel of the Workers' Compensation Board.

(7) whether the policy includes a family deductible applicable to the claim.

The AAA is required to appoint an arbitrator for a hearing within fifteen days of its receipt of the dispute from the insurance department. The award must be rendered within fifteen days of the close of the hearings.

Regular AAA Arbitration of Economic Issues

Questions of basic economic loss, such as amount of wage loss benefits or reasonable expenses, are submitted to "regular" AAA arbitration procedures. Under the regulations, the parties are provided a list of four arbitrators, from which one strike may be made. The AAA selects the arbitrator from among the names remaining on the list.

The hearing must be held within twenty-one days of the arbitrator's appointment, unless the parties agree otherwise. Again, the award must be mailed within fifteen days.

Health Service Arbitration

Disputes involving health service matters are referred to the Health Service Arbitration forum for resolution. This panel must decide whether fees for medical services comply with the fee schedule, whether hospitalization, treatment, or services were excessive or unnecessary, and whether medical injuries sustained were caused by the accident.

Health Service Arbitrations are scheduled within twenty-one days of their submission. The panel is composed of three persons, designated by the chairperson, one person selected from each of the following areas: (1) persons nominated by the chairperson and appointed by the Superintendent of the Insurance Department who are qualified to resolve health service disputes; (2) persons nominated by the insurance industry who are qualified to resolve health service disputes; and (3) representatives of the state and county professional societies and hospital associations.

HSA cases are usually decided on the basis of documents. Personal appearances are not necessary, although persons having a direct interest in the arbitration are entitled to attend. The award is made and delivered within fifteen days of the completion of the hearing.

Insurance Department Arbitration

Where the only issue is whether the claim for benefits was overdue when it was paid by the insurer, the dispute is referred to the Insurance Department Arbitration forum. IDA arbitrators are examiners or attorneys who regularly administer no-fault claims and are appointed by the superintendent. The matter is resolved solely on the basis of written submissions from the parties, and no oral arguments are permitted. The parties are provided twenty-one days within which to forward their submissions to the arbitrator, and the award is rendered and mailed within twenty-one days from the date set for filing of submissions.

AAA Awards

No-fault arbitration awards usually contain detailed opinions. The AAA publishes a monthly award reporting service, *New York No-Fault Arbitration Reports*, which summarizes interesting decisions and opinions and provides up-to-date information on other no-fault developments.

Qualifications of AAA Arbitrators

AAA no-fault arbitrators are experienced in negligence and insurance matters. They are all licensed to practice law in New York State. Arbitrators are paid a nominal fee for their services.

Attorney and Witness Fees

Arbitrators may award attorneys' fees to successful claimants. A fee schedule contained in the regulations governs the amount that may be awarded. Arbitrators are also empowered to award witness fees.

Appellate Procedure: Master Arbitration

Although it is not typical in arbitration, the New York no-fault arbitration system has its own review procedure. Awards can be appealed to a master arbitrator. The grounds for review go far beyond those applicable to traditional arbitration awards. They include:

(1) the statutory grounds for vacating an award contained in the New York arbitration law, except failure to follow procedures contained therein;
(2) that the award required an insurer to pay amounts in excess of policy limitations;
(3) that the award, in an expedited case, was incorrect, as a matter of law;
(4) that an attorney's fee awarded by the hearing arbitrator was not in accordance with the fee schedule; or
(5) that an AAA award was "inconsistent and irreconcilable" with a Health Service Award involving the same injuries.

The regulations require that an insurer pay all amounts not in dispute before submitting an issue for review by a master arbitrator. The master arbitrators, who serve at the superintendent's pleasure, are required to have been licensed to practice law in New York for at least fifteen years. Review by a master arbitrator is based solely on submitted documents unless the master arbitrator requires oral argument. Only those matters that were the subject of the arbitration can be considered. Where the master award exceeds $5,000, exclusive of interest and attorneys' fees, the law permits a trial *de novo* in court.

MINNESOTA NO-FAULT ARBITRATION

A claimant in Minnesota can request arbitration of a no-fault dispute when a claim for benefits is denied by the insurer. The arbitration is heard by a single arbitrator mutually selected by the parties from a list supplied by the AAA. Arbitrators receive a fee of $100 for each half-day of hearing, and $50 in the event that a case is settled prior to a hearing. The arbitrator's fee is paid by the insurer but may be assessed as a cost by the arbitrator.

Under the Minnesota No-Fault Law, the arbitrator is encouraged to conciliate the claim prior to the arbitration hearing. Ten days prior to the scheduled date of hearings, the parties are asked by the arbitrator to stipulate to those facts that are not in dispute. If conciliation is unsuccessful, a hearing is held, usually at the arbitrator's office. The rules provide the arbitrator with subpoena power and authorize the arbitrator to permit any discovery allowable under court rules.

The hearing itself proceeds along the familiar lines of opening statements, presentation of witnesses and exhibits, cross-examinations, and summations. Consistent with other types of arbitration, strict conformity to rules of evidence is not required. The arbitrator is sole judge of the relevance and materiality of evidence. The award is due no later than thirty days after the close of the hearings, unless the parties agree otherwise.

NEW JERSEY NO-FAULT ARBITRATION

Effective in 1984, New Jersey's automobile insurance law was amended to require that all automobile insurers provide any claimant with the option of submitting a dispute concerning personal injury protection benefits to binding arbitration under the auspices of the AAA. Personal injury protection (PIP) benefits comprise compensation for direct economic loss (medical expenses, wage loss, funeral expenses). The benefits are the heart of the "no-fault" concept, in which the right to sue for pain and suffering is traded off for immediate compensation of out-of-pocket expenses. The value of arbitrating and thus quickly resolving disputes replaces the greater economic compensation of insurance claims. The system established incorporates several innovative features in an effort to make the process pliable to the needs of the parties.

Evidence may be presented by submission of documents only or at an oral hearing. Either side may request an oral hearing, but where there is no such request, arrangements are made for document submission. The party requesting the oral hearing pays a surcharge. Additionally, either party, for the purpose of attempting settlement, may request a prehearing conference with AAA administrative staff or a mediation conference.

A single arbitrator is administratively appointed from the rotating list of arbitrators selected by a balanced advisory committee of practitioners active in the field. Either side may object to the appointment of a specific arbitrator for cause.

Parties make their own arrangements for stenographers, if desired, and pay the stenographer directly. Arbitrators are compensated at the rate of $100 per case, split evenly by the parties. Arbitrators are compensated at the rate of $50 for any hearing dates postponed less than 24 hours prior to the time of the scheduled hearing, payable by the party causing the postponement.

In accordance with the law, where the claimant prevails, the arbitrator must direct the insurer to pay all the costs of the proceedings, including reasonable attorneys' fees to be determined in accordance with a schedule of hourly rates for services performed, as prescribed by the Supreme Court of New Jersey.

Other provisions of the automobile insurance law provide for the establishment of court-administered arbitration for the liability portion of the disputes not covered under PIP. Formulation of the procedures is to be accomplished by each of the county assignment judges. It is intended that disputes valued at under $15,000 be subject to mandatory arbitration. For disputes of greater value, arbitration is an option.

These two arbitration systems are part of an overall embracing of the arbitration process by the New Jersey court system and the state legislature. Additional alternatives to litigation are anticipated, with study being done on the concept of the "multidoor courthouse," where disputants are directed to the particular forum best equipped to dispose of the conflict.

ALTERNATIVE DISPUTE RESOLUTION PROGRAM

Responding to the expressed need of the insurance industry for a simple, inexpensive, and expeditious way to resolve liability claims, the American Arbitration Association prepared Alternative Dispute Resolution (ADR) Procedures for the industry, the claimants, and claimants' counsel. Initiated in mid-1983 on a pilot basis, the ADR program speeds up claims resolution and helps control litigation costs.

The ADR program is entirely voluntary. Both insurers and claiming parties are invited to submit cases. Cases are filed by submission to arbitration or to nonbinding mediation, at the parties' option; there need not be a previous contractual arrangement between the parties to use the program. Insurers or claimants list with the AAA cases that they would be willing to submit under the ADR procedures. The AAA then serves as intermediary, explaining the program to the other party with an invitation to submit the case to either mediation or arbitration. If there is agreement, the AAA appoints the neutral and proceeds to schedule the matter.

The arbitrators and mediators selected by the AAA for this program are qualified, experienced, neutral attorneys with an understanding of current legal and business practices. They are required to inform the AAA of any circumstances that might prevent a prompt hearing or create a presumption of bias. The AAA is authorized to replace neutrals when necessary.

The costs of the ADR program are reasonable. There is an administrative fee of $100 per party, plus a suggested compensation fee of $250 for the neutral, to be paid equally by the parties. The exact compensation rate for the neutral is arranged by the AAA with the parties before the hearings.

There is no limit on the amount of claim that may be submitted to the program. The average claim in the pilot program was for approximately $10,000, but many claims were substantially greater.

Case Selection

Parties are urged to exhaust their own direct negotiation efforts prior to submitting a case to the program. When there are multiple parties, all parties must agree to the submission. Generally, cases submitted concern matters where the insurer acknowledges some liability. Although there is no limit on the amount of claim, the parties may wish to limit, in the submission, the dollar amount an arbitrator can award.

Examples of the types of issues that have been submitted include:

- Rear-end collision with a truck
- A "slip and fall" case that had been in suit for ten years
- Dispute between neighbors over destruction of trees on property
- Passenger on bus injured when bus made a sudden stop
- Claimant was guest at hotel and a heavy steel fire door closed quickly, crushing her finger between the door and the door jamb
- Claimant struck by clothes rack blown over during sidewalk sale
- False arrest of shopper at a department store
- Claimant fell and was injured in a neighbor's swimming pool

Resolution of the Dispute

The results of the pilot program show that mediation, the more informal process, is selected more often as the means of settlement than arbitration. The mediator's role is to assist the parties in negotiating their own settlement. A mediator does not have the authority to make a binding decision or award.

The mediator will work with both sides toward establishing realistic, acceptable claims and offers. When the parties reach agreement, they should reduce the terms to writing and exchange releases. They may also request that the agreement be put in the form of a Consent Award, for which the AAA will make the arrangements.

If there are any issues not resolved in mediation, the parties may wish to submit them to arbitration for a final, binding determination.

If arbitration is the settlement technique selected under the ADR procedures, hearings will be held to provide the arbitrator with the information necessary to decide the dispute. After listening to the evidence and arguments, the arbitrator declares the hearing closed. Under the ADR Procedures, the arbitrator has 30 days from that time within which to render a binding award.

The award is usually a brief statement directing one or both parties to provide specific relief. It is not accompanied by a written opinion unless the parties and the arbitrator agree that an opinion is desirable.

The power of the arbitrator ends with the making of the award. Once it is made, an award may not be clarified or modified by the arbitrator unless the parties mutually agree in writing to reopen the proceedings and to restore the power of the arbitrator, or unless the law provides otherwise.

CONCLUSION

Arbitration of insurance claims has proven to be an attractive alternative to litigation. Claimants with meritorious cases can be compensated sooner, and the time and expense of processing claims can be reduced. Finally, the public's perception of the justice system is enhanced when the system works efficiently.

Uninsured motorist arbitration has been in operation for more than twenty years. And no-fault arbitration has become an established part of the claims system in many jurisdictions. As other states begin to modernize their systems for compensating injured persons, they should take advantage of the impartial services of the AAA.

In addition, as the ADR program indicates, new procedures are being continuously tested to provide claimants with the best possible systems for resolving their insurance disputes.

ACCIDENT CLAIMS ARBITRATION RULES (INCLUDING MEDIATION)

As Amended and in Effect July 1, 1985

1. Agreement of Parties–The parties make these Rules a part of their arbitration agreement whenever a policy of insurance or applicable Insurance Department regulation provides for arbitration by the American Arbitration Association (AAA) in connection with a dispute involving a motor vehicle liability claim. These Rules and any amendment thereof shall apply in the form obtaining at the time the arbitration is initiated.

2. Administrator–When the parties agree to arbitrate under these Rules they thereby authorize the AAA to act hereunder. The duties of the AAA under these Rules may be carried out through such representatives as the AAA may direct.

3. Panel of Neutral Arbitrators–The American Arbitration Association shall establish and maintain an Accident Claims Panel of neutral Arbitrators made up of attorneys with negligence experience. Each of the AAA regional offices will maintain an Advisory Committee, made up of equal numbers of at least three members of the defense bar and/or the insurance industry and three members of the plaintiff's bar, which will approve the qualifications of the members of that Panel. Each Committee shall meet at least once a year.

4. Initiation under an Arbitration Provision in a Policy–When the conditions precedent contained in the insurance policy or state insurance department regulations have been complied with, arbitration may be initiated by filing a written Demand for Arbitration. The Demand shall be served by U.S. certified mail–return receipt requested. When filed by an insured, it shall be directed to the claims office of the insurer under whose policy arbitration is sought, at the office where the claim has been discussed or the office of the insurer closest to the residence of the insured.

The Demand shall set forth the following information: (1) name, address, and telephone number of the insured person(s) and of the filing attorney; (2) name and address of policyholder, and policy number; (3) identity and location of claims office of insurer, if known, the claim file number, if known, and name of individual with whom the claim was discussed; (4) date and location of accident; (5) nature of dispute and injuries alleged; (6) amount of UM policy limits and amount claimed thereunder; (7) address of AAA regional office where copies of Demand are being filed.

Three copies of the above Demand must be filed with an AAA regional office at the same time, with a copy of the parts of the policy or regulations relating to the dispute, including the arbitration provisions, together with the administrative filing fee.

The AAA will acknowledge receipt of the Demand to all parties. The insurer(s) shall have thirty calendar days within which to affirmatively deny coverage or to raise an issue as to applicable policy limits. If no such procedure is initiated, it will be assumed that there is no objection to arbitration and that the claim is denied.

Where the insurer moves in court to contest coverage, administration will be suspended until that issue is determined. Arbitrators may only decide contested issues of coverage where ordered to do so by a court, or where authorized by law, or where both parties so agree in writing.

5. Change of Claim—If any party desires to make any new or different claim, such claim shall be made in writing and filed with the AAA and a copy thereof mailed to the other party. After the Arbitrator is appointed, no new or different claim may be submitted except with the consent of the Arbitrator.

6. Initiation under a Submission—Parties to an already existing dispute may commence an arbitration under these Rules by filing at any office of the AAA three copies of a written agreement to arbitrate (Submission), setting forth the information specified in Section 4.

7. Fixing of Locality—Either the county of residence of the insured or the county where the accident occurred may be designated by the insured as the locale in which the hearing is to be held. Only if all parties agree, shall the hearing be held in some other locale.

8. Designation of Arbitrators—Cases may be heard by a single Arbitrator appointed from the Accident Claims Panel. However, where any party requests that the case be heard by three Arbitrators, and local law does not provide otherwise, the insured will select one Arbitrator and the insurer will select another. The two Arbitrators will then select a neutral Arbitrator from a list of six members of the Accident Claims Panel submitted by the AAA.

If a party does not select its Arbitrator within twenty calendar days, its right to select a party-selected Arbitrator will have been waived, and the AAA will proceed with the selection of the neutral Arbitrator. In that situation, the matter may be heard by the neutral Arbitrator and the single party-selected Arbitrator.

When a neutral Arbitrator is appointed by the AAA or selected by the Arbitrators appointed by the parties, the AAA will submit a list of six members of the Accident Claims Panel, from which the parties or their Arbitrators shall select. Each party shall have the right to strike two names from each such list on a peremptory basis and to challenge the appointment of a neutral Arbitrator for reasonable cause filed within twenty days of the notice of appointment.

9. Qualification of Arbitrators—No person shall serve as a neutral Arbitrator in any arbitration in which that person has any financial or personal interest. A neutral Arbitrator shall disclose any circumstances likely to create a presumption of bias which might disqualify him or her as an impartial Arbitrator. Either party may advise the AAA of any reason why a neutral Arbitrator should withdraw or be disqualified from serving. If a neutral Arbitrator should resign, be disqualified, or be unable to perform the duties of the office, the AAA shall appoint a replacement in accordance with the provisions of Section 8. If an Arbitrator selected by one of the parties shall be unable to serve, that party shall select a replacement Arbitrator, unless such right has been waived.

10. Time and Place—The Arbitrator shall fix the time and place for each hearing. At least twenty calendar days prior to the first scheduled hearing, the AAA shall mail notice thereof to each party, unless a party waives such notice.

11. Representation by Counsel—Any party may be represented at the hearing by counsel.

12. Stenographic Record—Any party wishing a stenographic record shall make such arrangements directly with the stenographer and shall notify the other parties of such arrangements in advance of the hearing. The requesting party or parties shall pay the cost of such record.

13. Interpreter—Any party wishing an interpreter shall make all arrangements directly with an interpreter and shall assume the costs of such service.

14. Attendance at Hearings–Persons having a direct interest in the arbitration are entitled to attend hearings. The Arbitrator shall otherwise have the power to require the retirement of any witness or witnesses during the testimony of other witnesses. It shall be discretionary with the Arbitrator to determine the propriety of the attendance of any other persons.

15. Adjournments–The Arbitrator for good cause may adjourn the hearing upon the request of a party or upon the Arbitrator's own initiative, and shall grant such adjournment when all of the parties agree thereto.

16. Oaths–Before proceeding, each Arbitrator may take an oath of office, and if required by law, shall do so. The Arbitrator has discretion to require witnesses to testify under oath and shall do so if requested by either party.

17. Majority Decision–Whenever there are more than two Arbitrators, a majority vote shall be sufficient for all of the decisions of the Arbitrators, including the Award.

18. Order of Proceedings–A hearing shall be opened by the filing of the oath of the Arbitrator, where required, and by recording the place, time and date of hearing, the presence of the Arbitrator and parties, and the receipt by the Arbitrator of the Demand or Submission.

The Arbitrator may, at the beginning of the hearing, ask for statements clarifying the issues involved. The complaining party may then present its claim, proofs, and witnesses, who shall submit to questions or other examination. Defending parties may then present their defense, proofs, and witnesses, who shall submit to questions or other examination. The Arbitrator has the discretion to vary this procedure but shall afford full and equal opportunity to all parties for the presentation of any material or relevant proofs.

Exhibits, when offered by either party, may be received in evidence by the Arbitrator. The names and addresses of all witnesses and exhibits in the order received shall be made a part of the record.

19. Arbitration in the Absence of a Party–Unless the law otherwise provides, the arbitration may proceed in the absence of any party who, after due notice, fails to be present or fails to obtain an adjournment. The Arbitrator shall require the party present to submit such evidence as he or she may require for the making of an Award, and will ordinarily offer the absent party an opportunity to appear at a subsequent hearing.

20. Evidence–The parties may offer such evidence as they desire and shall produce such additional evidence as the Arbitrator may deem necessary to an understanding and determination of the dispute. When the Arbitrator is authorized by law to subpoena witnesses or documents, this may be done upon the Arbitrator's own initiative or upon the request of any party. The Arbitrator shall be the judge of the relevancy and materiality of the evidence offered, and conformity to legal rules of evidence shall not be necessary. All evidence shall be taken in the presence of all the Arbitrators and all the parties except parties in default and parties or party-selected Arbitrators who have waived the right to be present. Any party who intends to offer any medical report or record at the hearing must provide the other party with a copy at least twenty days in advance thereof.

21. Evidence by Affidavit or Document–The Arbitrator may receive and consider the evidence of witnesses by affidavit, but shall give it only such weight as the Arbitrator deems it entitled to after consideration of any objections made to its admission.

If the parties agree that documents are to be submitted to the Arbitrator after the hearing, they shall be filed with the AAA for transmission to the Arbitrator. All parties shall be afforded opportunity to examine such documents.

22. Closing of Hearings–The Arbitrator shall specifically inquire of all parties whether they have any further evidence. If they do not, the Arbitrator shall declare the hearings closed. If briefs or documents are to be filed, the hearings shall be declared closed as of the final date set by the Arbitrator for receipt of such briefs or documents. The time limit within which the Arbitrator is required to make the Award shall commence to run upon the closing of the hearings.

23. Reopening of Hearings–The hearings may be reopened upon the Arbitrator's own motion, or upon application of a party for good cause shown, at any time before the Award is made.

24. Waiver of Rules–Any party who proceeds with the arbitration after knowledge that any provision or requirement of these Rules has not been complied with and who fails to state objection thereto in writing shall be deemed to have waived the right to object.

25. Extensions of Time–The parties may modify any period of time by mutual agreement. The AAA for good cause may extend any period of time established by these Rules except the time for making the Award. The AAA shall advise the parties of any such extension of time and its reason therefor.

26. Serving of Notices–With the exception of the Demand, which shall be served by U.S. certified mail–return receipt requested, each party shall be deemed to have consented that any other papers, notices, or process necessary or proper for the continuation of an arbitration under these Rules, and for any court action in connection therewith or for the entry of judgment on any Award made thereunder, may be served upon such party (a) by mail addressed to such party or its attorney at its last known address, or (b) by personal service, within or without the State wherein the arbitration has been or is to be held, provided that reasonable opportunity to be heard with regard thereto has been granted such party. The AAA is not a necessary party in judicial proceedings relating to the arbitration.

27. Communication with the Arbitrator–There shall be no direct communication between parties and the Arbitrator other than at oral hearings. Any other oral or written communication from the parties to the Arbitrator shall be directed to the AAA for transmittal to the Arbitrator.

28. Time of Award–The Arbitrator shall render the Award promptly and, unless otherwise agreed by the parties, not later than thirty days from the date of the close of the hearings or the reopened hearings.

29. Form of Award–The Award shall be in writing and shall be signed by the sole Arbitrator or by a majority if there be more than one. It shall be executed in the manner required by law.

30. Scope of Award–The Arbitrator shall render a decision determining whether the insured person has a right to receive any damages under the policy, and the amount thereof, not in excess of the applicable policy limits. The award shall not contain a determination as to issues of coverage except as provided in Section 4 above.

31. Award upon Settlement–If the parties settle their dispute during the course of the arbitration, the Arbitrator, upon their request, may set forth the terms of the agreed settlement in an Award.

32. Delivery of Award to Parties–Parties shall accept as legal delivery of the Award the placing of the Award or a true copy thereof in the mail, addressed to such party or its attorney at its last known address, or personal service of the Award, or other manner which may be prescribed by law.

33. Expenses–The expenses of witnesses for either side shall be paid by the party producing such witnesses. All other expenses of the arbitration, including required travelling and other expenses of the Arbitrator and the AAA and the expenses of any witness or the cost of any proofs produced at the direct request of the Arbitrator, shall be borne equally by the parties unless they agree otherwise.

34. Applications to Court and Exclusion of Liability–(a) No judicial proceedings by a party relating to the subject matter of the arbitration or mediation shall be deemed a waiver of the party's right to arbitrate.

(b) Neither the AAA nor any Arbitrator or Mediator in a proceeding under these Rules is a necessary party in judicial proceedings relating to the arbitration or mediation.

(c) Parties to these Rules shall be deemed to have consented that judgment upon the arbitration award may be entered in any Federal or State Court having jurisdiction thereof.

(d) Neither the AAA nor any Arbitrator or Mediator shall be liable to any party for any act or omission in connection with any arbitration or mediation conducted under these Rules.

35. Interpretation and Application of Rules–The Arbitrator shall interpret and apply these Rules insofar as they relate to the Arbitrator's powers and duties. When there is more than one Arbitrator and a difference arises among them concerning the meaning or application of any Rules relating to their powers and duties, it shall be decided by a majority vote. If that is unobtainable, either an Arbitrator or a party may refer the question to the AAA for final decision. All other Rules shall be interpreted and applied by the AAA.

AMERICAN ARBITRATION ASSOCIATION RULES FOR NEW YORK STATE NO-FAULT ARBITRATION AND NO-FAULT EXPEDITED ARBITRATION

Effective for Requests Filed with the New York State Insurance Department on and after September 1, 1985 for Disputes Involving First Party Benefits Arising Out of Accidents Occurring on and after December 1, 1977 and Disputes Involving Additional First Party Benefits Arising Out of Accidents Occurring on and after January 1, 1982

PART I. AAA EXPEDITED ARBITRATION

1. The Insurance Department shall refer to the American Arbitration Association (AAA) all requests for arbitration when resolution of any of the following issues is a condition precedent to payment of first party benefits and/or additional first party benefits:

(a) whether a policy was in force on the date of the accident;

(b) whether the applicant qualified as an "eligible injured person" under the policy or as a "qualified person" pursuant to Article 52 of the Insurance Law;

(c) whether the applicant was excluded from coverage under the policy conditions or exclusions;

(d) whether the applicant violated policy conditions, resulting in exclusion from coverage;

(e) whether the applicant's injuries arose out of the "use or operation" of a motor vehicle or a motorcycle;

(f) whether a valid assignment of no-fault benefits exists or whether the absence of same precludes the applicant's standing in the arbitration; or

(g) whether the policy includes a family deductible as provided for in Section 5103(c) of the Insurance Law, which is applicable to the applicant's claim.

2. The AAA procedures contained in Part II of these Rules shall be applicable to AAA Expedited Arbitrations, subject to the following:

(i) Existence or termination of policy. AAA Expedited Arbitrations involving 11 NYCRR 65.16(c) (3) (i) (a) (whether a policy was in force on the date of the accident) shall be heard by an AAA arbitrator who is a member of a roster of arbitrators who, based upon their legal background and experience, are designated by the Superintendent for this purpose. The AAA shall appoint all other expedited arbitrators by selecting, in sequence, from the AAA's existing panel of no-fault arbitrators within the general locale of the applicant's residence, or, where requested in writing by the applicant prior to transmittal of the dispute to the AAA, within the general locale of the applicant's attorney's principal place of business.

(ii) The AAA shall appoint all expediting arbitrators and schedule a hearing to be held within 15 calendar days of receipt by the AAA from the Insurance Department of the request for arbitration. The arbitrator shall, within 15 calendar days after the conclusion of the arbitration hearing, render a written award in a format prescribed by the Superintendent.

(iii) If the arbitrator finds for the applicant, the insurer shall have 15 calendar days after the date of mailing of the award to either appeal the award to a master arbitrator, or accept the arbitrator's resolution(s) of the issue(s) and process the claim pursuant to 11 NYCRR 65.15.

PART II. AAA ARBITRATION

1. Coordination of Arbitrators–Where one of the issues is within the jurisdiction of the Health Service Arbitration (H.S.A., the forum designated to resolve disputes involving health services rendered in New York State) and the remaining issues involving the same issue(s) of fact are within the jurisdiction of AAA arbitration, the Insurance Department shall not forward the matter to the AAA until the Health Service Arbitration has rendered an award and forwarded it to the Insurance Department. The AAA arbitrator shall consider the H.S.A. award when resolving the disputed elements of basic economic loss which are the subject of the AAA arbitration. Notwithstanding the above, the Department may forward the case to both the H.S.A. and AAA forums, concurrently, where the issues to be resolved by the H.S.A. forum are not relevant to the dispute which will be subject to AAA arbitration, and resolution by the H.S.A. is not necessary in order to resolve the AAA dispute.

2. Notice–Upon receipt of the request for arbitration from the Insurance Department, the AAA shall send to the insurer written notice that arbitration has been requested and shall bill the insurer $300. The AAA shall return the $300 filing fee to an insurer if the arbitration does not result in an award to the applicant or the entire award is reversed by a master arbitrator. For the purpose of this paragraph, consent awards resulting in a payment to the applicant shall be considered awards. The notice shall state the names of the applicant and the policyholder (if applicable), the arbitration file number, and the insurer's file number as set forth on the request for arbitration.

3. Consolidation–The AAA shall, except when impracticable, consolidate disputes for which a request for arbitration has been received, if the claims involved arose out of the same accident and involve common issues of fact.

4. Appointment of Arbitrator–After the notice required by Part II, Rule 2 has been mailed, an arbitrator shall be appointed by the AAA in the following manner: The AAA shall select in sequence the next four names, within the general locale of the applicant's residence, or where requested in writing by the applicant prior to transmittal of the dispute to the AAA, within the general locale of the applicant's attorney's principal place of business, from the AAA's existing panel of no-fault arbitrators and submit these names to each party to the arbitration. If there are more than two parties to an arbitration, the AAA shall submit to the parties a list of names equal to the number of parties, plus one. Each party to the arbitration shall have the right to strike one arbitrator from the list. The AAA shall maintain a file containing the professional background of each member of its panel of no-fault arbitrators. The information contained therein shall be available to any party to the arbitration upon written or oral request. The right to strike shall be exercised within 8 calendar days after the mailing of the list of arbitrators by the AAA. The AAA shall select the arbitrator from those remaining on the list. No arbitrator shall serve in more than 25 no-fault arbitrations in any one calendar year.

5. Qualifications of the Arbitrator–Every arbitrator appointed for a hearing held in New York State shall be a licensed attorney of this State, and for a hearing held outside of New York State shall be a licensed attorney in the State or Canadian province where the hearing is held. No person shall serve as an arbitrator in any arbitration in which such person has any financial or personal interest. An arbitrator shall disclose to the AAA any circumstances likely to create an appearance of bias or which might disqualify such arbitrator. Upon receipt of such information, the AAA shall immediately disclose it to the parties. If a party challenges an arbitrator, the specific grounds for the challenge shall be submitted in writing. The AAA shall determine whether the arbitrator should be disqualified and shall inform the parties of its decision, which shall be conclusive. If an arbitrator should resign, be disqualified, or be otherwise unable to perform the duties of the office, the AAA shall appoint another arbitrator to the case.

6. Oaths—The arbitrator shall take an annual oath of office. The arbitrator shall require all witnesses to testify under oath or affirm that their statements are true under the penalties of perjury.

7. Time and Place of Arbitration—The arbitration hearing shall be held in the arbitrator's office or any other appropriate place in the general locale of the applicant's residence or other locale agreed upon by the parties. The arbitrator shall fix the time and place for such hearing. At least 12 calendar days prior to the hearing, the AAA shall mail a notice of hearing to each party, and to the party's designated representative, if any. Unless otherwise agreed to by the parties, the hearing shall be scheduled to be held within 21 calendar days of the date of the appointment of the arbitrator. The parties to the arbitration shall not directly contact the arbitrator at any time prior to or subsequent to the hearing, but may submit material intended for the arbitrator to the AAA.

8. Postponements and Adjournments—The AAA or the arbitrator, for good cause shown, may postpone or adjourn the hearing upon request of a party or upon the arbitrator's own initiative, and shall postpone or adjourn when all the parties agree thereto. Each party may request one adjournment without the payment of an adjournment fee. There shall be an adjournment fee of $25 payable to the AAA by the party requesting any subsequent adjournment. Such fee shall be used to defray the cost of administration of the AAA forum.

9. Representation at Arbitration—Any party may be represented by an attorney.

10. Designated Representative—The "designated representative" of any party is the attorney of any party or any other person designated by a party in writing to the AAA.

11. Record of Proceedings—A stenographic record of the arbitration proceedings will not be required. However, a party requesting such a record shall inform the other party or parties of such intent, make the necessary arrangements, and pay the cost thereof directly to the person or agency making such record. Any other party or parties to the arbitration shall be entitled to a copy of such record upon agreeing to share the cost of the total stenographic expense. Whether or not a stenographic record of the proceedings is made, the arbitrator shall, at a minimum, record the names and addresses of all parties and witnesses and the exhibits offered by each party.

12. Attendance at Hearings—Persons having a direct interest in the arbitration are entitled to attend hearings. It shall be discretionary with the arbitrator to determine the propriety of the attendance of any other person.

13. Evidence—The arbitrator shall be the judge of the relevancy and materiality of the evidence offered, and strict conformity to legal rules of evidence shall not be necessary. The arbitrator may subpoena witnesses or documents upon the arbitrator's own initiative or upon the request of any party, when the issues to be resolved necessarily require such witnesses or documents.

14. Arbitration in the Absence of a Party—The arbitration may proceed in the absence of any party, who, after due notice, fails to be present or fails to obtain a postponement or adjournment. An award shall not be made in favor of an appearing party solely on the default of another party. The arbitrator shall require the appearing party to submit such evidence as may be required for the making of an award. The arbitrator may require the appearance of a party at the hearing if the arbitrator determines that the party's appearance is necessary to realize a fair and just resolution of the dispute and to afford all parties due process.

15. Time of Award–The award shall be made and delivered no later than 15 calendar days from the date the hearing is completed.

16. Form and Scope of Award–The award shall be in writing in a format approved by the Superintendent. It shall state the issues in dispute and contain the arbitrator's findings and conclusions based on the Insurance Law and the Insurance Department Regulations. It shall be signed by the arbitrator and shall be transmitted to the parties by the AAA, with a copy to the Insurance Department. The award shall contain a decision on all issues submitted to the arbitrator by the parties. In the event that the applicant prevails in whole or in part on the claim, the arbitrator shall also direct the insurer to:

(a) reimburse the applicant for the amount of the filing fee, unless the filing fee had already been returned to the applicant pursuant to an earlier award;
(b) if due under Section 5106 of the Insurance Law, pay a reasonable attorney's fee in accordance with the limitations set forth in Rule 23 below;
(c) in an award of interest, the arbitrator shall direct the insurer to compute the amount due for each element of first party benefits in dispute, commencing 30 days after proof of claim therefor was received by the insurer and ending with the date of payment of the award, subject to the provisions of 11 NYCRR 65.15(g) (3) (stay of interest).

17. Award upon Settlement–If the parties settle their dispute during the course of arbitration, the arbitrator shall set forth the terms of the agreed settlement in an award which shall provide that the parties agree that the settlement is final and binding and shall not be subject to review by a master arbitrator or by a court. If an attorney's fee is due under Section 5106 of the Insurance Law, such fee shall be awarded in accordance with the limitations set forth in Rule 23 below. The award shall be signed by the arbitrator and shall be transmitted to the parties by the AAA, with a copy to the Insurance Department.

18. Delivery of Award to Parties–The parties shall accept as delivery of the award the placing of the award or a true copy thereof in the mail, addressed to the parties or their designated representatives at their last known addresses, or by any other form of service permitted by law. The AAA shall note on such award or transmittal letter thereof the date of mailing and keep a record of same.

19. Interpretation and Application of Procedures–The arbitrator shall interpret and apply these procedures insofar as they relate to the arbitrator's powers and duties. All other procedures shall be administered by the AAA, subject to consultation with and approval by the Superintendent.

20. Alternative Legal Remedies–The AAA should not be made a party to a court proceeding relating to an arbitration award unless the AAA's presence as a party is pertinent to the issues raised in the litigation. The AAA shall transmit to the Superintendent copies of any legal papers served upon AAA or an arbitrator, relating to any stay or appeal of an arbitration.

21. Payment of Award—Insurers shall, within 21 calendar days of the date of mailing of the award, either pay the amounts set forth in the award or, where grounds exist, appeal to the master arbitrator as provided for in 11 NYCRR 65.17, which appeal shall stay payment of the award. The award need not be confirmed into judgment.

22. Arbitrator's Fee—An arbitrator shall be compensated in the amount of $80 for each case, which shall be paid by the insurer. If the insurer prevails in whole, the fee of the arbitrator shall be charged to the expense of administering the AAA arbitration system.

23. Limitations on Attorney's Fees Pursuant to Section 5106 of the Insurance Law—The following limitations shall apply to the payment by insurers of applicant's attorney's fees for services necessarily performed in the resolution of no-fault disputes:

(i) If an arbitration was initiated or a court action was commenced by an attorney on behalf of an applicant and the claim or portion thereof was not denied or overdue at the time the arbitration proceeding was initiated or the action was commenced, no attorney's fees shall be granted.

(ii) The minimum attorney's fee payable pursuant to this Regulation shall be $55.

(iii) *Disputes subject to AAA Expedited Arbitration:* Subject to the provisions of (i) and (ii) above, an attorney's fee shall be limited as follows:

(a) For preparatory services relating to the arbitration forum or court, the attorney shall be entitled to receive a fee of up to $60 per hour, subject to a maximum fee of $1,200, and, in addition,

(b) an attorney shall be entitled to receive a fee of up to $75 per hour for each personal appearance before the arbitrator or court.

(iv) *Disputes subject to AAA Arbitration:* Subject to the provisions of (i) and (ii) above, an attorney's fee shall be limited as follows:

(a) For preparatory services relating to the arbitration forum or court, the attorney shall be entitled to receive a fee of up to $40 per hour, subject to a maximum fee of $400, and, in addition,

(b) an attorney shall be entitled to receive a fee of up to $65 per hour for each personal appearance before the arbitration forum or court;

(c) however, except as provided in (ii) above, in no event shall the attorney's fee exceed the amount of first party benefits plus interest thereon awarded to the applicant.

(v) Notwithstanding the above limitations, if the arbitrator(s) or a court determines that the issues in dispute were of such a novel and/or unique nature as to require extraordinary skills or services, the arbitrator(s) or court may award an attorney's fee in excess of the limitations set forth above. An excess fee award must describe in detail the specific novel and/or unique nature of the dispute which justifies the award. An excess award by an arbitrator shall be appealable to a master arbitrator.

(vi) If a dispute involving an overdue or denied claim is resolved either before arbitration is initiated or before a court action is commenced, the claimant's attorney shall be entitled to a fee of $55, which shall be full compensation from the insurer for the attorney's services with respect to such claim.*

(vii) If a dispute involving an overdue or denied claim is resolved by the parties after

*Attorneys should be aware of the Appellate Division Rules prohibiting contingent fees in connection with the collection of first party no-fault benefits (22 NYCRR 603.7(e) (7), 691.20(e) (7), and 806.12(f)).

it has been forwarded by the Insurance Department to the appropriate arbitration forum or after a court action has been commenced, the claimant's attorney shall be entitled to a fee which shall be computed in accordance with the limitations set forth in this Rule.

(viii) No attorney shall demand, request, or receive from the insurer any payment or fee in excess of the fees permitted by this paragraph.*

24. Witness Fees–(i) Whenever a witness fee is determined by the arbitrator to be payable, it shall be paid by the forum hearing the arbitration and the cost thereof shall be charged as an administrative expense of the particular arbitration forum.

(ii) The arbitrator shall not approve the payment of a fee to a witness appearing on behalf of an applicant or an assignee unless the witness was subpoenaed by the arbitrator or, prior to appearance, the witness's presence was determined by the arbitrator to be necessary for the resolution of the dispute. Provided, however, that no witness fee shall be payable to a person who is a party to the arbitration.

(iii) Any witness fee awarded pursuant to (i) and (ii) above shall be determined as follows:

(a) If the witness is testifying as an expert, the fee shall be calculated on the basis of such witness's documented usual and customary hourly charge for an appearance, plus necessary verified disbursements.

(b) Any other witness shall only be entitled to reimbursement for verified expenses and economic losses necessarily incurred in connection with an appearance before the arbitrator.

---

*Attorneys should be aware of the Appellate Division Rules prohibiting contingent fees in connection with the collection of first party no-fault benefits (22 NYCRR 603.7(e) (7), 691.20(e) (7), and 806.12(f)).

ALTERNATIVE DISPUTE RESOLUTION PROCEDURES

Effective April 1, 1984

1. Agreement of Parties–These Alternative Dispute Resolution Procedures shall apply whenever the parties have agreed to use them. By mutual agreement, in writing, the parties may modify any provision.

2. Initiation of Alternative Dispute Resolution Procedures–Cases may be initiated by a joint submission in writing, containing a brief description of the dispute with the names and addresses of the parties.

3. Appointment of Neutral–The AAA shall appoint a neutral attorney, knowledgeable in the area of the dispute. The parties shall agree in advance whether the neutral is authorized to issue a binding decision as an arbitrator. When the parties agree that such a decision will be binding, they are deemed to have consented that judgment upon such an award may be entered in any court having jurisdiction. If not authorized to issue a binding decision, the neutral will serve the parties as a mediator.

4. Qualifications of Neutrals–No person shall serve as a neutral in any matter in which that person has any financial or personal interest in the result of the proceeding. Prior to accepting appointment, a person being considered for such appointment shall disclose any circumstances likely to prevent a prompt hearing or to create a presumption of bias. Upon receipt of such information, the AAA will either replace that person or communicate the information to the parties for comment. Thereafter, the AAA may disqualify that person. Vacancies shall be filled in accordance with Section 3 of these procedures.

5. Time and Place of Mediation Conference or Arbitration Hearing–The neutral shall set the date, time, and place of the first conference or hearing with the parties, seven (7) days advance notice of which shall be given by the AAA to the parties. If the matter is to be mediated, the mediator will arrange an appropriate format with the parties.

6. Representation by Counsel–Any party may be represented at the conference or hearing by counsel or other representative.

7. Adjournment–Conferences or hearings may be adjourned by the neutral for good cause.

8. No Stenographic Record–There shall be no stenographic record of any such proceeding.

9. Arbitration Hearing–A hearing may be conducted by the arbitrator in a manner which permits a fair presentation of the case by the parties. Normally, the hearing shall be completed within one day. Only for good cause shown may the arbitrator schedule an additional hearing.

10. Evidence–The arbitrator shall be the sole judge of the relevance and materiality of the evidence offered.

11. Close of Hearing–The arbitrator shall ask whether the parties have any further proofs or testimony to offer. Upon determining that the presentations are concluded, the arbitrator shall declare the hearing closed.

12. Award–The award shall be in writing and shall be signed by the arbitrator. It shall be rendered promptly and, unless otherwise stipulated, not later than thirty (30) days following the close of the hearing. Any settlement reached by the parties may be incorporated in such an award.

13. Delivery of Award to Parties – The parties shall accept as legal delivery of the award the placing of the award or a true copy thereof in the mail by the AAA, addressed to such party at its last known address or to its attorney, or personal service of the award, or the filing of the award in any manner which may be prescribed by law.

14. Expenses – The expenses of witnesses for any party shall be paid by the party producing such witnesses.

15. Interpretation and Application of Procedures – The neutral shall interpret and apply these procedures insofar as they relate to the neutral's powers and duties. All other procedures shall be interpreted and applied by the AAA.

16. Judicial Proceedings and Immunity – Neither the AAA nor any neutral serving in a proceeding under these procedures is a necessary party in judicial proceedings relating to the arbitration or mediation. Neither the AAA nor any neutral serving under these procedures shall be liable to any party for any act or omission in connection with this service.

BIBLIOGRAPHY

American Arbitration Association. *Accident Claims Arbitration Rules (Including Mediation): As Amended and in Effect July 1, 1985.* New York: 1985.

______. *Alternative Dispute Resolution in Action*. New York: 1984.

______. *Alternative Dispute Resolution Procedures: Effective April 1, 1984.* New York: 1984.

______. *Alternative Dispute Resolution Procedures for Life and Health Claims: Effective January 1, 1985.* New York: 1985.

______. *American Arbitration Association Rules for New York State No-Fault Arbitration and No-Fault Expedited Arbitration: Effective for Requests Filed with the New York State Insurance Department on and after September 1, 1985 for Disputes Involving First Party Benefits Arising Out of Accidents Occurring on and after December 1, 1977 and Disputes Involving Additional First Party Benefits Arising Out of Accidents Occurring on and after January 1, 1982.* New York: 1985.

______. *Arbitration of Uninsured Motorist Claims*. New York: 1985.

______. *A Legal Course Outline on New York No-Fault Arbitration*. New York: March 1985.

______. *A Manual for Accident Claims Arbitrators.* New York: 1985.

______. *A Manual for New York No-Fault Arbitrators: For Accidents Occurring on or after December 1, 1977 and Filed with the New York State Insurance Department on and after January 2, 1981.* New York: 1984.

______. *Procedures: New York State No-Fault Master Arbitration Procedures.* New York: 1985.

American Insurance Association. *Summary of Selected Laws and Regulations Relating to Automobile Insurance.* New York: 1982.

"Arbitration of Uninsured Motorist Claims." *Lawyers' Arbitration Letter*, vol. 6, no. 3 (September 1981), pp. 1–7.

Friedman, George H. "Amendments Coming in Uninsured Motorist Arbitration Rules." *New York Law Journal*, June 14, 1985, p. 1.

______. "Arbitration of No-Fault Claims." In *No-Fault and Uninsured Motorist Automobile Insurance. Volume 1*, pp. 15-1–15-109. New York: Matthew Bender, 1984.

Hines, Bernard L. *Insurance Arbitration: A Guide to Insurance Industry Forums.* New York: Board of Governors–Insurance Arbitration Forums, 1981.

Krochock, Richard H. "UM Arbitration: Practical Considerations in Representing Insurer." *For the Defense*, vol. 25, no. 9 (September 1983), pp. 6–7.

Lerner, Richard E., and Richard Naimark. "Arbitration of No-Fault Auto Insurance Claims." *New Jersey Law Journal*, May 10, 1979, p. 1.

McLucas, Robert J. "Alternative Dispute Resolution: The Travelers' Experience." *The Arbitration Journal*, vol. 39, no. 2 (June 1984), pp. 55–57.

New York No-Fault Arbitration Reports. New York: American Arbitration Association, 1977–present (ongoing publication).

New York State Insurance Department. "Regulations Implementing the Comprehensive Automobile Insurance Act." 11 NYCRR 65.1 *et seq.*

Schermer, Irvin E. *Automobile Liability Insurance: No-Fault Insurance, Uninsured Motorists, Compulsory Coverage.* 2d ed. New York: Clark Boardman Co., 1974–present (ongoing publication).

Weitz, Harvey. *The No-Fault Handbook: New York State*. 3d ed. New York: New York State Trial Lawyers Association, 1981.

Widiss, Alan I. *Uninsured and Underinsured Motorist Insurance*. 2d ed. Cincinnati: Anderson, 1985.

Woodroof, M. G. III, John R. Fonseca, and Alphonse M. Squillante. *Automobile Insurance and No-Fault Law.* Rochester: Lawyers Co-operative Publishing, 1974. Has cumulative supplement pocket part issued September 1982.

CHAPTER 5

INTERNATIONAL ARBITRATION—A SMORGASBORD OF SYSTEMS

An understanding of arbitration should be part of the working knowledge of every person doing business abroad or with foreign interests operating in the United States. Arbitration clauses are frequently included in contracts in international trade because both American and foreign parties have shown a strong preference for submitting their disputes to arbitration. They use arbitration because they can avoid the formalities, complexities, and uncertainties of foreign court proceedings.

Unfortunately, because international arbitration clauses often are defective, problems can surface. The parties may fail to designate an agency to administer the arbitration, or they may not have specified appropriate rules or procedures. Defective arbitration arrangements often result in unnecessary litigation.

In general, using a broad arbitration clause covering every dispute can greatly reduce the need for clarifying litigation. On the other hand, the parties may wish to decide in advance that only certain issues are subject to arbitration. In such a case, the parties should specify which terms and conditions in the contract are to be covered.

In international trade, there has been a trend toward clauses that provide for administration by a recognized, impartial institution under a definite set of rules. Such a procedure helps to eliminate potential conflicts. The agency arranges for the filing of papers, the appointment of arbitrators, the filling of any vacancies caused by the death or disability of an arbitrator, and the details of the hearing.

When an American business person does work abroad, the foreign party may suggest using one or more of the international arbitration systems available in other countries. It is important that the U.S. lawyer be knowledgeable about these systems. Foreign practices vary from U.S. procedures and may be less attractive to an American party. In general, however, they do provide a recognized process that is, in most cases, better for resolving business controversies than going to foreign courts.

Some of the leading international systems abroad are the London Court of Arbitration, the Court of Arbitration of the International Chamber of Commerce in Paris, and the arbitration facilities of the Stockholm Chamber of Commerce. The need for such services is expanding. Competition among arbitration agencies should lead to better service and enhance the use of arbitration in the worldwide business community. A list of international arbitration institutions is printed at the end of this chapter.

When parties decide to use arbitration, the important choice will be *where* and *how* to arbitrate. The nature of the contract, the kind of project involved, and the preferences of the spokespersons will determine that choice. The realities of the industry, the expectations of the interests involved, and the cultural standards of their society must also be considered. The contract specifications and the political and social setting within which the work may take place are important considerations.

The arbitration clause may be the last item to be discussed. The selection of an arbitration locale and a particular arbitration mechanism may not even be talked about before the deal is closed. The prime negotiators may agree on the principle but leave the procedure to the lawyers. The selection of the forum is a matter for the attorneys.

An arbitration clause can be a two-edged sword. If your client is the claimant, you want to be able to enforce the obligations of your client's contract. If your party is the respondent, you may rejoice in interminable delays. Not every advocate wants a prompt award.

The location of the arbitration may determine the procedural law of the case, shaping the process. Specifying the locale and the applicable law often lends certainty to the process. For example, in the United States, contracts usually specify that the arbitrator's award is subject to confirmation in court. In the absence of such a clause, courts may refuse to enforce an award. If an international contract provides for arbitration in the U.S., this kind of provision may be advisable. If the arbitration is in a country without such a rule, the provision may not be appropriate, because, under the New York Convention on the Recognition and Enforcement of Foreign Arbitral Awards, confirmation in the courts of the forum is not required. In fact, a foreign arbitration award may be easier to enforce in some countries than a court judgment.

Trade executives have used arbitration to resolve international trade disputes for many years. As a result, the concept of arbitration is already well accepted in other countries. Foreign traders are familiar with the process and expect an arbitration clause to appear in trade contracts. Disagreement will not arise over whether to use arbitration, but foreign business people are likely to have fixed opinions as to the situs of the arbitration, the method of choosing arbitrators, and the procedural rules to be applied.

The arbitration clause in international contracts should select the tribunal that best suits the mutual needs of the parties. Some questions can be anticipated. The following checklist of items can help you decide what arbitration provisions should be inserted in an international contract.

DESIGNATION OF ARBITRAL INSTITUTION

Many different types of international arbitration systems exist. Some are set within a particular national legal structure and are shaped by its traditions. Others are international in scope. Potential problems resulting from this diversity of systems can be minimized by designating a familiar arbitration agency to administer your case.

Parties are not required to utilize the services of arbitration agencies. Such agencies, however, have been used increasingly in order to obtain impartial administrative services and the benefit of orderly rules and an established panel of arbitrators. When the contracting parties choose such an institution, they often designate that institution's rules of procedure. If they provide that the arbitration will be in accordance with the rules of an institution, it is understood that the case will be administered by that agency.

The rules of most arbitral institutions contain certain basic provisions: (1) a method of initiating arbitration through the filing of a notice; (2) the appointment of arbitrators, with procedures for substitution and challenge; (3) rules covering such matters as the submission of documents, representation by counsel, witnesses, fees, and security for costs; (4) ordering a transcript, if desired; and (5) the award, including its communication to the parties and its possible modification.

The international caseload of the American Arbitration Association has been increasing. The AAA handles hundreds of international cases annually, many of them involving substantial sums. In addition, many international cases flow through international tribunals in other countries.

International arbitration provides many options. Counsel must decide whether to arbitrate, and *where* and *how*. Should they refer to an institutional system? Which one? Among the relevant considerations are the arbitration preferences of the client, the range of authority to be delegated to the arbitrator, the amount of institutional involvement desired, the hearing procedure, what criteria the arbitrator should consider, whether the arbitrator should give reasons in the award, and the costs of the process. It is recommended that arbitrators be selected who are experienced in the particular industry.

Arbitration agencies will play an ever-greater role. As agencies attempt to expand their services, they need to be more responsive to the procedural preferences of lawyers and business people. The American Arbitration Association administers cases under its Supplementary Procedures for International Commercial Arbitration. If parties wish to use these procedures, it is necessary to so specify in the contract.

ARBITRATION CONVENTIONS

The 1958 Convention on the Recognition and Enforcement of Foreign Arbitral Awards, adopted in New York by the United Nations Conference on International Commercial Arbitration, is a multilateral treaty that encourages the use of arbitration for resolving international commercial disputes. The parties may be governments, private citizens, or corporations. The Convention is applicable to all systems of arbitration, either *ad hoc* or administered by an institution. The Convention provides for the enforcement of arbitration clauses in contracts, as well as for the enforcement of awards.

There are no rules or permanent panels of arbitrators specified by the Convention. An award, if not voluntarily honored, may be enforced by means of a judgment obtained in the court of the contracting state. It is not subject to review by that court on the merits, but rather, as described in the Convention, on grounds of fairness, public policy, and due process.

The United Nations Commission on International Trade Law (UNCITRAL) sponsors a set of arbitration rules for use on a worldwide basis to provide uniformity in international arbitrations. The AAA is prepared to serve as appointing agency under these rules and to provide its traditional administrative services. The UNCITRAL rules provide for a simple notice of arbitration; a listing procedure for appointment of arbitrators, with a challenge and replacement process; and an informal statement of claim procedure, with the tribunal empowered to determine its own jurisdiction, to manage the hearings, and to protect the interests of the parties. Following the continental procedure, arbitrators must give their reasons. Arbitrators' fees are to be reasonable, taking into account the amount of money involved, the complexity of the subject matter, the time spent, and other circumstances. Some parties have referred to the UNCITRAL rules in their contracts, requesting that the AAA serve as appointing authority and provide administrative services.

PREARBITRATION PROCEDURES

Some international arbitration procedures include provisions for discovery, fact-finding, or conciliation to help resolve the dispute early in the process.

American lawyers have a high regard for discovery procedures, but business people worry about the cost in terms of both money and time. Similarly, a fact-finding process can help define the issues but may cause delay and increase costs.

In some Far Eastern cultures, business people believe that disagreements should be resolved through friendly discussions or conciliation. Arbitration is used only as a last resort and is regarded with the same disapproval as taking a case to court. People try very hard to settle their disagreements. Conciliation can be particularly helpful when a cultural gap exists between the parties or when each side hopes to resolve the dispute without disrupting future business opportunities.

APPOINTMENT OF ARBITRATORS

Parties may wish to specify whether their case is to be heard before a single arbitrator or before three neutral arbitrators. In some situations, parties still utilize the method of designating "party-appointed" arbitrators, who may or may not participate in the selection of the third neutral arbitrator. In international arbitration, party-appointed arbitrators may expect to be neutral, rather than serving as advocates for the parties that appointed them. The parties should decide in advance whether the other party's arbitrator will be impartial. Parties can use a single neutral arbitrator or three neutral arbitrators selected from institutional lists rather than the party-appointed arbitrator system. Multiple arbitrator panels should be used only where the amount of claims is large or where the parties want to include arbitrators from different disciplines or industries.

The question of nationality should also be taken into account in international arbitration, both to avoid national bias and to obtain arbitrators who are familiar with the cultural, legal, or commercial traditions that may be involved in the case.

PLACE OF HEARING

Usually the arbitration clause should designate where the hearing will take place. This may prove difficult – for example, when the parties are located in distant parts of the globe. Traveling to the country of the other party for an arbitration case can be expensive. Sometimes parties have dealt with this problem by specifying a "home-on-home" arrangement under which the party initiating the arbitration must go to the other's country. Or parties may agree upon a neutral third-country location.

It may be desirable to designate a major city in the United States because of the availability of experienced arbitrators and the national network of AAA regional offices. The AAA administers international cases between parties from all over the world. Its reputation and prestige are internationally recognized, and foreign parties often agree upon a site in the United States.

It is possible to handle an international arbitration case in the United States in the European manner. If the parties desire, they can exchange documents. They can appoint foreign arbitrators. Parties can arbitrate in exactly the same way as in Europe. The AAA will follow the preferences of the parties and is prepared to provide administrative services under any reasonable and fair arrangement requested by the parties.

LANGUAGE

In some cases involving international transactions, a party may prefer that the hearing be held in his or her native language. If so, this should be specified in the arbitration agreement to avoid any subsequent dispute. The parties should also try to obtain an arbitrator who is comfortable in that language. If the language of the arbitration is not one that both parties share, expensive translation facilities may be required.

TIME LIMITS

Where the arbitration clause refers to an administrative agency, the time limits incorporated in that agency's rules become part of the arbitration agreement. If there is no such designation, it may be necessary to specify time limits for various actions. For example, time limits commonly apply to the arbitrator selection process. Time limits within which an award must be rendered after the close of hearings should be imposed upon the arbitrator.

APPLICABLE LAW

The arbitration laws of most jurisdictions permit parties to designate their own arbitration procedure by inserting special provisions in the contract or selecting preestablished institutional rules. Where the arbitration clause has gaps, the local law may provide backup provisions. For example, the United States Arbitration Act states that where no method is provided for naming an arbitrator, the federal court will designate the arbitrator. Such a provision is not always available in other jurisdictions.

The local arbitration law may also determine whether attachment, preliminary injunction, or other helpful remedies are available. In some jurisdictions, neither the arbitrators nor the courts can provide such assistance. This aspect of the local procedure should be investigated by counsel in advance.

The selected procedures may conflict with the local law. For example, an arbitration clause may specify that the arbitrators shall be nationals of a third country, but local law may not permit foreign arbitrators. Counsel should be aware of such problems in advance; otherwise such a dispute may have to be resolved in court–exactly the predicament parties wish to avoid by selecting the arbitration process.

International contracts often specify which law shall be applicable. The law may be separate from the arbitration clause, or the arbitration clause itself may tell the arbitrators which law they should consider. In other situations, the parties may wish to have the dispute determined on the basis of trade practice and custom.

The selection of applicable law should be determined based on an analysis of the contract involved. Counsel for the parties should be familiar with that law. If the parties want the arbitrators to consider trade usages, they may include a statement to that effect. In many European countries, there is a practice of giving arbitrators the power to decide as *amiables compositeurs;* that is, without obligation to observe the rules of law but subject to the rules of "natural justice" or the fundamental principles of commercial law. In addition, some contracts direct the arbitrator to decide the matter according to what is just and equitable in the circumstance. In this case, the strict rules of law would not necessarily be observed.

The choice of locale for the arbitration may affect the applicable law. If no law is specified in the arbitration agreement, the law of the forum, procedural and substantive, may be applied.

COSTS AND EXPENSES

Parties to commercial arbitration pay their own legal fees and other costs of preparation. In international arbitration, arbitrators generally charge a per diem fee, negotiated with the parties in advance. This may be shared equally by the parties. Where an administrative agency is involved, fee discussions are carried out by that agency. Parties should settle the terms of the arbitrators' compensation at an early stage. In addition, an administrative charge, which will vary in accordance with the rules, is made by the agency.

ENTRY OF JUDGMENT

In the United States, it is prudent for parties to include language in the arbitration clause authorizing the courts to enter judgment on the award. Without such a clause, some federal courts have refused to enforce arbitration awards. The clause recommended by AAA includes a provision that "judgment upon the award may be entered in any court having jurisdiction thereof." Some parties have been unable to obtain judgments on awards in the absence of such a provision.

In 1970, the United States became a party to the 1958 Convention on the Recognition and Enforcement of Foreign Arbitral Awards. Congress added a new part to the Federal Arbitration Act to effectuate this treaty and to provide easy access to U.S. courts. Under the Convention, the winning party may take an award directly to the participating country where the respondent has property, procure a judgment confirming it, and obtain enforcement of the judgment therein. In addition, the United States has bilateral commercial treaties with some countries that are not members of the New York Convention. These treaties enable either party to seek enforcement of an arbitration award in the other party's country.

In general, there is no right to appeal an arbitration award. Parties may wish to provide for such an appeal. For example, under the arbitration rules of the copra industry, an award can be appealed to a board of arbitration that reviews the decision of the original panel.

In 1979, the English law was amended and should be reviewed by anyone planning to arbitrate in Great Britain. For certain types of cases, the law now permits parties to agree in advance to avoid appeals on legal issues.

ENFORCEMENT OF AN AWARD

Enforcing an international arbitration award may present difficulties. Fortunately, most developed countries have accepted the New York Convention, including most places where an American company is likely to do business.

When both parties are nationals of countries that are signatories to the Convention, the following paragraph can be included in the arbitration provision: "The parties acknowledge that this agreement and any award rendered pursuant to it shall be governed by the 1958 Convention on the Recognition and Enforcement of Foreign Arbitral Awards."

Even if the country of the foreign party is not a signatory to the New York Convention and there is no bilateral treaty applicable, it may still be possible for the parties to specify enforcement under the law of a state that provides appropriate enforcement procedures.

DEFAULT

If one of the parties fails to appear at a hearing, the arbitrator has the power to proceed on the basis of the evidence taken from one party. At least, this is the case under AAA rules.

If it were possible for a party to nullify the process by failing to appear at a hearing, the arbitration clause would be ineffectual. Most agency rules authorize the arbitrator to proceed in such a case. If the parties are not using an administrative agency, they should specify that the arbitrator has such powers. Under the New York Convention, the award may be enforced despite a party's failure to appear.

AAA: AN INTERNATIONAL ARBITRATION RESOURCE

Lawyers and business people should know how to draft arbitration clauses in international agreements. They should learn how to arbitrate. The AAA has emerged as an important resource for the American business community. The AAA's Eastman Arbitration Library contains a comprehensive collection of arbitration laws, rules, and regulations, as well as a collection of international arbitration cases. The AAA represents the U.S. interests at many international conferences where other national arbitration agencies are present. In New York City, the Association's legal staff maintains up-to-date information on foreign arbitration rules and institutions.

WORLD ARBITRATION INSTITUTE

The World Arbitration Institute, established in 1983, is a program of the AAA, cosponsored by the New York City and State Bar Associations, the Court of Arbitration of the ICC, the Inter-American Commercial Arbitration Commission, the Parker School of Foreign and Comparative Law at Columbia University, the Society of Maritime Arbitrators, Inc., and the American Association of Exporters and Importers. It is located at the New York headquarters of the AAA.

The purpose of the World Arbitration Institute is to publicize and explain the facilities in New York for handling international commercial arbitrations. Its activities include the publication of a newsletter and the organization and sponsoring of conferences. The Institute also acts as a clearinghouse for information.

CONCLUSION

Arbitration has become increasingly useful for companies engaged in international business activities, particularly U.S. firms. The United States not only recognizes and enforces arbitration agreements and awards, but it is part of an international network of countries that have similar policies. The New York Convention encourages the use of contractual arbitration in international trade.

There is growing cooperation among arbitration agencies. The International Chamber of Commerce in Paris and the London Court of Arbitration have contributed greatly to the practice of arbitration. Foreign Trade Arbitration Commissions of the Socialist countries also recognize the benefits of arbitration. Here in the United States, the AAA helps the business community to use arbitration effectively.

Arbitration in international trade may seem complicated to some American business people. But it offers an efficient dispute settlement process, if care is taken in selecting an administrative agency, a convenient locale, and a legal system that meets the expectations of the parties. As one law school professor wrote several years ago, "Arbitration is power." Arbitration gives parties the right to place their international business disputes in trustworthy hands for an appropriate, impartial determination. When properly designed, arbitration can significantly reduce the risk of unanticipated arbitrary determinations. It is important that American and foreign business people be informed about this subject.

MAJOR ARBITRAL INSTITUTIONS

AUSTRALIA
Institute of Arbitrators Australia
26 Brisbane Avenue
Barton, ACT, 2600

AUSTRIA
Arbitration Centre of the Federal Economic Chamber
Wiedner Hauptstrasse 63
P.O. Box 190
A-1045 Vienna

BULGARIA
Arbitration Court at the Bulgarian Chamber of Commerce and Industry
11-A Stamboliiski Boulevard
Sofia

CANADA
Arbitrators' Institute of Canada, Inc.
Suite 411
234 Eglinton Avenue East
Toronto, Ontario M4P 1K5

CHINA (PEOPLE'S REPUBLIC)
China Council for the Promotion of International Trade
4, Tai Ping Chiao Street
Beijing

CZECHOSLOVAKIA
Arbitration Court of the Chamber of Commerce and Industry of Czechoslovakia
Argentinská 38
170 05 Prague 7

EGYPT
Asian-African Legal Consultative Committee, Regional Centre for Commercial Arbitration at Cairo
c/o Egyptian Society for International Law
16, Ramses Street
Cairo

FINLAND
Board of Arbitration of the Central Chamber of Commerce of Finland
Fabianinkatu 14a
00100 Helsinki 10

FRANCE
Arbitration Court at the International Chamber of Commerce
38, Cours Albert Ier
75008 Paris

GERMANY (DEMOCRATIC REPUBLIC)
Arbitration Court at the Chamber of Foreign Trade of the German Democratic Republic
Am Kupfergraben 7
P.O. Box 70
1080 Berlin

GERMANY (FEDERAL REPUBLIC)
German Arbitration Institute
P.O. Box 100 447
Kolumbastrasse 5
D-5000 Köln 1

German Arbitration Committee
Adenauerallee 148
P.O. Box 1446
D-5300 Bonn 1

GREECE
Greek Arbitration Association
102 Solonos Street
Athens 144

HONG KONG
Arbitration Committee of the Hong Kong General Chamber of Commerce
Swire House
9th Floor
Chater Road

HUNGARY
Arbitration Court at the Hungarian Chamber of Commerce
Kossuth Lajos tér 6-8
1389 Budapest V.

INDIA
The Indian Council of Arbitration
Federation House
New Delhi-110001

INDONESIA
Indonesian National Arbitration Board
Jalan Merdeka Timur 11
4 Jakarta-Pusat

ITALY
Italian Arbitration Association
5, Via XX Settembre
00187 Roma

JAPAN
Japan Commercial Arbitration Association
2-2, Marunouchi 3-chome
Chiyoda-ku
Tokyo

KOREA
Korean Commercial Arbitration Board
World Trade Centre
P.O. Box 681
10-1, 2-ka, Hoehyon-dong, Chung-ku
Seoul

MALAYSIA
Asian-African Legal Consultative Committee, Regional Centre for Arbitration at Kuala Lumpur
576, Jalan Clifford
Kuala Lumpur

THE NETHERLANDS
Netherlands Arbitration Institute
Oppert 34
3011 HV Rotterdam
P.O. Box 22105 (correspondence)
3003 DC Rotterdam

PAKISTAN
Commercial Arbitration Tribunal, Federation of Pakistan Chambers of Commerce and Industry
Share-a-Firdousi
Main Clifton
Karachi-6

POLAND
Arbitration Court at the Polish Chamber of Foreign Trade
Trebaçka 4
P.O. Box 361
00-074 Warsaw

International Court of Arbitration for Marine and Inland Navigation, Gdynia
Ul. Pulaskiego 6
81-368 Gdynia

ROMANIA
Arbitration Commission of the Chamber of Commerce and Industry of the Socialist Republic of Romania
Blvd. N. Bâlcescu 22
Bucharest 70122

SPAIN
Spanish Arbitration Association
Plaza San Amaro 1
Madrid 20

SWEDEN
Arbitration Institute of the Stockholm Chamber of Commerce
P.O. Box 16050
S-103 22 Stockholm 16

SWITZERLAND
Basel Chamber of Commerce
St. Alban-Graben 8
4001 Basel

Berne Chamber of Commerce
Gutenbergstrasse 1
3011 Berne

Geneva Chamber of Commerce and Industry
4, Bd. du Théâtre
1204 Geneva

Zürich Chamber of Commerce
Bleicherweg 5
P.O. Box 4031
8022 Zürich

UNION OF SOVIET SOCIALIST REPUBLICS
U.S.S.R. Chamber of Commerce and Industry
K-3 Kuibyshev Street 6
101000 Moscow

UNITED KINGDOM
Chartered Institute of Arbitrators, Inc.
69-75 Cannon Street
London EC4N 5BH

UNITED STATES
American Arbitration Association
140 West 51st Street
New York, N.Y. 10020

Society of Maritime Arbitrators
Suite 1200
26 Broadway
New York, N.Y. 10004

YUGOSLAVIA
Foreign Trade Arbitration Court at the Economic Chamber of Yugoslavia
Knez Mihajlova Street 10
11000 Belgrade

SUPPLEMENTARY PROCEDURES FOR INTERNATIONAL COMMERCIAL ARBITRATION

1. Non-National Arbitrators – In cases where the parties are of different nationalities or residents of different countries, the list of arbitrators may include the names of persons who are nationals of neither country. At the request of either party, and if the applicable rules permit, the neutral arbitrator(s) will be appointed from among the nationals of a country other than that of any of the parties. Consideration will be given to an arbitrator's fluency in the language to be used in the proceedings.

2. Communications – Parties may prefer that correspondence be transmitted through the arbitration administrator. Oral or written communications from a party to the arbitral tribunal – except at hearings – can be directed to the AAA, which will transmit them to the arbitrator(s) and to the other party(s). For purposes of compliance with applicable time requirements, any written communication shall be deemed to have been received by the addressee when received by the AAA. When transmitting communications to a party, the AAA will do so to the address furnished by the party.

3. Exchange of Documents – At the request of any party, the AAA will make arrangements for the exchange of documentary evidence or lists of witnesses between the parties. In international cases, it is important that parties know in advance what will transpire at the hearing. By cooperating in an exchange of relevant information, the parties can avoid unnecessary delays.

4. Documents to Arbitrator in Advance – In international cases, it is customary for an arbitrator to be provided with copies of the initiating documents and supplementary documents in advance of the first hearing. The AAA will make arrangements for such an exchange if it does not delay the proceedings.

5. Hearings – The AAA will assist in establishing the date, time, and place of hearings, giving advance notice thereof to the parties pursuant to the applicable rules. The AAA will attempt to schedule consecutive hearings to reduce the need for unnecessary travel. The AAA will provide a room for hearings in one of the regional offices of the AAA. If a hearing room is not available, the AAA will arrange a facility elsewhere.

6. Language of the Arbitration – If the parties have not agreed on the language of the arbitration and have not designated a method for deciding that question, the AAA can determine the language to be used in the proceedings. Consideration will be given to the nationality of the parties, their counsel and potential witnesses, and to the location of the hearings. Upon request, the AAA can make arrangements for the services of interpreters at hearings.

7. Opinions – Parties in international cases often expect arbitrators to provide a written opinion explaining the reasons for their award. The AAA can make arrangements for such an opinion in consultation with the parties and the arbitrators.

8. Fees of Arbitrators and Deposits – Ordinarily, arbitrators on international cases are compensated. The AAA can make arrangements for the arbitrators' fees, and for necessary advance deposits for such fees, in consultation with the parties and the arbitrators. The administrative fees of the AAA are separate and apart from the fees of the arbitrators.

AMERICAN ARBITRATION ASSOCIATION PROCEDURES FOR CASES UNDER THE UNCITRAL ARBITRATION RULES

To facilitate the conduct of arbitration cases that the parties have agreed to conduct under the UNCITRAL Arbitration Rules, the American Arbitration Association will:

1. Perform the functions of the appointing authority as set forth in the UNCITRAL Arbitration Rules whenever the AAA has been so designated by the parties either in the arbitration clause of their contract or in a separate agreement.
2. Perform administrative services when called for by the contract, or when requested by all parties or by the arbitral tribunal.

SERVICES AS APPOINTING AUTHORITY

1. Appointment of Sole or Presiding Arbitrator—When requested to appoint a sole or presiding arbitrator, the AAA will follow the list procedure set forth in the UNCITRAL Arbitration Rules (Article 6(3)). The AAA has extensive experience in using the list procedure because it utilizes a similar procedure to conduct cases under various other rules.

In selecting arbitrators, the AAA will utilize its extensive panel of arbitrators for commercial cases. That panel includes qualified persons of many different nationalities having varied professional and business backgrounds. The AAA will carefully consider the nature of the case, as described in the Notice of Arbitration, in order to include in the list persons having appropriate professional or business experience and language ability.

When appointing a sole or presiding arbitrator under the UNCITRAL Rules, the AAA will follow its usual practice and, upon request of either party, designate a person of a nationality other than the nationalities of the parties, unless otherwise provided by written agreement of the parties.

2. Appointment of a "Second" Arbitrator in Three-Arbitrator Cases—Under Article 7 of the UNCITRAL Arbitration Rules, when three arbitrators are to be appointed, each party is to appoint one arbitrator, but if a party fails to do so, the other party may request that the appointment of the second arbitrator be made by the appointing authority.

In accordance with the UNCITRAL Arbitration Rules, the AAA, when appointing a second arbitrator, will exercise its discretion and will not utilize the list procedure. The second arbitrator to be appointed under Article 7(2)(a) shall be impartial and independent of either party.

3. Decisions on Challenges to Arbitrators—Under Article 10 of the UNCITRAL Arbitration Rules, all arbitrators—including those appointed by one party—are required to be impartial and independent. Article 10 provides that any arbitrator may be challenged if circumstances exist that give rise to justifiable doubts as to the arbitrator's impartiality or independence.

Article 12 of the UNCITRAL Arbitration Rules requires that all contested challenges be decided by the appointing authority. When deciding challenges at the request of any party, the AAA will appoint a special committee to make the decision, consisting of three persons, a majority of whom will be of nationalities different than that of either party.

In deciding challenges, the AAA and any such committee will be guided by the principles set forth in the Code of Ethics for Arbitrators in Commercial Disputes, a code jointly adopted by the AAA and the American Bar Association.

4. Appointment of Substitute Arbitrators–The UNCITRAL Arbitration Rules provide that a substitute arbitrator will be appointed if an arbitrator dies or resigns during an arbitration proceeding, or if a challenge against him is sustained (Articles 12(2) and 13). In such cases, the AAA will perform the same function in appointing a substitute arbitrator as described above with respect to other arbitrators.

5. Consultation on Fees of Arbitrators–The UNCITRAL Arbitration Rules provide that the fees of arbitrators shall be reasonable in amount, taking into consideration the amount in dispute, the complexity of the subject matter, the time spent by the arbitrators, and any other relevant circumstances of the case (Article 39(2)). The Rules provide that parties may request the appointing authority to provide to the arbitrators and parties a statement setting forth the basis for establishing fees that is customarily followed in cases in which the appointing authority acts (Article 39(3)). The AAA has no schedule of fees for arbitrators, but it will furnish a statement concerning customary fees based on its experience in administering large numbers of cases.

ADMINISTRATIVE SERVICES

Upon the request of all parties or the arbitral tribunal, the AAA will provide the following administrative services:

1. Communications–The experience of major arbitration agencies suggests that arbitrations are best served when communications–except at hearings–are transmitted through the arbitration administrator. Upon request, all oral or written communications from a party to the arbitral tribunal–except at hearings–may be directed to the AAA, which will transmit them to the arbitral tribunal and to the other party.

Agreement by the parties that the AAA shall administer a case constitutes consent by the parties that, for purposes of compliance with time requirements of the UNCITRAL Arbitration Rules, any written communications shall be deemed to have been received by the addressee when received by the AAA. When transmitting communications to a party, the AAA will do so to the addresses set forth in the Notice of Arbitration or such other address as has been furnished by a party in writing to the AAA.

2. Hearings–Upon request, the AAA will assist the arbitral tribunal to establish the date, time, and place of hearings, giving such advance notice thereof to the parties as the tribunal may determine pursuant to the UNCITRAL Arbitration Rules (Article 25, paragraph 1).

3. Hearing Rooms–The AAA will provide a room for hearings in the offices of the AAA. If a hearing room is not available in the offices of the AAA, the AAA will arrange a hearing room elsewhere. The cost of hearing rooms outside AAA offices will be billed separately and not included in the fee for administrative services.

4. Stenographic Transcripts–Any party wishing a stenographic record shall make such arrangements directly with the stenographer and shall notify the other parties of such arrangements in advance of the hearing. The requesting party or parties shall pay the cost of such record.

5. Interpretation–Any party wishing an interpreter shall make all arrangements directly with an interpreter and shall assume the costs of such service.

6. Fees of Arbitrators and Deposits–Upon request, the AAA will make all arrangements concerning the amounts of the arbitrators' fees, and advance deposits to be made on account of such fees in consultation with the parties and the arbitrators. The AAA does not fix the amount of fees of arbitrators and has no schedule for arbitrators in international commercial cases.

7. Other Services–Upon request, the AAA will consider providing other appropriate administrative services.

BIBLIOGRAPHY

Aksen, Gerald. "Dispute Settlement under U.S.-China Trade Agreement." *New York Law Journal*, August 9, 1979, p. 1.

American Arbitration Association. *Commercial Arbitration Rules: As Amended and in Effect April 1, 1985.* New York: 1985.

______. *New Strategies for Peaceful Resolution of International Business Disputes.* Dobbs Ferry, N.Y.: Oceana Publications, 1971.

______. *Procedures for Cases under the UNCITRAL Arbitration Rules.* New York: 1976.

______. *Supplementary Procedures for International Commercial Arbitration.* New York: 1985.

______. *Survey of International Arbitration Sites.* New York: American Arbitration Association, 1984.

Arbitration and the Law: AAA General Counsel's Annual Report. New York: American Arbitration Association, 1981–present (ongoing publication).

Associazione Italiana per L'Arbitrato. *Arbitrage Commercial; Essais in Memoriam Eugenio Minoli. Commercial Arbitration; Essays in Memoriam Eugenio Minoli.* Roma: Unione Tipografico-Editrice Torinese, 1974.

Berg, Albert Jan van den. *The New York Arbitration Convention of 1958: Toward a Uniform Judicial Interpretation.* Deventer: Kluwer, 1981.

Bos, Maarten, ed. *The Present State of International Law and Other Essays.* Deventer: Kluwer, 1973.

Butler, William E., comp. and ed. *Soviet Commercial and Maritime Arbitration.* Dobbs Ferry, N.Y.: Oceana Publications, 1980–present (ongoing publication).

Cherian, Joy. *Investment Contracts and Arbitration: The World Bank Convention on the Settlement of Investment Disputes.* Leyden: Sijthoff, 1975.

Craig, W. Laurence, William W. Park, and Jan Paulsson. *International Chamber of Commerce Arbitration.* Dobbs Ferry, N.Y.: Oceana Publications, 1984–present (ongoing publication).

David, Rene. *Arbitration in International Trade*. Deventer: Kluwer Law and Taxation Publishers, 1985.

Delaume, Georges R. *Transnational Contracts. Applicable Law and Settlement of Disputes (A Study in Conflict Avoidance).* Prepared under the auspices of the Parker School of Foreign and Comparative Law. Dobbs Ferry, N.Y.: Oceana Publications, 1978.

Gaja, Giorgio, comp. and ed. *New York Convention*. Dobbs Ferry, N.Y.: Oceana Publications, 1978–present (ongoing publication).

Goldscheider, Robert, and Michael de Haas, eds. *Arbitration and the Licensing Process*. New York: Clark Boardman, 1981.

Hoellering, Michael F. "International Arbitration: A Survey of Recent Cases." *New York Law Journal*, May 12, 1983, p. 1.

______. "International Commercial Arbitration: A Peaceful Method of Dispute Settlement." *The Arbitration Journal*, vol. 40, no. 4 (December 1985), pp. 19–26.

______. "*Mitsubishi*: Arbitrability and Antitrust Claims." *New York Law Journal*, August 19, 1985, p. 1.

International Chamber of Commerce. *Arbitration Law in Europe.* Paris: 1981.

______. *International Arbitration: 60 Years on a Look at the Future.* Paris: ICC Publishing, 1984.

"International Commercial Arbitration." *Lawyers' Arbitration Letter*, vol. 1, no. 12 (December 1975), pp. 1–10.

International Council for Commercial Arbitration. *International Handbook on Commercial Arbitration.* Deventer: Kluwer Law and Taxation Publishers, 1984–present (ongoing publication).

______. *Yearbook Commercial Arbitration.* Deventer: Kluwer, 1976–present (ongoing publication).

Jackson, David C. *The "Conflicts" Process: Jurisdiction and Choice in Private International Law*. Dobbs Ferry, N.Y.: Oceana Publications, 1975.

Lew, Julian D. M. *Applicable Law in International Commercial Arbitration: A Study in Commercial Arbitration Awards.* Dobbs Ferry, N.Y.: Oceana Publications, 1978.

McClelland, Arden Guy. "International Arbitration: A Practical Guide for Effective Use of the System for Litigation of Transnational Commercial Disputes." *International Lawyer*, vol. 12, no. 1 (Winter 1978), pp. 83–103.

Report on Delocalized Arbitration. *The Arbitration Journal*, vol. 39, no. 3 (September 1984), pp. 58–60.

Schmitthoff, Clive M., ed. *International Commercial Arbitration.* Dobbs Ferry, N.Y.: Oceana Publications, 1974–present (ongoing publication).

Schultsz, Jan C., and Albert Jan van den Berg, eds. *The Art of Arbitration: Essays on International Arbitration, Liber Amicorum Pieter Sanders, 12 September 1912–1982.* Deventer: Kluwer, 1982.

Wetter, J. Gillis. *The International Arbitral Process: Public and Private*. Dobbs Ferry, N.Y.: Oceana Publications, 1979.

APPENDIX

CODE OF ETHICS FOR ARBITRATORS IN COMMERCIAL DISPUTES

PREAMBLE

The use of commercial arbitration to resolve a wide variety of disputes has grown extensively and forms a significant part of the system of justice which our society relies upon for the fair determination of legal rights. Persons who act as commercial arbitrators therefore undertake serious responsibilities to the public as well as to the parties. These responsibilities include important ethical obligations.

Few cases of unethical behavior by commercial arbitrators have arisen. Nevertheless, the American Bar Association and the American Arbitration Association believe that it is in the public interest to set forth generally accepted standards of ethical conduct for the guidance of arbitrators and parties in commercial disputes. By establishing this Code, the sponsors hope to contribute to the maintenance of high standards and continued confidence in the process of arbitration.

There are many different types of commercial arbitration. Some cases are conducted under arbitration rules established by various organizations and trade associations, while others are carried on without such rules. Although most cases are arbitrated pursuant to voluntary agreement of the parties, certain types of disputes are submitted to arbitration by reason of particular laws. This Code is intended to apply to all such proceedings in which disputes or claims are submitted for decision to one or more arbitrators appointed in a manner provided by an agreement of the parties, by applicable arbitration rules or by law. In all such cases the persons who have the power to decide should observe fundamental standards of ethical conduct. In this Code all such persons are called "arbitrators," although in some types of cases they may be called "umpires" or may have some other title.

Various aspects of the conduct of arbitrators, including some matters covered by this Code, may be governed by agreements of the parties, by arbitration rules to which the parties have agreed, or by applicable law. This Code does not take the place of, or supersede, any such agreements, rules and laws and does not establish any new or additional grounds for judicial review of arbitration awards.

While this Code is intended to provide ethical guidelines in many types of arbitration, it does not form part of the arbitration rules of the American Arbitration Association or of any other organization, nor is it intended to apply to mediation or conciliation. Labor arbitrations are governed by the "Code of Professional Responsibility for Arbitrators of Labor-Management Disputes," not by this Code.

Arbitrators, like judges, have the power to decide cases. However, unlike full-time judges, arbitrators are usually engaged in other occupations before, during and after the time they serve as arbitrators. Often arbitrators are purposely chosen from the same trade or industry as the parties in order to bring special knowledge to the task of deciding. This Code recognizes these fundamental differences between arbitrators and judges.

In some types of arbitration there are three, or more, arbitrators. In these cases, it is sometimes the practice for each party, acting alone, to appoint one arbitrator and for the other arbitrator(s) to be designated by those two, or by the parties, or by an independent institution or individual. The sponsors of this Code believe that it is preferable for parties to agree that all arbitrators should comply with the same ethical standards. However, it is recognized that there is a long-established practice in some types of arbitration for those arbitrators who are appointed by one party, acting alone, to be governed by special ethical considerations. Those special considerations are set forth in the last section of the Code, headed "Ethical Considerations Relating to Arbitrators Appointed by One Party."

Although this Code is sponsored by the American Arbitration Association and the American Bar Association, its use is not limited to arbitrations administered by the AAA or to cases in which the arbitrators are lawyers. Rather, it is presented as a public service to provide guidance in all types of commercial arbitration.

CANON I.
AN ARBITRATOR SHOULD UPHOLD THE INTEGRITY AND FAIRNESS OF THE ARBITRATION PROCESS

A. Fair and just processes for resolving disputes are indispensable in our society. Commercial arbitration is an important method for deciding many types of disputes. In order for commercial arbitration to be effective, there must be broad public confidence in the integrity and fairness of the process. Therefore, an arbitrator has a responsibility not only to the parties but also to the process of arbitration itself, and must observe high standards of conduct so that the integrity and fairness of the process will be preserved. Accordingly, an arbitrator should recognize a responsibility to the public, to the parties whose rights will be decided, and to all other participants in the proceeding. The provisions of this Code should be construed and applied to further these objectives.

B. It is inconsistent with the integrity of the arbitration process for persons to solicit appointment for themselves. However, a person may indicate a general willingness to serve as an arbitrator.

C. Persons should accept appointment as arbitrators only if they believe that they can be available to conduct the arbitration promptly.

D. After accepting appointment and while serving as an arbitrator, a person should avoid entering into any financial, business, professional, family or social relationship, or acquiring any financial or personal interest, which is likely to affect impartiality or which might reasonably create the appearance of partiality or bias. For a reasonable period of time after the decision of a case, persons who have served as arbitrators should avoid entering into any such relationship, or acquiring any such interest, in circumstances which might reasonably create the appearance that they had been influenced in the arbitration by the anticipation or expectation of the relationship or interest.

E. Arbitrators should conduct themselves in a way that is fair to all parties and should not be swayed by outside pressure, by public clamor, by fear of criticism or by self-interest.

F. When an arbitrator's authority is derived from an agreement of the parties, the arbitrator should neither exceed that authority nor do less than is required to exercise that authority completely. Where the agreement of the parties sets forth procedures to be followed in conducting the arbitration or refers to rules to be followed, it is the obligation of the arbitrator to comply with such procedures or rules.

G. An arbitrator should make all reasonable efforts to prevent delaying tactics, harassment of parties or other participants, or other abuse or disruption of the arbitration process.

H. The ethical obligations of an arbitrator begin upon acceptance of the appointment and continue throughout all stages of the proceeding. In addition, wherever specifically set forth in this Code, certain ethical obligations begin as soon as a person is requested to serve as an arbitrator and certain ethical obligations continue even after the decision in the case has been given to the parties.

CANON II.
AN ARBITRATOR SHOULD DISCLOSE ANY INTEREST OR RELATIONSHIP LIKELY TO AFFECT IMPARTIALITY OR WHICH MIGHT CREATE AN APPEARANCE OF PARTIALITY OR BIAS

Introductory Note:

This Code reflects the prevailing principle that arbitrators should disclose the existence of any interests or relationships which are likely to affect their impartiality or which might reasonably create the appearance that they are biased against one party or favorable to another. These provisions of the Code are intended to be applied realistically so that the burden of detailed disclosure does not become so great that it is impractical for persons in the business world to be arbitrators, thereby depriving parties of the services of those who might be best informed and qualified to decide particular types of cases.*

This Code does not limit the freedom of parties to agree on anyone they choose as an arbitrator. When parties, with knowledge of a person's interests and relationships, nevertheless desire that individual to serve as an arbitrator, that person may properly serve.

Disclosure:

A. Persons who are requested to serve as arbitrators should, before accepting, disclose:

(1) Any direct or indirect financial or personal interest in the outcome of the arbitration;

---

*In applying the provisions of this Code relating to disclosure, it may be helpful to recall the words of the concurring opinion in a case decided by the United States Supreme Court, that arbitrators "should err on the side of disclosure" because "it is better that the relationship be disclosed at the outset when the parties are free to reject the arbitrator or accept him with knowledge of the relationship." At the same time, it must be recognized that "an arbitrator's business relationships may be diverse indeed, involving more or less remote commercial connections with great numbers of people." Accordingly, an arbitrator "cannot be expected to provide the parties with his complete and unexpurgated business biography," nor is an arbitrator called upon to disclose interests or relationships which are merely "trivial." (Concurring opinion in *Commonwealth Coatings Corp. v. Continental Casualty Co.*, 393 US 145, 151–152, 1968.)

(2) Any existing or past financial, business, professional, family or social relationships which are likely to affect impartiality or which might reasonably create an appearance of partiality or bias. Persons requested to serve as arbitrators should disclose any such relationships which they personally have with any party or its lawyer, or with any individual whom they have been told will be a witness. They should also disclose any such relationships involving members of their families or their current employers, partners or business associates.

B. Persons who are requested to accept appointment as arbitrators should make a reasonable effort to inform themselves of any interests or relationships described in Paragraph A above.

C. The obligation to disclose interests or relationships described in Paragraph A above is a continuing duty which requires a person who accepts appointment as an arbitrator to disclose, at any stage of the arbitration, any such interests or relationships which may arise, or which are recalled or discovered.

D. Disclosure should be made to all parties unless other procedures for disclosure are provided in the rules or practices of an institution which is administering the arbitration. Where more than one arbitrator has been appointed, each should inform the others of the interests and relationships which have been disclosed.

E. In the event that an arbitrator is requested by all parties to withdraw, the arbitrator should do so. In the event that an arbitrator is requested to withdraw by less than all of the parties because of alleged partiality or bias, the arbitrator should withdraw unless either of the following circumstances exists:

(1) If an agreement of the parties, or arbitration rules agreed to by the parties, establishes procedures for determining challenges to arbitrators, then those procedures should be followed; or

(2) If the arbitrator, after carefully considering the matter, determines that the reason for the challenge is not substantial, and that he or she can nevertheless act and decide the case impartially and fairly, and that withdrawal would cause unfair delay or expense to another party or would be contrary to the ends of justice.

CANON III.
AN ARBITRATOR IN COMMUNICATING WITH THE PARTIES SHOULD AVOID IMPROPRIETY OR THE APPEARANCE OF IMPROPRIETY

A. If an agreement of the parties, or any applicable arbitration rules referred to in that agreement, establishes the manner or content of communications between the arbitrator and the parties, the arbitrator should follow those procedures notwithstanding any contrary provisions of the following Paragraphs B and C.

B. Unless otherwise provided in applicable arbitration rules or in an agreement of the parties, arbitrators should not discuss a case with any party in the absence of each other party, except in any of the following circumstances:

(1) Discussions may be had with a party concerning such matters as setting the

time and place of hearings or making other arrangements for the conduct of the proceedings. However, the arbitrator should promptly inform each other party of the discussion and should not make any final determination concerning the matter discussed before giving each absent party an opportunity to express its views.

(2) If a party fails to be present at a hearing after having been given due notice, the arbitrator may discuss the case with any party who is present.

(3) If all parties request or consent that such discussion take place.

C. Unless otherwise provided in applicable arbitration rules or in an agreement of the parties, whenever an arbitrator communicates in writing with one party, the arbitrator should at the same time send a copy of the communication to each other party. Whenever an arbitrator receives any written communication concerning the case from one party which has not already been sent to each other party, the arbitrator should do so.

CANON IV.
AN ARBITRATOR SHOULD CONDUCT THE PROCEEDINGS FAIRLY AND DILIGENTLY

A. An arbitrator should conduct the proceedings in an evenhanded manner and treat all parties with equality and fairness at all stages of the proceedings.

B. An arbitrator should perform duties diligently and conclude the case as promptly as the circumstances reasonably permit.

C. An arbitrator should be patient and courteous to the parties, to their lawyers and to the witnesses and should encourage similar conduct by all participants in the proceedings.

D. Unless otherwise agreed by the parties or provided in arbitration rules agreed to by the parties, an arbitrator should accord to all parties the right to appear in person and to be heard after due notice of the time and place of hearing.

E. An arbitrator should not deny any party the opportunity to be represented by counsel.

F. If a party fails to appear after due notice, an arbitrator should proceed with the arbitration when authorized to do so by the agreement of the parties, the rules agreed to by the parties or by law. However, an arbitrator should do so only after receiving assurance that notice has been given to the absent party.

G. When an arbitrator determines that more information than has been presented by the parties is required to decide the case, it is not improper for the arbitrator to ask questions, call witnesses, and request documents or other evidence.

H. It is not improper for an arbitrator to suggest to the parties that they discuss the possibility of settlement of the case. However, an arbitrator should not be present or otherwise participate in the settlement discussions unless requested to do so by all parties. An arbitrator should not exert pressure on any party to settle.

I. Nothing in this Code is intended to prevent a person from acting as a mediator or conciliator of a dispute in which he or she has been appointed as arbitrator, if requested to do so by all parties or where authorized or required to do so by applicable laws or rules.

J. When there is more than one arbitrator, the arbitrators should afford each other the full opportunity to participate in all aspects of the proceedings.

CANON V.
AN ARBITRATOR SHOULD MAKE DECISIONS IN A JUST, INDEPENDENT AND DELIBERATE MANNER

A. An arbitrator should, after careful deliberation, decide all issues submitted for determination. An arbitrator should decide no other issues.

B. An arbitrator should decide all matters justly, exercising independent judgment, and should not permit outside pressure to affect the decision.

C. An arbitrator should not delegate the duty to decide to any other person.

D. In the event that all parties agree upon a settlement of the issues in dispute and request an arbitrator to embody that agreement in an award, an arbitrator may do so, but is not required to do so unless satisfied with the propriety of the terms of settlement. Whenever an arbitrator embodies a settlement by the parties in an award, the arbitrator should state in the award that it is based on an agreement of the parties.

CANON VI.
AN ARBITRATOR SHOULD BE FAITHFUL TO THE RELATIONSHIP OF TRUST AND CONFIDENTIALITY INHERENT IN THAT OFFICE

A. An arbitrator is in a relationship of trust to the parties and should not, at any time, use confidential information acquired during the arbitration proceeding to gain personal advantage or advantage for others, or to affect adversely the interest of another.

B. Unless otherwise agreed by the parties, or required by applicable rules or law, an arbitrator should keep confidential all matters relating to the arbitration proceedings and decision.

C. It is not proper at any time for an arbitrator to inform anyone of the decision in advance of the time it is given to all parties. In a case in which there is more than one arbitrator, it is not proper at any time for an arbitrator to inform anyone concerning the deliberations of the arbitrators. After an arbitration award has been made, it is not proper for an arbitrator to assist in any post-arbitration proceedings, except as may be required by law.

D. In many types of arbitration it is customary practice for the arbitrators to serve without pay. However, in some types of cases it is customary for arbitrators to receive compensation for their services and reimbursement for their expenses. In cases in which any such payments are to be made, all persons who are requested to serve, or who are serving as arbitrators, should be governed by the same high standards of integrity and fairness as apply to their other activities in the case. Accordingly, such persons should scrupulously avoid bargaining with parties over the amount of payments or engaging in any communications concerning payments which would create an appearance of coercion or other impropriety. In the absence of governing provisions in the agreement of the parties or in rules agreed to by the parties or in applicable law, certain practices relating to payments are generally recognized as being preferable in order to preserve the integrity and fairness of the arbitration process. These practices include:

(1) It is preferable that before the arbitrator finally accepts appointment the basis of payment be established and that all parties be informed thereof in writing.

(2) In cases conducted under the rules or administration of an institution which is available to assist in making arrangements for payments, the payments should be arranged by the institution to avoid the necessity for communication by the arbitrators directly with the parties concerning the subject.

(3) In cases where no institution is available to assist in making arrangements for payments, it is preferable that any discussions with arbitrators concerning payments should take place in the presence of all parties.

CANON VII. ETHICAL CONSIDERATIONS RELATING TO ARBITRATORS APPOINTED BY ONE PARTY

Introductory Note:

In some types of arbitration in which there are three arbitrators it is customary for each party, acting alone, to appoint one arbitrator. The third arbitrator is then appointed either by agreement of the parties or of the two arbitrators, or, failing such agreement, by an independent institution or individual. In some of these types of arbitration, all three arbitrators are customarily considered to be neutral and are expected to observe the same standards of ethical conduct. However, there are also many types of tripartite arbitration in which it has been the practice that the two arbitrators appointed by the parties are not considered to be neutral and are expected to observe many—but not all—of the same ethical standards as the neutral third arbitrator. For the purposes of this Code, an arbitrator appointed by one party who is not expected to observe all of the same standards as the third arbitrator is referred to as a "non-neutral arbitrator." This Canon VII describes the ethical obligations which non-neutral party-appointed arbitrators should observe and those which are not applicable to them.

In all arbitrations in which there are two or more party-appointed arbitrators, it is important for everyone concerned to know from the start whether the party-appointed arbitrators are expected to be neutrals or non-neutrals. In such arbitrations, the two party-appointed arbitrators should be considered non-neutrals unless both parties inform the arbitrators that all three arbitrators are to be neutral, or, unless the contract, the applicable arbitration rules, or any governing law requires that all three arbitrators are to be neutral.

It should be noted that in cases where the arbitration is conducted outside the United States the applicable law may require that all arbitrators be neutral. Accordingly, in such cases the governing law should be considered before applying any of the following provisions relating to non-neutral party-appointed arbitrators.

A. *Obligations Under Canon I:*

Non-neutral party-appointed arbitrators should observe all of the obligations of Canon I to uphold the integrity and fairness of the arbitration process, subject only to the following provisions:

(1) Non-neutral arbitrators may be predisposed toward the party who appointed them but in all other respects are obligated to act in good faith and with integrity and fairness. For example, non-neutral arbitrators should not engage in delaying tactics or harassment of any party or witness and should not knowingly make untrue or misleading statements to the other arbitrators.

(2) The provisions of Canon I-D relating to relationships and interests are not applicable to non-neutral arbitrators.

B. *Obligations Under Canon II:*

Non-neutral party-appointed arbitrators should disclose to all parties, and to the other arbitrators, all interests and relationships which Canon II requires be disclosed. Disclosure as required by Canon II is for the benefit not only of the party who appointed the non-neutral arbitrator, but also for the benefit of the other parties and arbitrators so that they may know of any bias which may exist or appear to exist. However, this obligation is subject to the following provisions:

(1) Disclosure by non-neutral arbitrators should be sufficient to describe the general nature and scope of any interest or relationship, but need not include as detailed information as is expected from persons appointed as neutral arbitrators.

(2) Non-neutral arbitrators are not obligated to withdraw if requested to do so by the party who did not appoint them, notwithstanding the provisions of Canon II-E.

C. *Obligations Under Canon III:*

Non-neutral party-appointed arbitrators should observe all of the obligations of Canon III concerning communications with the parties, subject only to the following provisions:

(1) In an arbitration in which the two party-appointed arbitrators are expected to appoint the third arbitrator, non-neutral arbitrators may consult with the party who appointed them concerning the acceptability of persons under consideration for appointment as the third arbitrator.

(2) Non-neutral arbitrators may communicate with the party who appointed them concerning any other aspect of the case, provided they first inform the other arbitrators and the parties that they intend to do so. If such communication occurred prior to the time the person was appointed as arbitrator, or prior to the first hearing or other meeting of the parties with the arbitrators, the non-neutral arbitrator should at the first hearing or meeting, disclose the fact that such communication has taken place. In complying with the provisions of this paragraph, it is sufficient that there be disclosure of the fact that such communication has occurred without disclosing the content of the communication. It is also sufficient to disclose at any time the intention to follow the procedure of having such communications in the future and there is no requirement thereafter that there be disclosure before each separate occasion on which such a communication occurs.

(3) When non-neutral arbitrators communicate in writing with the party who appointed them concerning any matter as to which communication is permitted

under this Code, they are not required to send copies of any such written communications to any other party or arbitrator.

D. *Obligations Under Canon IV:*

Non-neutral party-appointed arbitrators should observe all of the obligations of Canon IV to conduct the proceedings fairly and diligently.

E. *Obligations Under Canon V:*

Non-neutral party-appointed arbitrators should observe all of the obligations of Canon V concerning making decisions, subject only to the following provision:

(1) Non-neutral arbitrators are permitted to be predisposed toward deciding in favor of the party who appointed them.

F. *Obligations Under Canon VI:*

Non-neutral party-appointed arbitrators should observe all of the obligations of Canon VI to be faithful to the relationship of trust inherent in the office of arbitrator, subject only to the following provision:

(1) Non-neutral arbitrators are not subject to the provisions of Canon VI-D with respect to any payments by the party who appointed them.

CHECKLIST FOR COMMERCIAL ARBITRATION*

This is a brief summary of commercial arbitration principles and procedure in general. There are specialized rules for various types of commercial arbitrations, and these rules may differ in certain respects from the general commercial arbitration rules referred to in this checklist. These specialized rules should be consulted when dealing with such cases.

Modern arbitration statutes have been enacted in 46 states plus Puerto Rico and the District of Columbia. Of these, 31 have adopted the Uniform Arbitration Act in whole or in part. Features of modern statutes include: enforcement of agreements to arbitrate future disputes; judicial authority to compel arbitration pursuant to an arbitration agreement; power to stay litigation for an arbitrable dispute; judicial authority to appoint arbitrators where a party refuses to do so; and limited judicial review of arbitral awards.

The following abbreviations are used in this checklist: CAR: *Commercial Arbitration Rules of the American Arbitration Association* (April 1985); UAA: Uniform Arbitration Act; and USC: United States Code.

Nature of arbitration as contrasted with judicial proceedings.

A. Particular arbitrator with expertise selected for specific dispute, instead of permanent tribunal for all disputes. (CAR § 5)

B. Substantive principles of law not necessarily followed. (*Burchell* v. *Marsh*, 58 US (17 How.) 344 (1854))

C. Proceedings private and usually without recorded transcript. (CAR § 23)

D. Arbitrators not bound by rules of evidence. (CAR §§ 31, 32)

E. Reasons need not be given in support of determination. (CAR §§ 42, 43)

F. Award subject to limited appellate review. (9 USC § 10; UAA § 12; *Wilko* v. *Swan*, 346 US 427, 98 L Ed 168, 74 S Ct 182 (1953))

G. Proceedings expeditious and relatively inexpensive. (CAR Administrative Fee Schedule, p. 17)

Areas of dispute adaptable to arbitration.

A. General commercial disputes:
   1. Contracts.
      a. Interpretation.
      b. Performance.
   2. Accounting.
   3. Intra-business disputes.
   4. Matters of trade custom and usage.

---

*Prepared by the American Arbitration Association. Reprinted with permission from LEGAL CHECKLISTS, published by Callaghan & Co., 3201 Old Glenview Road, Wilmette, Illinois 60091.

5. Valuation issues.
6. Small claims.

B. Specialized commercial disputes:
1. Construction.
2. Home owners warranty.
3. Textile.
4. Seed and grain.
5. International.
6. No-fault.
7. Real estate valuation.
8. Uninsured motorist.
9. Maritime.
10. Fats and oils.
11. Patent validity and infringement. 35 USC § 294. See also American Arbitration Association Patent Arbitration Rules (December 1, 1985).

Methods of obtaining arbitration of disputes.

A. Future disputes.
Contract provisions suggested by American Arbitration Association:

Any controversy or claim arising out of or relating to this contract, or any breach thereof, shall be settled in accordance with the Rules of the American Arbitration Association and judgment upon the award may be entered in any Court having jurisdiction thereof.

B. Existing disputes.
Submission form suggested by American Arbitration Association:

We, the undersigned parties, hereby agree to submit to arbitration under the... Arbitration Rules of the American Arbitration Association the following controversy: (describe dispute briefly and state amount involved).

We further agree that the above controversy be submitted to (one) (three) Arbitrator(s) selected from the panels of Arbitrators of the American Arbitration Association.

We further agree that we will faithfully observe the agreement and the Rules and that we will abide by and perform any award and that a judgment of any Court having jurisdiction may be entered upon the award.

C. Variations on suggested arbitration clause. Parties may vary suggested clause to address matters discussed in C of next section.

Prerequisites to arbitration.

A. Arbitrable controversy.
1. Justiciable dispute or one subject to judicial action.
2. Dispute the resolution of which would not contravene public policy. (*Wilko* v. *Swan*, 346 US 427, 98 L Ed 168, 74 S Ct 182 (1953))

B. Formal writing.
   1. Contract clause providing for arbitration of future disputes (UAA § 1; CAR § 1), or
   2. Submission of a pending dispute. (UAA § 1; CAR § 9)

C. Arbitration procedure.
   1. Locale. (CAR § 11)
   2. Method of selecting arbitrators (9 USC § 5; UAA § 3; CAR § 12–16), and of filling vacancies. (UAA § 3; CAR § 20)
      a. Arbitrator must disclose any information about circumstances likely to affect impartiality. (CAR § 19) (*Commonwealth Coatings Corp.* v. *Continental Casualty Co.*, 393 US 145, 21 L Ed 2d 305, 89 S Ct 337 (1968), *reh'g denied*, 393 US 1112, 21 L Ed 2d 812, 89 S Ct 848 (1969))
   3. Number of arbitrators. (9 USC § 5; CAR § 17)
      a. Generally one arbitrator unless otherwise agreed by parties. (*Id.*)
   4. Time, place of hearing. (UAA § 5(a); CAR § 21)
      a. Generally set by arbitrator. (*Id.*)
      b. Pre-hearing conference may be available. (CAR § 10)
   5. Provision for costs and fees. (UAA § 10; CAR §§ 43, 48–51)
   6. Provision as to whether judgment may be entered on award. (UAA § 11)
   7. Arbitration may be available on a class basis for some jurisdictions. (*Keating* v. *Superior Court* (*Southland*), 645 P2d 1192, 183 Cal Rptr 360 (1982))

Initiation of arbitration proceedings.

A. Without court order.
   1. Demand for arbitration filed by one party to dispute, listing names of parties, contract involved, nature of claim, remedy sought. (CAR § 7)
   2. Submission agreement. (CAR § 9; Form C-1)
   3. Demand and answering statement/counterclaim are like pleadings and ordinarily define and limit scope of arbitrable issues. (CAR § 8)
      a. No new or different claims after filing period without consent of arbitrator. (*Id.*)

B. By court order.
   1. If either party refuses to arbitrate, the other party may apply for a court order compelling arbitration. (9 USC § 4; UAA § 2(a))
   2. Under U.S. Arbitration Act, notice of application for court order must be served in accordance with Federal Rules of Civil Procedure. (9 USC § 4)

C. Stay of action.
   1. If one party brings judicial action of an arbitrable issue, other party may obtain a stay in court in which action is brought. (9 USC § 3; UAA § 2(c))
   2. Failure of party to seek a stay may result in waiver of right to arbitrate. (9 USC §§ 3, 4)

Issues available to party opposing arbitration.

A. Party opposing arbitration may raise:

1. Questions of fact.
   a. No valid contract or submission for arbitration exists.
   b. Other party has failed to comply with conditions precedent to arbitration.
   c. No issue referable to arbitration agreement exists.
2. Questions of law.
   a. Existence of bona fide controversy.
   b. Waiver.
      (1) By filing judicial action.
      (2) By answering or counterclaiming to judicial action.
      (3) Other conduct inconsistent with arbitration.
   c. Illegal contract.
   d. Contract impossible of performance.
   e. Existence of subsequent written contract superseding, or releasing parties from requirements of, arbitration contract.

B. If substantial issue of fact exists, court in which action to enforce right to arbitration is brought will proceed with trial on such issue. (9 USC § 4; UAA § 2(b))
   1. Court hearing is similar to hearing on motion for summary judgment. (9 USC § 4; UAA § 2(b))
   2. Party opposing arbitration may seek jury trial under U.S. Arbitration Act. (9 USC § 4)

C. Ordinarily, participation in the selection of arbitrators or in any proceedings before them constitutes a waiver of the issue of validity of the arbitration submission or contract.
   1. Party seeking to raise issues opposing arbitration should avoid any participation in the arbitration proceedings.
   2. When party claims arbitrators were improperly selected, it should not continue with arbitration, in order to avoid a charge of waiver.

D. Section 2 of Federal Arbitration Act (9 USC § 2) precludes states from requiring judicial proceeding to resolve issues that parties have agreed to resolve by arbitration. (*Southland Corp.* v. *Keating*, __US__, 79 L Ed 2d 1, 104 S Ct 852 (1984))

Arbitration hearing.

A. Parties may be represented by attorneys. (UAA § 6; CAR § 22)

B. Hearings are ordinarily set promptly. (UAA § 5(a); CAR § 21)

C. Notice of hearing must be given to all parties. (*Id.*)

D. Arbitrators may be empowered to proceed in the absence of party that fails to appear. (UAA § 5(a); CAR § 30)

E. All parties having a direct interest in the case may attend. (UAA § 5(b); CAR § 25)

F. Arbitrator may adjourn hearing for good cause shown. (UAA § 5(a); CAR § 26)

G. Arbitrator has power to subpoena witnesses. (9 USC § 7; UAA § 7(a); CAR § 31)

H. Rules of evidence do not control, although sometimes relevant as guides. (CAR §§ 31, 32)

1. Arbitrator empowered to vary hearing procedure. (CAR § 29)

I. Party bringing the arbitration generally opens and closes hearing. (*Id.*)

J. No stenographic record kept unless requested by one or more parties. (CAR § 23)

K. Refusal of arbitrator to hear material evidence may constitute ground for vacating award. (9 USC § 10(c); UAA § 12(a)(4))

L. Party that proceeds with arbitration after knowledge that rules have not been complied with and fails to state objection in writing, is deemed to have waived right to object. (CAR § 38)

M. No ex parte communication by party with arbitrator. (CAR § 40(a))

N. Parties may stipulate to vary procedure.

O. Arbitrator may declare hearings closed if satisfied that record is complete. (CAR § 35)

Arbitration award.

A. Award must be rendered within specified time after close of hearings. (UAA § 8(b); CAR § 41)

B. Award must be in writing (9 USC § 13(b); UAA § 8(a); CAR § 42), signed by a majority. (UAA § 5(c); CAR § 28)

C. Interest is assessable at discretion of arbitrator. (CAR § 43)

D. Award may be confirmed by court, if either party so desires (9 USC § 13; UAA § 11), within one year after award. (9 USC § 9)

E. Award may be vacated by court only:
   1. If procured by corruption, fraud, or undue means. (9 USC § 10(a); UAA § 12(a)(1))
   2. Because of partiality or corruption of the arbitrator. (9 USC § 10(b); UAA § 12(a)(2))
   3. Where the arbitrator:
      a. Refused to hear pertinent or material evidence. (9 USC § 10(c); UAA § 12(a)(4))
      b. Refused to postpone hearing upon sufficient cause shown. (9 USC § 10(c); UAA § 12 (a)(4))
      c. Was guilty of other misbehavior prejudicing the rights of parties. (9 USC § 10(c); UAA § 12(a)(4))
      d. Exceeded powers. (9 USC § 10(d); UAA § 12(a)(3))
      e. Imperfectly executed powers. (9 USC § 10(d))

F. An award may be modified or corrected by a court:
   1. Where there was a miscalculation of figures or a mistake in description of person, thing, or property. (9 USC § 11(a); UAA § 13(a)(1))
   2. Where arbitrator awarded upon a matter not submitted to arbitration. (9 USC § 11(b); UAA § 13(a)(2))
   3. Where the award is imperfect in form. (9 USC § 11(c); UAA § 13(a)(3))

G. Arbitrator may be empowered to modify award for reasons set forth in (F), above, upon timely application by party. (UAA § 9)

Effect of arbitration judgment.

A. Res judicata applies to every arbitration award confirmed by a court. (*Rembrandt Industries* v. *Hodges International*, 38 NY2d 502, 381 NYS2d 451, 344 NE2d 383 (1970))

B. An appeal from a confirmed award is limited to defects in the arbitration procedure as outlined above. (9 USC § 10)

Liability of arbitrators.

A. Arbitrators immune from *civil* liability for damages arising out of their conduct as arbitrators. (*Hill* v. *Aro*, 263 F Supp 324 (ND Ohio 1967); see also CAR § 47(B); but see *Baar* v. *Tigerman*, 140 Cal App 3d 979, 189 Cal Rptr 834 (1983), holding that an arbitrator may be liable for breaching contract to render timely award.)

B. Arbitrators not liable for acts or omissions. (CAR § 47)

Liability of administering agencies.

A. Administering agencies generally immune from civil liability for damages arising out of their conduct in administration of arbitrations. (*Corey* v. *New York Stock Exchange*, 493 F Supp 51 (WD Mich 1980), *aff'd*, 691 F2d 1205 (CA6 1982); see also CAR § 47(B))

Alternatives to traditional arbitration.

A. Expedited procedures.
   1. Under CAR § 7(b), par 2, expedited procedures are applied where the total claim of any party does not exceed $15,000, exclusive of interest and costs.
   2. Parties accept all notices from American Arbitration Association by telephone (confirmed later in writing).
   3. Five names submitted on American Arbitration Association list of arbitrators; each party may strike up to two names.
   4. Hearing set by telephone; confirmed later in writing. Seven-day notice given.
   5. Award rendered within five days of close of hearing.

B. Mini-trial.
   1. Confidential, nonbinding settlement procedure. See Hoellering, The Mini-Trial, 37:4 *Arb J* 48 (1982).
   2. Abbreviated discovery.
   3. Case presented by counsel, usually in one day, to the mini-trial judge who has been mutually selected by the parties. Key executives involved in dispute are present.
   4. Judge issues nonbinding advisory decision, with written opinion detailing strengths and weaknesses in parties' cases.
   5. Parties attempt to settle dispute after receipt of judge's decision and opinion.

C. Mediation.
   1. Nonbinding process.
   2. Mediator may suggest ways of resolving the dispute but cannot impose a settlement on the parties. (AAA Commercial Mediation Rules § 10 (September 1984))

3. Mediator authorized to conduct ex parte caucuses with the parties. (*Id.*)
4. Disclosures made at mediation sessions may not be used in future arbitrations or litigations. (*Id.* § 12)
5. No stenographic record kept. (*Id.* § 13)
6. Mediator immune from liability for any act or omission in connection with the mediation. (*Id.* § 15)

International arbitration.

A. Important to specify that arbitration is desired and what rules should govern (e.g., UNCITRAL Arbitration Rules, Rules of Conciliation and Arbitration of the International Chamber of Commerce).

B. Consider giving arbitrator broad authority.

C. Specify number, nationality, and qualifications of arbitrators.

D. Choose language.

E. Specify governing law. Important to make it clear that law chosen applies to merits of dispute, not just to choice of law question. Sometimes parties stipulate lex mercatoria (international law merchant).

F. Consider authorizing arbitrator to be "amiable compositeur." Arbitrator decides disputes using equitable principles.

G. Waiver of sovereign immunity if contract involves nation or national agency.

H. Place of arbitration. Best to select place where court intervention unlikely. Choice might be left to institution dealing with arbitration if fear that political climate might change by time dispute occurs.
   1. Advisable to choose country party to the 1958 New York Convention on Recognition and Enforcement of Foreign Arbitral Awards.
   2. 1961 European Convention on International Commercial Arbitration.
   See Park, Arbitration of International Contract Disputes, 39 *Bus Law* 1783 (1984).

References:

Aksen, Gerald. "What You Need to Know About Arbitration Law; A 'Triality' of Research." *Forum*, vol. 10, no. 2 (Winter 1975), pp. 793–804.

American Arbitration Association. *American Arbitration Association Mini–Trial Procedures.* New York: 1985.

______. *Commercial Arbitration Rules of the American Arbitration Association: As Amended and in Effect April 1, 1985*. New York: 1985.

______. *Commercial Mediation Rules of the American Arbitration Association. Effective September 1, 1984.* New York: 1984.

______. *Lawyers' Arbitration Letter.* New York: American Arbitration Association, 1973–present (ongoing publication).

______. *Manual for Commercial Arbitrators.* New York: 1983.

______. *Supplementary Procedures for International Commercial Arbitration.* New York: 1985.

______. *Uniform Arbitration Act* (reprint). New York: 1983.

American Arbitration Association and American Bar Association. *Code of Ethics for Arbitrators in Commercial Disputes*. New York: 1977.

Domke, Martin. *The Law and Practice of Commercial Arbitration*. Rev. ed. Wilner. Wilmette, Ill.: Callaghan & Co., 1984.

Friedman, George H. "Correcting Arbitrator Error: The Limited Scope of Judicial Review." *The Arbitration Journal*, vol. 33, no. 4 (Dec. 1978), pp. 9–16.

Gibbons, Margaret, and Linda M. Miller, eds. *Construction Arbitration: Selected Readings.* New York: American Arbitration Association, 1981.

Goldberg, George E. *A Lawyer's Guide to Commercial Arbitration*. Philadelphia: American Law Institute–American Bar Association, 1977.

Williston, Samuel. *A Treatise on the Law of Contracts*. Vol. 16, 3d ed., Walter H. E. Jaeger. Rochester: Lawyers Co-operative Publishing, 1976.

SIGNIFICANT COURT DECISIONS

Amtorg Trading Corp. v. *Camden Fibre Mills*, 304 N.Y. 519, 109 N.E.2d 606 (1952): a company that agreed to do business with a trading agent for a foreign country waived the right to assert that the arbitrators could not be impartial because they were controlled by a foreign country.

Anaconda v. *American Sugar Refining Co.*, 332 U.S. 42 (1944): the statutory remedy provided in the United States Arbitration Act (9 U.S.C. § 1 *et seq.*) for libel and seizure in admiralty cases cannot be eliminated by the agreement of the parties.

Astoria Medical Group v. *Health Insurance Plan of Greater New York*, 11 N.Y.2d 128, 227 N.Y.S.2d 401 (1962): established criteria by which to judge a party-appointed arbitrator.

Baar v. *Tigerman*, 189 Cal. Rptr. 834 (App. 1983): an arbitrator who breaches his or her contract by failing to render a timely award is not protected by the doctrine of quasi-judicial immunity. Arbitration associations performing ministerial functions, as well, are not immune from suit.

Bernhardt v. *Polygraphic Company of America*, 350 U.S. 198 (1956): the Federal Arbitration Act applied to two types of claims: (1) admiralty and (2) those involving interstate commerce.

The Breman v. *Zapata Off Shore Co.*, 407 U.S. 1 (1972): a forum selection clause may not be disregarded solely on the ground of *forum non conveniens.*

Commonwealth Coatings Corp. v. *Continental Casualty Co.*, 393 U.S. 145 (1968): established a standard for determining the extent to which the United States Arbitration Act requires disclosure of the arbitrator's prior business relationships with either party to the arbitration agreement. Arbitrators must not only be unbiased but must avoid the appearance of bias.

Dean Witter Reynolds, Inc. v. *Byrd*, __U.S.__, 105 S. Ct. 1238 (1985): it is error for a federal district court to deny a motion to compel arbitration of arbitrable state law claims because they are intertwined with nonarbitrable federal law claims. Rather, the courts must compel arbitration of arbitrable claims at the request of a party to the agreement where there is a valid agreement to arbitrate, under the U.S. Arbitration Act (9 U.S.C. § 1 *et seq.*).

Dormitory Authority of the State of New York v. *Span Electric Corp.*, 18 N.Y.2d 114, 271 N.Y.S.2d 983 (1966): the state itself is not insulated against the operation of an arbitration clause because the power to contract implies the power to agree to arbitrate.

Ericksen, Arbuthnot, McCarthy, Kearney & Walsh v. *100 Oak Street*, 35 Cal. 3d 312, 197 Cal. Rptr. 581, 673 P.2d 251 (1983): under a broad arbitration clause, unless the parties specifically exclude from arbitration claims of fraud in the inducement of the contract, as distinguished from fraud in the inducement of the arbitration clause itself, claims are arbitrable.

Florasynth, Inc. v. *Pickholz*, 598 F. Supp. 17 (S.D.N.Y. 1984), *aff'd*, 750 F.2d 171 (2d Cir. 1984): under the Federal Arbitration Act, motions to vacate arbitration awards must be brought within the three-month limitation period specified in the statute. Such motions will not be timely when brought in answer to a motion to confirm made after the three-month period has expired.

H. W. Moseley v. *Electronic & Missile Facilities*, 374 U.S. 167 (1963): fraud in the inducement of the arbitration clause is an issue for the court to decide.

Just In-Material Designs, Ltd. v. *I.T.A.D. Associates, Inc.*, 61 N.Y.2d 882, 464 N.E.2d 1188, 474 N.Y.S.2d 47 (1984), *aff'g* 94 A.D.2d 103, 463 N.Y.S.2d 202 (1983): retention without objection for a reasonable period of time of a sales note executed by a broker authorized to act for both parties establishes an agreement to arbitrate, where the sales note contains an arbitration provision.

Kalman Floor Co., Inc. v. *Jos. L. Muscarelle, Inc.*, 196 N.J. Super. 16, 481 A.2d 553 (1984): the American Arbitration Association has the right to submit the consolidation question to the arbitrator without party consent or judicial decree.

Merit Insurance Co. v. *Leatherby Insurance Co.*, 714 F.2d 673 (7th Cir. 1983): an arbitration award will not be set aside for allegations of arbitrator bias unless the bias is adequately proven.

Mitsubishi Motors Corp. v. *Soler Chrysler-Plymouth, Inc.*, __U.S.__, 105 S. Ct. 3346 (1985): antitrust claims raised in cases involving international trade are arbitrable despite a domestic public policy reserving antitrust matters to the courts.

Moses H. Cone Memorial Hospital v. *Mercury Construction Corp.*, __U.S.__, 103 S. Ct. 927 (1983): the district court abused its discretion in granting a stay of the federal court proceedings pending resolution of the issue of arbitrability in the state court, and the stay order was appealable.

Prima Paint Corp. v. *Flood & Conklin Manufacturing Co.*, 388 U.S. 395 (1967): as long as the arbitration clause was not fraudulently induced, the question of fraud in the inducement of the contract was for the arbitrators, not the courts, to decide, under the U.S. Arbitration Act.

Scherk v. *Alberto-Culver Co.*, 417 U.S. 506 (1974): an international contract for the sale of stock was arbitrable under the Convention on the Recognition and Enforcement of Foreign Arbitral Awards. The holding in *Wilko* v. *Swan* does not apply to "truly international contracts."

Silverman v. *Benmor Coats, Inc.*, 61 N.Y.2d 299, 461 N.E.2d 1261, 473 N.Y.S.2d 774 (1984): under a broad arbitration clause, questions of fraud in inducement are for the arbitrator, except as related to the arbitration clause itself. Arbitration will be stayed only if the entire controversy is nonarbitrable.

Southland Corp. v. *Keating*, __U.S.__, 104 S. Ct. 852 (1984): the U.S. Arbitration Act creates federal substantive law that is applicable in both federal and state courts and supersedes conflicting state law in transactions evidencing commerce, under the Supremacy Clause of the U.S. Constitution.

Wilko v. *Swan*, 346 U.S. 427 (1953): a domestic contract for the sale of securities that is challenged on the ground of fraud is not subject to arbitration.

Willoughby Roofing & Supply Co., Inc. v. *Kajima International, Inc.*, 598 F. Supp. 353 (N.D. Ala. 1984): under a broad arbitration clause, arbitrators have authority to award punitive damages, and such awards do not violate public policy.

York International v. *Alabama Oxygen Co., Inc.*, __U.S.__, 104 S. Ct. 1260 (1984), *rev'g Ex Parte Alabama Oxygen Co., Inc.*, 433 So. 2d 1158 (Ala. 1983): the Supreme Court summarily reversed a decision of the Alabama Supreme Court that the U.S. Arbitration Act does not preempt contradictory state law in state courts, even if the transaction involves interstate commerce.

THE UNITED STATES ARBITRATION ACT

Title 9, U.S. Code Sections 1-14, first enacted February 12, 1925 (43 Stat. 883), codified July 30, 1947 (61 Stat. 669), and amended September 3, 1954 (68 Stat. 1233). Chapter 2 added July 31, 1970 (84 Stat. 692).

Chapter 1.—GENERAL PROVISIONS

Section 1. Maritime transactions and commerce defined; exceptions to operation of title.
Section 2. Validity, irrevocability, and enforcement of agreements to arbitrate.
Section 3. Stay of proceedings where issue therein referable to arbitration.
Section 4. Failure to arbitrate under agreement; petition to United States court having jurisdiction for order to compel arbitration; notice and service thereof; hearing and determination.
Section 5. Appointment of arbitrators or umpire.
Section 6. Application heard as motion.
Section 7. Witnesses before arbitrators; fees; compelling attendance.
Section 8. Proceedings begun by libel in admiralty and seizure of vessel or property.
Section 9. Award of arbitrators; confirmation; jurisdiction; procedure.
Section 10. Same; vacation; grounds; rehearing.
Section 11. Same; modification or correction; grounds; order.
Section 12. Notice of motions to vacate or modify; service; stay of proceedings.
Section 13. Papers filed with order on motions; judgment; docketing; force and effect; enforcement.
Section 14. Contracts not affected.

Chapter 2.—CONVENTION ON THE RECOGNITION AND ENFORCEMENT OF FOREIGN ARBITRAL AWARDS

Section 201. Enforcement of Convention.
Section 202. Agreement or award falling under the Convention.
Section 203. Jurisdiction; amount in controversy.
Section 204. Venue.
Section 205. Removal of cases from State courts.
Section 206. Order to compel arbitration; appointment of arbitrators.
Section 207. Award of arbitrators; confirmation; jurisdiction; proceeding.
Section 208. Chapter 1; residual application.

CHAPTER 1.–GENERAL PROVISIONS

Section 1. "MARITIME TRANSACTIONS" AND "COMMERCE" DEFINED; EXCEPTIONS TO OPERATION OF TITLE–"Maritime transactions," as herein defined, means charter parties, bills of lading of water carriers, agreements relating to wharfage, supplies furnished vessels or repairs of vessels, collisions, or any other matters in foreign commerce which, if the subject of controversy, would be embraced within admiralty jurisdiction; "commerce," as herein defined, means commerce among the several States or with foreign nations, or in any Territory of the United States or in the District of Columbia, or between any such Territory and another, or between any such Territory and any State or foreign nation, or between the District of Columbia and any State or Territory or foreign nation, but nothing herein contained shall apply to contracts of employment of seamen, railroad employees, or any other class of workers engaged in foreign or interstate commerce.

Section 2. VALIDITY, IRREVOCABILITY, AND ENFORCEMENT OF AGREEMENTS TO ARBITRATE–A written provision in any maritime transaction or a contract evidencing a transaction involving commerce to settle by arbitration a controversy thereafter arising out of such contract or transaction, or the refusal to perform the whole or any part thereof, or an agreement in writing to submit to arbitration an existing controversy arising out of such a contract, transaction, or refusal, shall be valid, irrevocable, and enforceable, save upon such grounds as exist at law or in equity for the revocation of any contract.

Section 3. STAY OF PROCEEDINGS WHERE ISSUE THEREIN REFERABLE TO ARBITRATION–If any suit or proceeding be brought in any of the courts of the United States upon any issue referable to arbitration under an agreement in writing for such arbitration, the court in which such suit is pending, upon being satisfied that the issue involved in such suit or proceeding is referable to arbitration under such an agreement, shall on application of one of the parties stay the trial of the action until such arbitration has been had in accordance with the terms of the agreement, providing the applicant for the stay is not in default in proceeding with such arbitration.

Section 4. FAILURE TO ARBITRATE UNDER AGREEMENT; PETITION TO UNITED STATES COURT HAVING JURISDICTION FOR ORDER TO COMPEL ARBITRATION; NOTICE AND SERVICE THEREOF; HEARING AND DETERMINATION–A party aggrieved by the alleged failure, neglect, or refusal of another to arbitrate under a written agreement for arbitration may petition any United States district court which, save for such agreement, would have jurisdiction under Title 28, in a civil action or in admiralty of the subject matter of a suit arising out of the controversy between the parties, for an order directing that such arbitration proceed in the manner provided for in such agreement. Five days' notice in writing of such application shall be served upon the party in default. Service thereof shall be made in the manner provided by the Federal Rules of Civil Procedure. The court shall hear the parties, and upon being satisfied that the making of the agreement for arbitration or the failure to comply therewith is not in issue, the court shall make an order directing the parties to proceed to arbitration in accordance with the terms of the agreement. The hearing and proceedings, under such agreement, shall be within the district in which the petition for an order directing such arbitration is filed. If the making of the arbitration agreement or the failure, neglect, or refusal to perform the same be in issue, the court shall proceed summarily to the trial thereof. If no jury trial be demanded by the party alleged to be in default, or if the matter in dispute is within admiralty jurisdiction, the court shall hear and determine such issue. Where such an issue is raised, the party alleged to be in default may, except in cases of admiralty, on or before the return day of the notice of application, demand a jury trial of such issue, and upon such demand the court shall make an order referring the issue or issues to a jury in the manner provided by the Federal Rules of Civil Procedure, or may specially call a jury for that purpose. If the jury find that no agreement in writing for arbitration was made or that there is no default in proceeding thereunder, the proceeding shall be dismissed. If the jury find that an agreement for arbitration was made in writing and that there is a default in proceeding thereunder, the court shall make an order summarily directing the parties to proceed with the arbitration in accordance with the terms thereof.

Section 5. APPOINTMENT OF ARBITRATORS OR UMPIRE—If in the agreement provision be made for a method of naming or appointing an arbitrator or arbitrators or an umpire, such method shall be followed; but if no method be provided therein, or if a method be provided and any party thereto shall fail to avail himself of such method, or if for any other reason there shall be a lapse in the naming of an arbitrator or arbitrators or umpire, or in filling a vacancy, then upon the application of either party to the controversy the court shall designate and appoint an arbitrator or arbitrators or umpire, as the case may require, who shall act under the said agreement with the same force and effect as if he or they had been specifically named therein; and unless otherwise provided in the agreement the arbitration shall be by a single arbitrator.

Section 6. APPLICATION HEARD AS MOTION—Any application to the court hereunder shall be made and heard in the manner provided by law for the making and hearing of motions, except as otherwise herein expressly provided.

Section 7. WITNESSES BEFORE ARBITRATORS; FEES; COMPELLING ATTENDANCE—The arbitrators selected either as prescribed in this title or otherwise, or a majority of them, may summon in writing any person to attend before them or any of them as a witness and in a proper case to bring with him or them any book, record, document, or paper which may be deemed material as evidence in the case. The fees for such attendance shall be the same as the fees of witnesses before masters of the United States courts. Said summons shall issue in the name of the arbitrator or arbitrators, or a majority of them, and shall be signed by the arbitrators, or a majority of them, and shall be directed to the said person and shall be served in the same manner as subpoenas to appear and testify before the court; if any person or persons so summoned to testify shall refuse or neglect to obey said summons, upon petition the United States court in and for the district in which such arbitrators, or a majority of them, are sitting may compel the attendance of such person or persons before said arbitrator or arbitrators, or punish said person or persons for contempt in the same manner provided on February 12, 1925, for securing the attendance of witnesses or their punishment for neglect or refusal to attend in the courts of the United States.

Section 8. PROCEEDINGS BEGUN BY LIBEL IN ADMIRALTY AND SEIZURE OF VESSEL OR PROPERTY—If the basis of jurisdiction be a cause of action otherwise justiciable in admiralty, then, notwithstanding anything herein to the contrary the party claiming to be aggrieved may begin his proceeding hereunder by libel and seizure of the vessel or other property of the other party according to the usual course of admiralty proceedings, and the court shall then have jurisdiction to direct the parties to proceed with the arbitration and shall retain jurisdiction to enter its decree upon the award.

Section 9. AWARD OF ARBITRATORS; CONFIRMATION; JURISDICTION; PROCEDURE—If the parties in their agreement have agreed that a judgment of the court shall be entered upon the award made pursuant to the arbitration, and shall specify the court, then at any time within one year after the award is made any party to the arbitration may apply to the court so specified for an order confirming the award, and thereupon the court must grant such an order unless the award is vacated, modified, or corrected as prescribed in sections 10 and 11 of this title. If no court is specified in the agreement of the parties, then such application may be made to the United States court in and for the district within which such award was made. Notice of the application shall be served upon the adverse party, and thereupon the court shall have jurisdiction of such party as though he had appeared generally in the proceeding. If the adverse party is a resident of the district within which the award was made, such service shall be made upon the adverse party or his attorney as prescribed by law for service of notice of motion in an action in the same court. If the adverse party shall be a nonresident, then the notice of the application shall be served by the marshal of any district within which the adverse party may be found in like manner as other process of the court.

Section 10. SAME; VACATION; GROUNDS; REHEARING—In either of the following cases the United States court in and for the district wherein the award was made may make an order vacating the award upon the application of any party to the arbitration—

(a) Where the award was procured by corruption, fraud, or undue means.

(b) Where there was evident partiality or corruption in the arbitrators, or either of them.

(c) Where the arbitrators were guilty of misconduct in refusing to postpone the hearing, upon sufficient cause shown, or in refusing to hear evidence pertinent and material to the controversy; or of any other misbehavior by which the rights of any party have been prejudiced.

(d) Where the arbitrators exceeded their powers, or so imperfectly executed them that a mutual, final, and definite award upon the subject matter submitted was not made.

(e) Where an award is vacated and the time within which the agreement required the award to be made has not expired the court may, in its discretion, direct a rehearing by the arbitrators.

Section 11. SAME; MODIFICATION OR CORRECTION; GROUNDS; ORDER—In either of the following cases the United States court in and for the district wherein the award was made may make an order modifying or correcting the award upon the application of any party to the arbitration—

(a) Where there was an evident material miscalculation of figures or an evident material mistake in the description of any person, thing, or property referred to in the award.

(b) Where the arbitrators have awarded upon a matter not submitted to them, unless it is a matter not affecting the merits of the decision upon the matter submitted.

(c) Where the award is imperfect in matter of form not affecting the merits of the controversy.

The order may modify and correct the award, so as to effect the intent thereof and promote justice between the parties.

Section 12. NOTICE OF MOTIONS TO VACATE OR MODIFY; SERVICE; STAY OF PROCEEDINGS—Notice of a motion to vacate, modify, or correct an award must be served upon the adverse party or his attorney within three months after the award is filed or delivered. If the adverse party is a resident of the district within which the award was made, such service shall be made upon the adverse party or his attorney as prescribed by law for service of notice of motion in an action in the same court. If the adverse party shall be a nonresident then the notice of the application shall be served by the marshal of any district within which the adverse party may be found in like manner as other process of the court. For the purposes of the motion any judge who might make an order to stay the proceedings in an action brought in the same court may make an order, to be served with the notice of motion, staying the proceedings of the adverse party to enforce the award.

Section 13. PAPERS FILED WITH ORDER ON MOTIONS; JUDGMENT; DOCKETING; FORCE AND EFFECT; ENFORCEMENT—The party moving for an order confirming, modifying, or correcting an award shall, at the time such order is filed with the clerk for the entry of judgment thereon, also file the following papers with the clerk:

(a) The agreement; the selection or appointment, if any, of an additional arbitrator or umpire; and each written extension of the time, if any, within which to make the award.

(b) The award.

(c) Each notice, affidavit, or other paper used upon an application to confirm, modify, or correct the award, and a copy of each order of the court upon such an application.

The judgment shall be docketed as if it was rendered in an action.

The judgment so entered shall have the same force and effect, in all respects, as, and be subject to all the provisions of law relating to, a judgment in an action; and it may be enforced as if it had been rendered in an action in the court in which it is entered.

Section 14. CONTRACTS NOT AFFECTED—This title shall not apply to contracts made prior to January 1, 1926.

CHAPTER 2.—CONVENTION ON THE RECOGNITION AND ENFORCEMENT OF FOREIGN ARBITRAL AWARDS

Section 201. ENFORCEMENT OF CONVENTION—The Convention on the Recognition and Enforcement of Foreign Arbitral Awards of June 10, 1958, shall be enforced in the United States courts in accordance with this chapter.

Section 202. AGREEMENT OR AWARD FALLING UNDER THE CONVENTION—An arbitration agreement or arbitral award arising out of a legal relationship, whether contractual or not, which is considered as commercial, including a transaction, contract, or agreement described in section 2 of this title, falls under the Convention. An agreement or award arising out of such a relationship which is entirely between citizens of the United States shall be deemed not to fall under the Convention unless that relationship involves property located abroad, envisages performance or enforcement abroad, or has some other reasonable relation with one or more foreign states. For the purpose of this section a corporation is a citizen of the United States if it is incorporated or has its principal place of business in the United States.

Section 203. JURISDICTION; AMOUNT IN CONTROVERSY—An action or proceeding falling under the Convention shall be deemed to arise under the laws and treaties of the United States. The district courts of the United States (including the courts enumerated in section 460 of title 28) shall have original jurisdiction over such an action or proceeding, regardless of the amount in controversy.

Section 204. VENUE—An action or proceeding over which the district courts have jurisdiction pursuant to section 203 of this title may be brought in any such court in which save for the arbitration agreement an action or proceeding with respect to the controversy between the parties could be brought, or in such court for the district and division which embraces the place designated in the agreement as the place of arbitration if such place is within the United States.

Section 205. REMOVAL OF CASES FROM STATE COURTS—Where the subject matter of an action or proceeding pending in a State court relates to an arbitration agreement or award falling under the Convention, the defendant or the defendants may, at any time before the trial thereof, remove such action or proceeding to the district court of the United States for the district and division embracing the place where the action or proceeding is pending. The procedure for removal of causes otherwise provided by law shall apply, except that the ground for removal provided in this section need not appear on the face of the complaint but may be shown in the petition for removal. For the purposes of Chapter 1 of this title any action or proceeding removed under this section shall be deemed to have been brought in the district court to which it is removed.

Section 206. ORDER TO COMPEL ARBITRATION; APPOINTMENT OF ARBITRATORS—A court having jurisdiction under this chapter may direct that arbitration be held in accordance with the agreement at any place therein provided for, whether that place is within or without the United States. Such court may also appoint arbitrators in accordance with the provisions of the agreement.

Section 207. AWARD OF ARBITRATORS; CONFIRMATION; JURISDICTION; PROCEEDING—Within three years after an arbitral award falling under the Convention is made, any party to the arbitration may apply to any court having jurisdiction under this chapter for an order confirming the award as against any other party to the arbitration. The court shall confirm the award unless it finds one of the grounds for refusal or deferral of recognition or enforcement of the award specified in the said Convention.

Section 208. CHAPTER 1; RESIDUAL APPLICATION—Chapter 1 applies to actions and proceedings brought under this chapter to the extent that chapter is not in conflict with this chapter or the Convention as ratified by the United States.

THE UNIFORM ARBITRATION ACT

ACT RELATING TO ARBITRATION AND TO MAKE UNIFORM THE LAW WITH REFERENCE THERETO

Section 1. VALIDITY OF ARBITRATION AGREEMENT–A written agreement to submit any existing controversy to arbitration or a provision in a written contract to submit to arbitration any controversy thereafter arising between the parties is valid, enforceable and irrevocable, save upon such grounds as exist at law or in equity for the revocation of any contract. This act also applies to arbitration agreements between employers and employees or between their respective representatives (unless otherwise provided in the agreement).

Section 2. PROCEEDINGS TO COMPEL OR STAY ARBITRATION–

(a) On application of a party showing an agreement described in Section 1, and the opposing party's refusal to arbitrate, the court shall order the parties to proceed with arbitration, but if the opposing party denies the existence of the agreement to arbitrate, the court shall proceed summarily to the determination of the issue so raised and shall order arbitration if found for the moving party, otherwise, the application shall be denied.

(b) On application, the court may stay an arbitration proceeding commenced or threatened on a showing that there is no agreement to arbitrate. Such an issue, when in substantial and bona fide dispute, shall be forthwith and summarily tried and the stay ordered if found for the moving party. If found for the opposing party, the court shall order the parties to proceed to arbitration.

(c) If an issue referable to arbitration under the alleged agreement is involved in action or proceeding pending in a court having jurisdiction to hear applications under subdivision (a) of this Section, the application shall be made therein. Otherwise and subject to Section 18, the application may be made in any court of competent jurisdiction.

(d) Any action or proceeding involving an issue subject to arbitration shall be stayed if an order for arbitration or an application therefor has been made under this Section or, if the issue is severable, the stay may be with respect thereto only. When the application is made in such action or proceeding, the order for arbitration shall include such stay.

(e) An order for arbitration shall not be refused on the ground that the claim in issue lacks merit or bona fides or because any fault or grounds for the claim sought to be arbitrated have not been shown.

Section 3. APPOINTMENT OF ARBITRATORS BY COURT–If the arbitration agreement provides a method of appointment of arbitrators, this method shall be followed. In the absence thereof, or if the agreed method fails or for any reason cannot be followed, or when an arbitrator appointed fails or is unable to act and his successor has not been duly appointed, the court on application of a party shall appoint one or more arbitrators. An arbitrator so appointed has all the powers of one specifically named in the agreement.

Section 4. MAJORITY ACTION BY ARBITRATORS–The powers of the arbitrators may be exercised by a majority unless otherwise provided by the agreement or by this act.

Section 5. HEARING—Unless otherwise provided by the agreement:

(a) The arbitrators shall appoint a time and place for the hearing and cause notification to the parties to be served personally or by registered mail not less than five days before the hearing. Appearance at the hearing waives such notice. The arbitrators may adjourn the hearing from time to time as necessary and, on request of a party and for good cause, or upon their own motion may postpone the hearing to a time not later than the date fixed by the agreement for making the award unless the parties consent to a later date. The arbitrators may hear and determine the controversy upon the evidence produced notwithstanding the failure of a party duly notified to appear. The court on application may direct the arbitrators to proceed promptly with the hearing and determination of the controversy.

(b) The parties are entitled to be heard, to present evidence material to the controversy and to cross-examine witnesses appearing at the hearing.

(c) The hearing shall be conducted by all the arbitrators but a majority may determine any question and render a final award. If, during the course of the hearing, an arbitrator for any reason ceases to act, the remaining arbitrator or arbitrators appointed to act as neutrals may continue with the hearing and determination of the controversy.

Section 6. REPRESENTATION BY ATTORNEY—A party has the right to be represented by an attorney at any proceeding or hearing under this act. A waiver thereof prior to the proceeding or hearing is ineffective.

Section 7. WITNESSES, SUBPOENAS, DEPOSITIONS—

(a) The arbitrators may issue (cause to be issued) subpoenas for the attendance of witnesses and for the production of books, records, documents and other evidence, and shall have the power to administer oaths. Subpoenas so issued shall be served, and upon application to the court by a party or the arbitrators, enforced, in the manner provided by law for the service and enforcement of subpoenas in a civil action.

(b) On application of a party and for use as evidence, the arbitrators may permit a deposition to be taken, in the manner and upon the terms designated by the arbitrators, of a witness who cannot be subpoenaed or is unable to attend the hearing.

(c) All provisions of law compelling a person under subpoena to testify are applicable.

(d) Fees for attendance as a witness shall be the same as for a witness in the ____________ Court.

Section 8. AWARD—

(a) The award shall be in writing and signed by the arbitrators joining in the award. The arbitrators shall deliver a copy to each party personally or by registered mail, or as provided in the agreement.

(b) An award shall be made within the time fixed therefor by the agreement or, if not so fixed, within such time as the court orders on application of a party. The parties may extend the time in writing either before or after the expiration thereof. A party waives the objection that an award was not made within the time required unless he notifies the arbitrators of his objection prior to the delivery of the award to him.

Section 9. CHANGE OF AWARD BY ARBITRATORS—On application of a party or, if an application to the court is pending under Sections 11, 12, or 13, on submission to the arbitrators by the court under such conditions as the court may order, the arbitrators may modify or correct the award upon the grounds stated in paragraphs (1) and (3) of subdivision (a) of Section 13, or for the purpose of clarifying the award. The application shall be made within twenty days after delivery of the award to the applicant. Written notice thereof shall be given forthwith to the opposing party, stating he must serve his objections thereto, if any, within ten days from the notice. The award so modified or corrected is subject to the provisions of Sections 11, 12 and 13.

Section 10. FEES AND EXPENSES OF ARBITRATION–Unless otherwise provided in the agreement to arbitrate, the arbitrators' expenses and fees, together with other expenses, not including counsel fees, incurred in the conduct of the arbitration, shall be paid as provided in the award.

Section 11. CONFIRMATION OF AN AWARD–Upon application of a party, the courts shall confirm an award, unless within the time limits hereinafter imposed grounds are urged for vacating or modifying or correcting the award, in which case the court shall proceed as provided in Sections 12 and 13.

Section 12. VACATING AN AWARD–

(a) Upon application of a party, the court shall vacate an award where:

(1) The award was procured by corruption, fraud or other undue means;

(2) There was evident partiality by an arbitrator appointed as a neutral or corruption in any of the arbitrators or misconduct prejudicing the rights of any party;

(3) The arbitrators exceeded their powers;

(4) The arbitrators refused to postpone the hearing upon sufficient cause being shown therefor or refused to hear evidence material to the controversy or otherwise so conducted the hearing, contrary to the provisions of Section 5, as to prejudice substantially the rights of a party; or

(5) There was no arbitration agreement and the issue was not adversely determined in proceedings under Section 2 and the party did not participate in the arbitration hearing without raising the objection;

But the fact that the relief was such that it could not or would not be granted by a court of law or equity is not ground for vacating or refusing to confirm the award.

(b) An application under this Section shall be made within ninety days after delivery of a copy of the award to the applicant, except that, if predicated upon corruption, fraud or other undue means, it shall be made within ninety days after such grounds are known or should have been known.

(c) In vacating the award on grounds other than stated in clause (5) of Subsection (a) the court may order a rehearing before new arbitrators chosen as provided in the agreement, or in the absence thereof, by the court in accordance with Section 3, or, if the award is vacated on grounds set forth in clauses (3), and (4) of Subsection (a) the court may order a rehearing before the arbitrators who made the award or their successors appointed in accordance with Section 3. The time within which the agreement requires the award to be made is applicable to the rehearing and commences from the date of the order.

(d) If the application to vacate is denied and no motion to modify or correct the award is pending, the court shall confirm the award.

Section 13. MODIFICATION OR CORRECTION OF AWARD–

(a) Upon application made within ninety days after delivery of a copy of the award to the applicant, the court shall modify or correct the award where:

(1) There was an evident miscalculation of figures or an evident mistake in the description of any person, thing or property referred to in the award;

(2) The arbitrators have awarded upon a matter not submitted to them and the award may be corrected without affecting the merits of the decision upon the issues submitted; or

(3) The award is imperfect in a matter of form, not affecting the merits of the controversy.

(b) If the application is granted, the court shall modify and correct the award so as to effect its intent and shall confirm the award as so modified and corrected. Otherwise, the court shall confirm the award as made.

(c) An application to modify or correct an award may be joined in the alternative with an application to vacate the award.

Section 14. JUDGMENT OR DECREE OF AWARD–Upon the granting of an order confirming, modifying or correcting an award, judgment or decree shall be entered in conformity therewith and be enforced as any other judgment or decree. Costs of the application and of the proceedings subsequent thereto, and disbursements may be awarded by the court.

*[**Section 15. JUDGMENT ROLL, DOCKETING**–

(a) On entry of judgment or decree, the clerk shall prepare the judgment roll consisting, to the extent filed, of the following:

(1) The agreement and each written extension of the time within which to make the award;

(2) The award;

(3) A copy of the order confirming, modifying or correcting the award; and

(4) A copy of the judgment or decree.

(b) The judgment or decree may be docketed as if rendered in an action.]

Section 16. APPLICATIONS TO COURT–Except as otherwise provided, an application to the court under this act shall be by motion and shall be heard in the manner and upon the notice provided by law or rule of court for the making and hearing of motions. Unless the parties have agreed otherwise, notice of an initial application for an order shall be served in the manner provided by law for the service of a summons in an action.

Section 17. COURT, JURISDICTION–The term "court" means any court of competent jurisdiction of this State. The making of an agreement described in Section 1 providing for arbitration in this State confers jurisdiction on the court to enforce the agreement under this Act and to enter judgment on an award thereunder.

Section 18. VENUE–An initial application shall be made to the court of the (county) in which the agreement provides the arbitration hearing shall be held or, if the hearing has been held, in the county in which it was held. Otherwise the application shall be made in the (county) where the adverse party resides or has a place of business or, if he has no residence or place of business in this State, to the court of any (county). All subsequent applications shall be made to the court hearing the initial application unless the court otherwise directs.

---

*Brackets and parentheses enclose language which the Commissioners suggest may be used by those states desiring to do so.

Section 19. APPEALS–

(a) An appeal may be taken from:

(1) An order denying an application to compel arbitration made under Section 2;

(2) An order granting an application to stay arbitration made under Section 2(b);

(3) An order confirming or denying confirmation of an award;

(4) An order modifying or correcting an award;

(5) An order vacating an award without directing a rehearing; or

(6) A judgment or decree entered pursuant to the provisions of this act.

(b) The appeal shall be taken in the manner and to the same extent as from orders or judgments in a civil action.

Section 20. ACT NOT RETROACTIVE–This act applies only to agreements made subsequent to the taking effect of this act.

Section 21. UNIFORMITY OF INTERPRETATION–This act shall be so construed as to effectuate its general purpose to make uniform the law of those states which enact it.

Section 22. CONSTITUTIONALITY–If any provision of this act or the application thereof to any person or circumstance is held invalid, the invalidity shall not affect other provisions or applications of the act which can be given without the invalid provision or application, and to this end the provisions of this act are severable.

Section 23. SHORT TITLE–This act may be cited as the Uniform Arbitration Act.

Section 24. REPEAL–All acts or parts of acts which are inconsistent with the provisions of this act are hereby repealed.

Section 25. TIME OF TAKING EFFECT–This act shall take effect__________.

MODERN ARBITRATION STATUTES IN THE UNITED STATES

United States Arbitration Act, 9 U.S.C. §1 et seq.

Alaska Stat. §09.43.010 et seq.* (4).
Ariz. Rev. Stat. §12-1501 et seq.* (4).
Ark. Stat. Ann. §34-511 et seq.* (2, 4, 7).
Cal. Code Civ. Proc. §1280 et seq.
Colo. Rev. Stat. §13-22-201 et seq.*
Conn. Gen. Stat. Ann. §52-408 et seq.
Del. Code Ann. Title 10, §5701 et seq.* (4).
D.C. Code Title 16, §16-4301 et seq.*
Fla. Stat. Ann. §682.01 et seq.
Ga. Code §9-9-80 et seq.†
Hawaii Rev. Stat. §658-1 et seq.*
Idaho Code §7-901 et seq.* (4).
Ill. Rev. Stat. Chap. 10, §101 et seq.*
Ind. Code Ann. §34-4-2-1 et seq.* (3, 5, 6).
Iowa Code §679A-1 et seq.*
Kan. Stat. §5-401 et seq.* (2, 4, 7).
Ky. Rev. Stat. Chap. 417, §1 et seq.* (2).
La. Rev. Stat. §9:4201 et seq.* (4).
Me. Rev. Stat. Ann. Title 14, §5927 et seq.* (8).
Md. Cts. & Jud. Proc. Code Ann. §3-201 et seq.* (4).
Mass. Ann. Laws Chap. 251, §1 et seq.* (4).
Mich. Comp. Laws §600.5001 et seq.
Minn. Stat. Ann. §572.08 et seq.*
Miss. Code Ann. §11-15-101 et seq.*†
Mo. Ann. Stat. §435.350 et seq.*
Mont. Code Ann. Ch. 27 [S.B. No. 110]* (2).
Nev. Rev. Stat. §38.015 et seq.*
N.H. Rev. Stat. Ann. §542:1 et seq.
N.J. Stat. Ann. §2A:24-1 et seq.

` Modern statutes are those enforcing agreements to arbitrate existing controversies and any arising in the future. Other state arbitration statutes (for example, Alabama) apply to existing controversies only. (Code of Alabama, Chap. 19.)

* Referred to as Uniform Arbitration Act. Numbers following the asterisk indicate statute exclusions as to: (1) Construction, (2) Insurance, (3) Leases, (4) Labor Contracts, (5) Loans, (6) Sales, (7) Torts, (8) Uninsured Motorists, (9) Doctors, Lawyers.

† Applicable to construction disputes only.

N.M. Stat. Ann. §44-7-1 et seq.*
N.Y. Civ. Prac. Law §7501 et seq.
N.C. Gen. Stat. §1-567.1 et seq.* (4).
Ohio Rev. Code Ann. §2711.01 et seq.
Okla. Stat. Ann. Title 15, §801 et seq.* (2, 4).
Or. Rev. Stat. §33.210 et seq.
Pa. Stat. Ann. Title 42, Chap. 73, §7301 et seq.*
R.I. Gen. Laws §10-3-1 et seq.
S.C. Code §15-48-10 et seq.* (2, 4, 7, 9).
S.D. Codified Laws §21-25A-1 et seq.* (2).
Tenn. Code Ann. §29-5-302 et seq.*
Tex. Rev. Civ. Stat. Ann. Title 10, Art. 224 et seq.* (1, 2, 4).
Utah Code Ann. §78-31-1 et seq.
Vt. Stat. Ann. Title 12, §5651 et seq.* (2).
Va. Code Ann. §8.01-577 et seq.
Wash. Rev. Code Ann. §7.04.010 et seq.
Wis. Stat. Ann. §788.01 et seq.
Wyo. Stat. §1-36-101 et seq.*
See also, P.R. Laws Ann. Title 32, §3201 et seq.

AMERICAN ARBITRATION ASSOCIATION REGIONAL OFFICES

ATLANTA (30361), India Johnson
1197 Peachtree Street, N.E., (404) 872-3022

BOSTON (02114), Richard M. Reilly
60 Staniford Street, (617) 367-6800

CHARLOTTE (28226), Mark Sholander
7301 Carmel Executive Park, (704) 541-1367

CHICAGO (60606), LaVerne Rollé
205 West Wacker Drive, (312) 346-2282

CINCINNATI (45202), Philip S. Thompson
2308 Carew Tower, (513) 241-8434

CLEVELAND (44115), Earle C. Brown
1127 Euclid Avenue, (216) 241-4741

DALLAS (75201), Helmut O. Wolff
1607 Main Street, (214) 748-4979

DENVER (80203), Mark Appel
1775 Sherman Street, (303) 831-0823

DETROIT (48226), Mary A. Bedikian
615 Griswold Street, (313) 964-2525

GARDEN CITY, NY (11530), Mark A. Resnick
585 Stewart Avenue, (516) 222-1660

HARTFORD (06106), Karen M. Jalkut
2 Hartford Square West, (203) 278-5000

KANSAS CITY, MO (64106), Neil Moldenhauer
1101 Walnut Street, (816) 221-6401

LOS ANGELES (90020), Jerrold L. Murase
443 Shatto Place, (213) 383-6516

MIAMI (33129), René Grafals
2250 S.W. 3rd Avenue, (305) 854-1616

MINNEAPOLIS (55402), James R. Deye
510 Foshay Tower, (612) 332-6545

NEW JERSEY (SOMERSET 08873), Richard Naimark
1 Executive Drive, (201) 560-9560

NEW YORK (10020), George H. Friedman
140 West 51st Street, (212) 484-4000

PHILADELPHIA (19102), Arthur R. Mehr
230 South Broad Street, (215) 732-5260

PHOENIX (85012), Deborah A. Krell
77 East Columbus, (602) 234-0950

PITTSBURGH (15222), John F. Schano
221 Gateway Four, (412) 261-3617

SAN DIEGO (92101), Dennis Sharp
530 Broadway, (619) 239-3051

SAN FRANCISCO (94108), Charles A. Cooper
445 Bush Street, (415) 981-3901

SEATTLE (98104), Neal M. Blacker
811 First Avenue, (206) 622-6435

SYRACUSE (13202), Deborah A. Brown
720 State Tower Building, (315) 472-5483

WASHINGTON, DC (20036), Garylee Cox
1730 Rhode Island Avenue, N.W., (202) 296-8510

WHITE PLAINS, NY (10601), Marion J. Zinman
34 South Broadway, (914) 946-1119

MEMBERSHIP IN THE AMERICAN ARBITRATION ASSOCIATION

The AAA administers more than 40,000 cases each year. Fees cover the major part of its administrative costs, but it requires further support to finance its membership services, research, and educational work. Foundations and major national organizations provide funds for special projects. AAA members include corporations, unions, trade associations, and law firms, as well as individuals interested in voluntary arbitration.

Members may consult with the AAA on special problems. Help can be given on the design or administration of grievance and arbitration systems. The experience of the AAA staff is unique in this regard.

Members also have access to the Association's Eastman Arbitration Library, which houses one of the most comprehensive collections on dispute settlement, and you are invited to use the AAA educational facilities. Seminars, films, pamphlets, and programs are designed to meet specific needs. Discounts are available to members.

Members of the Association receive *The Arbitration Journal* and *Arbitration Times* as part of their membership. Association members may also be entitled to receive a choice of award or court decision reporting service, depending on the type of membership they hold. Membership in the American Arbitration Association is open to all who are interested in voluntary out-of-court dispute settlement. Memberships range from individual to those for large companies and unions. Support for the Association is important in order to accomplish the goals that have been set.

For further information about becoming a member, please contact the Membership Department, AAA, 140 West 51st Street, New York, N.Y. 10020.